# For Self and Country

# Country

## A TRUE STORY
## *by* RICK EILERT

# FOR THE WOUNDED IN VIETNAM
## THE JOURNEY HOME TOOK
## MORE COURAGE
## THAN GOING
## INTO BATTLE

WILLIAM MORROW AND COMPANY • NEW YORK • 1983

This book is dedicated to the doctors, corpsmen, and nurses of the Navy Medical Corps, to my parents, to my wife, Cheryl, to my children, Kerrie and Scott, and to those brave men in all wars who endured the consequences of combat.

# Foreword

I WAS PRIVILEGED to know Lance Corporal Rick Eilert as a marine and as a human being, since I was his orthopedic surgeon at the time of his transfer to Great Lakes Naval Hospital. His story is not unique, but his sense of humor, courage, and facility in recall are exemplary.

The American involvement in Vietnam was grave and extensive. Opposition to the war ultimately split the country, forcing a president to decline to seek reelection. Despite these well-publicized differences at home, the American fighting man, typified by Rick Eilert, by and large continued to do his duty to the fullest extent of his ability. As Rick learned, one's duties and responsibilities to self and country are often more odious in a protracted rehabilitation-hospital setting than on a battlefield. But Rick is unique in that he recognized early the necessity for this story to be written as a talisman for the uncounted men whose stories, however important, will never be told.

When I was asked to write the Foreword to *For Self and Country*, I was profoundly honored. As a medical officer in Vietnam, I knew well the faces of the wounded and the depression that inevitably followed as the wounded fighting man gradually became aware of the awful finality of a crippling injury. The courage displayed in these circumstances was often of the highest kind, combined in this case with the rarest and most precious gift of all, the ability to laugh at oneself.

The opportunity to serve in the treatment and rehabilitation of men such as Rick remains one of my most precious memories. I would like to say to Rick Eilert and his comrades, on behalf of every American, that you have our sincerest thanks for a job well done. We are all in your debt.
*Semper Fidelis!*

BOONE BRACKETT, M.D.
Lieutenant Commander
U.S. Naval Reserve

# Acknowledgments

I WANT TO thank the many people who helped nurse me back to life and, later, helped me create this book.

Dr. Boone Brackett always treated his young patients with respect and dignity. He still works unceasingly to help heal our bodies and our spirits. Bill Corson, a fine combat commander who now is dedicated to the cause of wounded veterans, understood what I was trying to write and found an audience for me. My agent, John Cushman, and my editor, Bruce Lee, believed in me and my story, and I benefited from their assistance and wise counsel. Steve Markley and all the other men of Ward Three South shared the agony of our wounds and the confidences of our youth. The friendship of these men helped me carry my own load. Joe Fornelli and Dale Samuelson supplied the excellent art for this book. Finally, I thank the men of 3/26, especially Penna, Horne, Neely, Kuehnlein, Jones, Chief, Schott, Hawkins, Madison, and the young, freckle-faced, tattered corpsman, Doc Toner, who saved my life and was killed in action months later.

For all that you gave me, I rejoice; for all that we lost, I shall never forget.

# FOR SELF AND COUNTRY

# 1

MR AND MRS RICHARD L EILERT . . .
THIS IS TO CONFIRM THAT YOUR SON PRIVATE FIRST CLASS
RICHARD E EILERT USMC WAS INJURED 26 NOVEMBER 1967 IN
THE VICINITY OF THUA THIEN, REPUBLIC OF VIETNAM HE
SUSTAINED MULTIPLE FRAGMENTATION WOUNDS TO BOTH
LEGS, BOTH HANDS, BOTH ARMS AND FACE FROM A
HOSTILE EXPLOSIVE DEVICE WHILE ON PATROL. HE IS
PRESENTLY RECEIVING TREATMENT AT THE THIRD
MEDICAL BATTALION. HIS CONDITION AND PROGNOSIS
WERE GOOD. YOUR ANXIETY IS REALIZED AND YOU ARE
ASSURED THAT HE IS RECEIVING THE BEST OF CARE. HIS
MAILING ADDRESS REMAINS THE SAME
   WALLACE M GREENE JR GENERAL USMC COMMANDANT
OF THE MARINE CORPS

Sixteen years later I still dream about the night before I was wounded.

Our flatbed truck was speeding north on Highway 1. I tried to see the other faces, but rain was pouring down and it was pitch-black. Everyone on the truck had his poncho pulled up high, with only his helmet showing where his head was. They looked like turtles sitting on mounds of plastic.

The truck stopped. We gathered our gear and jumped to the roadside. It was then that I noticed more trucks parked behind ours. It was so dark I hadn't noticed them following us. Our whole company was there.

I looked around, trying to find a road sign or a piece of terrain that would give me an idea of where we were. We'd left Camp Evans, north of Hue, less than an hour ago so we were maybe ten kilometers north of there. Thua Thien Province for sure. I remembered hearing the captain tell us we would sweep west of Highway 1 up to Khe Sanh.

Each of the three platoons formed up quietly and moved off in a different direction, into the darkness.

My platoon started into the bush in single file. We walked all night through the storm to reach our checkpoint, where we'd stay until dawn. You couldn't see the man in front of you, so we held on to each other's belt loops. Never before had I seen such complete blackness. We fell all over each other. One minute we were on the walls of a dike; the next minute we'd fall five feet into the muddy waters of a rice paddy.

All of us knew Charlie wouldn't be foolish enough to sit out in the driving rain just to ambush us. We were the only ones dumb enough to be out in such miserable weather. Finally, after hours of crashing through bushes, elephant grass, and knee-deep paddies, we reached the checkpoint. My squad was lucky. We'd run the first patrol early after daybreak, so we could sleep the remainder of the night rather than stand watch. We dug in for the rest of the night. Sometime later the rain stopped and the moon shone through the clouds with little rays of light. I thought how beautiful a scene it was, almost like the paintings of Bethlehem the night Christ was born. The only difference was that the shepherds on this hillside carried M-16s instead of walking sticks. Suddenly the wind died and it became very still, a phenomenon I have observed only in that little country.

The leaves on the trees stopped swaying. I could hear raindrops falling from the leaves. Great swarms of mosquitoes attacked us, but even they made little noise. The only other sounds were of the men swatting at the bugs or turning over in the grass as they slept.

When I woke up the next morning I found that I'd wrapped my head in my poncho to keep off the mosquitoes. It was only sunrise, yet the air was warm, a sign that it would be very hot. The day before, the temperature had reached 105 degrees, which, along with the 85 percent humidity, made breathing difficult, especially when you had to carry a full pack, almost 90 pounds, along with a flak jacket.

Match, our lieutenant, called my squad over. He got that nickname because he was always scraping his teeth with a wooden match, and always had one dangling from his mouth, and also because he rathered the men call him that than "sir" in the bush. Officers made good targets and Match wanted as low a profile as possible.

Match laid a map down on the ground and pointed out the checkpoints and the direction he wanted the men to follow. Thompson was squad leader so most of the instructions were intended for him. However, I was walking point so my knowledge of the direction was important. Match continued his instructions as he folded up the map.

"All right, now listen up, all of you. They say there's a reinforced company in the area. I want you to find it and call in when you do. Don't engage them, just call in and we'll get an air strike on them. Understood?" Everyone nodded and filed out down the small knoll toward the river a mile or more to the north.

The air remained very still and the odors of decay and mold filled our nostrils as we moved cautiously along the path. It seemed to me that everything in this lousy country was dying from one thing or the other. The smell of decaying flesh was prominent almost all the time. My clothes were still covered with dried blood from carrying some wounded men two weeks before.

The trail wound through thick, six-foot-high jungle grass and a dense forest of bamboo with the branches twisted and intertwined. The many shades of green were beautiful, but that imposing foliage made me cautious. Parts of the trail were completely covered overhead by vines and twisted fallen branches. It seemed as though we were entering a cave.

For some, walking point was punishment for falling asleep on watch or goofing off on a work detail. At point you were alone. You walked fifteen meters ahead of the rest of the squad. You looked for signs of a booby trap or an ambush. Often you were the one who tripped the booby trap or walked into the barrel of Charlie's rifle before the enemy opened up the ambush. In a 15-second fire fight, the life expectancy of the point man was 0.8 seconds. Short-timers, men with just a few months left before they were to return home, avoided the point. So point fell to those less experienced or with less time in country. I was lucky. I had a great teacher, Gage. He walked point for ten weeks before he got killed at Con Tien during a mortar barrage. He showed me the signs to look for. Stones or sticks piled off the trail in a certain way indicated a booby trap or an ambush. A piece of green plastic meant a booby trap. I'd walked point now for over twelve weeks. I felt good out in front. I trusted my instincts and I was slow and careful. I'd found several booby traps before and, more important, the others trusted me.

Every two or three hundred meters I broke through thick brush, using a machete, to find a clearing. On several occasions I spotted civilians moving on the trails and occasional banana or fruit tree orchards. I was always leery of these people. Most likely some of them were only farmers by day, and the enemy by night.

The sun had dried the rain-soaked soil. Each step reduced the earth to a fine powder. The utilities we wore were covered with red dust and our combat boots were pink. The farther we moved away from the perimeter, the slower I went.

We were on a hill, surrounded by elephant grass, thick bushes, and more rolling hills covered with bamboo. We were at least two kilometers west of our platoon's position and the rice paddies we'd crossed the night before. Only gone two hours, but I was really tired.

The heat was so intense that sweat was dripping into my eyes, burning and fogging my vision. I'd walked point too long. I was becoming careless, paying less attention to the signs in the trail. My mind wandered to the cool Minnesota lake where my family vacationed during the summer.

The razor-sharp edges of the jungle grass snapped me back to reality, cutting chunks of flesh from my face, forearms, and hands. Four months in the Nam, three of them walking point, had left my body a mass of open, running sores and scars. I stopped, raising my arm high over my head and dropping it quickly to my side. I turned back to see that my signal was obeyed. It was. The squad was down off the trail. Staring ahead at the open trail I sensed something wrong in the stillness of the jungle heat. Looking back I saw Tommy, the squad leader, crawling forward.

"What's up, Rick?"

"This trail is the shits. I've spotted three man-traps, a fighting hole, and punji sticks on both sides of the trail in the last hundred meters. Something's up—it's so quiet you could hear a popcorn fart. If Charlie's going to pop an ambush, this is as good a place as any. We could backtrack to the fork and try the other trail."

"Want a butt?"

"Yeah. I'm going to call the CP and see what Match thinks."

Thompson signaled for the radio man to come forward. "How's it going, Rick?"

"Just out-fucking-standing, duffus. Get Match on the hook."

Red was a new man in the squad. All new men carried the radio, mostly because it weighed so much and also to familiarize them with squad and company radio procedure. Red's problem was that he wants action, and a jerk like that could get someone greased. Thompson made his call. "OK. We'll go back to the fork in the trail. Remember, Match wants no contact. Just find them and get out. . . . Red, got a light?" Red struck the match, lighting his cigarette, then Thompson's, then—without thinking—I took the third light. All three of us looked at each other.

Thompson stared at me. "Just walk point like you always did." Red seemed bewildered. "Hell, that's only superstition. You don't believe in that shit." But I knew only too well about three on a match.

I was thinking, *Christ, Oggy caught one right between the running lights not three minutes after, and Gordon had a bouncing Betty go up his ass and explode in his belly an hour after he got his third light. Why am I any different? After a while, duffus, you just know it's coming and there ain't shit you can do about it.*

"Let's bug out of here," I said. Now I could feel my heart pounding. The perspiration running down my hands made it difficult to grasp my rifle. I wheeled and started to double-back down the trail. "Keep them spread out," I told Thompson. I moved past the sprawling men on the trail and spotted the medical corpsman. "Doc, I hope you brought your shit today. We're going to need it." Doc only nodded. He'd seen too many men whose premonition of death had come true.

I moved back to the fork in the trail and the squad followed slowly behind me. Now they all knew about my ill fortune.

They kept the distance between themselves and me even greater than usual. I knew my job, but I just couldn't seem to concentrate. What had happened to the signs I'd always been so quick to see? Nothing was there. Nothing fit. I could feel the blood rushing through my veins, my heart pounding, the sweat pouring off me. Even the heat seemed more intense. I stopped, signaling everyone down. I knelt, thinking I'd heard a noise. Match had said there was a reinforced company in the area. Damn, why couldn't I be home cruising the greasy Macs, partying, anything except being here. I remembered the night Peaches told Doc not to bother bringing any of his gear—it wouldn't do any good. An hour later he got both his legs blown off by a mortar round. He, too, had known.

I broke off a long, flexible twig from a nearby bush, stripped the leaves from the stem, and measured it for size, waist high. I gave the signal to move out. As I moved I held the branch straight in front of me and two inches off the ground. If any trip wires lay across the path, the branch would snag the wire without setting off the booby trap. I'd learned this from a previous point man. Unfortunately, he'd been so preoccupied with watching for trip wires that he walked right into the barrel of some gook's rifle. With slow, deliberate motion, I moved no more than three paces at a time. The other squad members understood. They preferred to be moving at a snail's pace than walking point themselves. Besides, I knew I was good, real good.

I held my hand high, then dropped it. Everyone stopped. I'd spotted a clearing not twenty meters ahead, beyond several clumps of bushes. I signaled for Thompson to come up. He came like a shot, with Red humping the radio. "It's going to happen here, Tommy, I feel it. We make that clearing and the shit'll hit the fan."

Thompson grabbed the hook from Red's back. "Lima Two, this is Two Three Alpha."

"Two Three Alpha, this is Two Go."

"Two, this is Two Three Alpha. We are approximately one hundred meters west of Checkpoint Rosebud. Stand by, Willy Peter."

"Rog, Two Three Alpha. We read you five by five."

Thompson had sweat pouring down his face. His eyes showed no expression. "Rick, put C.L. on point. Just keep him out of that fucking clearing. He's never walked up front before. Besides, he's never seen action. Look, you're going on R and R in two weeks to meet your girl. C.L. has to take over then anyway. May as well learn now."

"Fine, get him up here and let's get it over with. Say, Tommy, what day is it? I mean the date?"

"It's November twenty-sixth."

I glanced down at my watch. "Eight minutes to twelve, November twenty-sixth. Damn, all this for twenty-five cents an hour." C.L. had made his way up to point. "Listen, C.L., there's a clearing ahead." I pointed to the area beyond several clumps of bushes in front of us. "All of these bushes have thorns. Try to find another place to break into the clearing, even if you have to break through all these damn thorny bushes. Don't pass through that opening in the clearing. I'll bet the mortgage money Charlie's got a booby trap in or around that opening. Whatever you do, don't go into that clearing."

C.L. nodded. He'd been in country only six weeks but he knew the mortality rate for point men was unreal. Now his time had come. If he was lucky enough to live today, there was always tomorrow.

I motioned the men to move out. Everyone got up quickly. There were only eight in the squad, and they all knew the importance of zero hesitation. The click of their weapons being turned to automatic in unison sounded like a large hammer on metal. C.L. moved slowly, trying to remember all I'd said and still concentrate on every move. When he came to the opening in the clearing he tried desperately to break through the thick brush on either side of the trail, but the bushes were long, thin thorns that cut and sliced his hands, arms, and face until blood flowed from the open gashes.

I could hear the commotion but could barely see C.L.'s form through a large bush between us. I continued moving until I lost sight of him. When I got to the opening of the clearing I spotted the thorny brush on either side of the trail. I saw drops of blood on the foliage. I realized that C.L. had entered the clearing and moved off to the left, still out of my sight. I hadn't heard any explosions or gunfire or screams, so I knew he was OK. If he'd gone through, it had to be all right. I passed through the opening and turned left immediately. There, about fifteen meters in front of me, was C.L. walking down a straight narrow path, high bushes on both sides, away from the clearing. C.L. continued down the path slowly and I followed. I shook my head. The fool had done what I told him not to, but we were moving away from the clearing. So I followed. In back of me the others came slowly, keeping a ten-meter distance between us.

The next few moments unfold in memory like a slow-motion movie, almost frame by frame. I step off with my right foot and look down. I spot a grenade just in front of me and off to the left, where I'm about to drop my left foot. In back of the grenade a C-ration can sits in the bushes. C.L. has tripped the wire attached to the grenade and pulled it from the can. It's *live.*

I know it's too late. I'm in the middle of taking a step. My left foot yet to hit the ground. My mind says, *Run, duck, evaporate;* but my body won't react fast enough. It's like sliding on ice. No way to stop and nowhere to go but in the direction gravity moves you. I feel a rush go through my body. I feel the stillness. My left foot touches earth. I start to take a running stride. The grenade explodes. Flames spew into my face, then there's the smell of burned gunpowder and burning flesh. My body lifts straight up. There's only blackness. I never hear the explosion. I scream, *"Oh, God!"* but no one can hear my cry over the noise of the blast.

I lay there, eyes closed, ears ringing, and felt a tingling sensation all over my body—then total numbness. *I'm dead. I'm fucking dead.*

As I opened my eyes smoke was pouring from the small crater to my left. My left leg was twisted around on top of my chest, the fatigues and flesh smoldering. My left arm was broken. Small, pulsating fountains of blood gushed from my leg and neck. I had to spit out the fragments of teeth and the blood to avoid choking. As the ringing subsided, the sound of gunfire was everywhere. It was automatic fire and lots of it. I lifted my head. I could see nothing but C.L. He was down, too. "Corpsman, corpsman! I can't move my legs!" I kept screaming. While I was watching C.L., another grenade landed nearby. It exploded before I could get my head down, tearing away more flesh, breaking my right leg, and opening a large gaping wound in my right arm. Again my ears were ringing. This time I spotted Charlie running up to C.L., sticking his weapon in his face, and firing; part of C.L.'s skull hit me in the face. While I was wiping blood from my face, Charlie cooly walked toward me and leveled his weapon at my chest.

I pulled what was left of my rifle to my side, but the barrel had been bent by the blast. I pulled out my knife. *Shit, I might as well be holding my dick.* I couldn't do anything. Now only about four meters away, Charlie lowered his weapon at my chest. Suddenly I heard a shot from behind. Charlie's neck opened wide and his head almost fell off, but his finger was still locked in a death grip on the trigger of his AK-47. One round scraped across my belly. A second hit the leg already on my chest, making it jump off to the side. Instantly Doc was kneeling beside me. He didn't say anything but worked feverishly, applying pressure bandages.

"Doc, do I still got my nuts?"

Ripping open my fly, Doc investigated quickly. "Yep, equipment's still there." Glenn ran up to help Doc. The firing seemed even more intense, maybe because the ringing in my ears was going away. Glenn wiped the blood out of my eyes. "Nice shooting, Doc," Glenn yelled. "In the six months you've been here I've seen you clean that damn forty-five only once, and then you dropped it in the river and just wiped it off so *you* wouldn't get wet. Shit, one shot and you blew that fucker's head clean off."

Doc, who was still hard at work, looked up. "Hell, stupid, I was aiming at his balls."

The firing was deafening. It was almost impossible to determine what direction it was coming from. Thompson must have called in mortars. The air was filled with whizzing shrapnel and loud explosions. I looked up and could see a helicopter, just as Gary jumped over me with his M-60 pumping away. For an instant all that was happening seemed unimportant, but now rounds began landing all around Doc. Glenn laid his body over mine so that no more rounds could hit me.

"Glenn, pray for me."

"Shit, Rick, you're going back to the world. Right, Doc?"

"Yeah, probably with one leg, but you are definitely getting the hell out of here."

The call for "Corpsman!" could be heard all around now, but Doc kept on working. Tommy came up with the radio. He'd already called in a med-i-vac chopper. "Rick, what's your med-i-vac number?"

"Thoo thee five nine thoo thoo thix," I said, spitting out more tooth fragments.

Thompson repeated the information into the radio. "Blood

type A. Eilert. Yeah, Eilert, Echo India Lima Echo Romeo Tango. Got it? Eilert." The firing seemed to subside after the call was made, but everyone realized that was because the chopper and the corpsman were all Charlie was really after, and as soon as the med-i-vac touched down all hell would break loose.

Doc, Glenn, and Thompson knew I'd lost a lot of blood. They had to keep me from going into shock, keep me awake. Thompson kicked me in the ass while Glenn and Doc tried to get me to start singing. I started with "I'm in Pieces, Bits and Pieces" by the Dave Clark Five. The pain became intolerable as the numbing sensation of the blast wore off.

"Doc, for God's sake, give me a shot . . . please."

"Rick, you know I can't give you anything because of your head wound. Just hold on a little longer."

I could feel life draining out of me. The faces of my dead friends flashed by as I felt myself passing out, only to be jolted back to consciousness by fits of pain and Thompson's boot. I looked up and saw the chopper circling, but the ringing in my ears muffled the noise of the engines. The sound of gunfire picked up. Tree branches and dirt were moving in every direction. Thompson waved orders to the squad while he guided the chopper in for a landing, knowing this was the most critical moment for everyone. Charlie was just waiting for the chopper to come in before opening up with all his firepower.

Doc lifted me up under the arms while Glenn grabbed me under the thighs. With all the blood on my legs, he had trouble getting a grip. I knew the chopper could break off at any time if the move looked too difficult to execute. "Bring that son of a bitch in. . . . Please, God, bring it in." The figures of the door gunners were visible now as the craft hovered overhead.

Thompson shouted to the pilot, "You come in right fucking now or we'll gun you down ourselves."

In they came, kicking up dirt and debris in all directions. The popping of rifle fire and automatic weapons could still be heard over the whirlwind of noise and flying shrapnel. At the instant the wheels touched down, Doc and Glenn bolted for the door of the chopper. The door gunner sprayed the jungle grass inches above their heads. I was flung in the door as Doc and Glenn bolted for cover. As soon as I was aboard, the chopper lifted off. The crew chief on board grabbed my belt and pulled me onto a stretcher close to the open hatch. The door gunner was still pumping rounds into the jungle below.

I rolled my head to the left. There was C.L.'s body in a heap on the floor next to me, his eyes open wide, his jaw gone. I turned my head away, only to see a river of my blood running out the door. It seemed that with each beat of my heart there was a surge of blood out the hatch. The crew chief and the door gunner tried to patch the holes still open on my legs and arms, but they seemed to be losing the battle. I tried to speak, but my throat was swollen and the blood rushing down my throat caused me to gag and puke more blood and busted teeth. The crew chief put his ear to my mouth. Still the words couldn't come. He smiled and wiped the blood from my face.

"We'll pick up a corpsman in Camp Evans and some plasma. You'll be OK." The chopper landed for just a moment. On jumped the corpsman and off we went. I felt the needle strike and saw the plasma bottle hung over my head. I heard the new-comer say he didn't think this grunt would make it.

*Jesus H. Christ, that's just what I needed to hear,* I thought to myself.

The pain was disappearing. I began to feel cold. Sleepiness started to set in. I knew I was fading fast. If I passed out, chances were I would never wake up. For some reason or other, death didn't scare me any longer and sleep seemed so inviting. My chest began to heave, my breath seemed short. My eyes closed for only a moment. When I tried to open them, everything was dark. *No shit, I'm fucking dead. Hell, this is boring,* I thought, *but no pain . . . at least no pain.* Suddenly I was awakened by a corpsman slapping my face. My eyes opened and the pain came charging back. I was out of the chopper being carried to a large hangar-type area, filled with the wounded. I was immediately taken to one of the four tables in the middle of the room. As I was set down, three corpsmen began to strip off my fatigues using scissors while another corpsman took my vital signs. I looked around. All the other tables were busy with the same procedure, the tattered clothing tossed on the floor, which was completely covered with blood. Around the room sat at least fifty less seriously wounded marines, watching the ghoulish scene before them. As I looked up at the ceiling, someone shoved his face into mine.

"Son, have you any last words to say to your God? I'm the chaplain. I'm going to give you the last rites."

I couldn't speak. I only shook my head and thought, *Who is this duffus sky pilot, and how does he know if I'm not Jewish? Last words to my God? Shit, I haven't even said good-bye to my girl friend, let alone God.*

The corpsman wiped the blood off my face. The sky pilot rubbed oil on my forehead. A doctor wrote something on a chart and talked to some other doctor about a "procedure."

"Please, Doc. Please give me something for the pain or knock me out—anything, just stop the pain," I pleaded.

"Easy, marine, just hold on a little longer. Take this man to X ray, STAT.

They wheeled me away into the X-ray room, where several civilian women sat waiting with children and other less severely wounded marines were holding up the walls. I felt embarrassed lying there on the gurney, stark-naked except for the bandages covering my wounds. A large corpsman pulled me from the gurney onto the X-ray table. He was so gruff about it that he didn't have anyone move my legs. I was on the X-ray table and my shattered legs were on the gurney. Oblivious to my pain, the corpsman simply pulled the torn parts over, took the pictures, and pulled me back onto the gurney while I screamed in agony.

Finally I looked up at him. "I'd love to kill you, mother fucker."

The X-ray tech looked back, saying, "Blow it out your ass, tough guy."

The rage I felt almost made the pain disappear. One of the waiting marines heard the exchange of words, came around the curtain, and gave the technician a vertical butt stroke in the teeth with his M-14. I just looked up and grinned as another corpsman pulled my gurney away, saying, "This is marine country. That's the last place to play tough. Hell, that marine just as soon killed him."

The corpsman wheeled me down the corridor to the OR. I heard an attendant say they'd get that marine tossed in jail for that little show. I laughed to myself. *Hell, that jarhead just as soon go to jail as go back in the bush and get killed. What fools*, I thought.

The corpsman noticed blood dripping from my stretcher and

quickly pushed his way through the corridors of wounded men to the operating room. I knew I was in big trouble and I fought off the urge to pass out. To go into shock now after holding on for so long seemed like quitting. There was no way this grunt would hang it up now. The pain was bad but it was dulled by the thoughts of finally going home to my family and friends, and most of all Cheryl.

"God, how I miss her," I said over and over.

In the operating room three corpsmen lifted me onto the table. I looked up, forced to squint because of the bright lights overhead. My head began to buzz. Suddenly, my vision gone, I slipped into a deep sleep. The anesthetic was fast acting. For the first time in months I was able to sleep.

Noise was the first sensation I was aware of as I started to come out from under the anesthetic. Muffled noises at first, which built up into whispers. I couldn't open my eyes. When I finally did, the figures before me were in a foggy mist. "How are you feeling, Eilert? Eilert, wake up!" the corpsman shouted. "Come on, sunshine, marine." My eyes opened again, more fully this time. I felt as groggy as I had when I drank a bottle of B & B at a fraternity party. I stared up at the ceiling, not wanting to look down at my feet. Hell, I knew I'd lost one leg for sure—probably the other one as well. It seemed that if I could put off looking at my missing limbs, somehow they would still at least be there, maybe a minute longer.

"Rick, I'm Kelly. I'm the corpsman on duty for tonight. I need to take your vital signs. Sorry I had to wake you, but we've been pretty worried about you. You almost bought the farm. Shit, you was on the table for twenty-one hours. That's beaucoup time under the knife, especially with all your wounds and blood loss. Do you need anything . . . anything at all?" I just shook my head. It was then that I noticed all the tubes in my arms, and two bumps at the foot of my rack. Tears welled up in my eyes. For the first time in the Nam I was going to cry. I still had my legs. *Oh, my God, my legs, I still have my legs. . . . Sweet Jesus, I still have my legs.*

Tears flowed down my cheeks.

"Kelly, where am I?" I asked, my mouth swollen with stitches.

"You're in Phu Bai. This is the field medical hospital," he chuckled.

The pain started to take hold again. At first my tears were for the joy of finding my legs still attached to my body. Soon they were for all the sleepless nights, for the dead and mangled forms of my very close and dear friends, for the chance to finally relax. I was going home . . . alive. The thought of ever getting out of the bush was a luxury no grunt could afford to think of. Hell, only two ways any marine went home—*intact* or *tacked in.* Sure, everyone always thought of home and Mom, and of course Susy Snatch and Rosy Rotten Crotch, but nobody really in his heart could believe it. When you first got here in this stinking country, it was a fantastic nightmare—just unreal. But now after one or two fire fights and Con Tien, the reality became Vietnam and the dream was home. It was as if home never really existed, as if you'd always been chopping your way through jungles and knowing that there was no living beyond the moment, or even just the second. Now finally, at last . . . to really be going home. *Shit,* I thought, *it's like winning the damn lottery.*

I could hear rain hitting the roof of the Quonset hut, that water-hitting-metal sound, like a rain on a helmet. All those nights on ambushes and LPs, sitting waist deep in water, soaked to the skin . . . hell, to the bone. *Good God,* I thought, *nobody in their right mind would go out on a night like this. Charlie is probably sitting in some hut with his lady, drinking whiskey and being all cozy and warm, and here these dumb jugheads sit getting rained on all night long without any sleep, only to go back to the perimeter in the morning and be Cook for a Day.*

The raindrops became steady, rhythmic. I could inhale the sweet smell of clean sheets. *Good God, clean dry sheets and a warm blanket to boot. If I was in the field now I would be wet and cold. Just think, I'm warm and dry.* My eyelids got heavy and merciful sleep came—that sweet kind of sleep that comes with feeling safe and going home.

# 2

MR. & MRS. RICHARD L. EILERT . . .
A REPORT RECEIVED THIS HEADQUARTERS REVEALS THAT
THE CONDITION OF YOUR SON, PRIVATE FIRST CLASS
RICHARD E. EILERT, U. S. M. C. HAS BEEN CHANGED TO
SERIOUS AND HIS PROGNOSIS REMAINS GOOD. YOUR
CONCERN IS REALIZED AND YOU ARE ASSURED THAT HE
CONTINUES TO RECEIVE THE BEST OF CARE. WHEN
FURTHER REPORTS CONCERNING HIS CONDITION ARE
AVAILABLE, YOU WILL BE INFORMED. HIS MAILING ADDRESS
REMAINS THE SAME.
> WALLACE M. GREENE, JR.
> GENERAL U.S.M.C.
> COMMANDANT OF THE MARINE CORPS.

I was wakened suddenly by two corpsmen scurrying around my rack. One was holding a bottle of blood high in the air over my head while the other frantically tried to find a vein to put the needle into. "What the hell is going on?"

"You must have rolled over during the night. You ripped the damn IV out of your arm. It's so dark over here nobody noticed until I slipped on a puddle of blood next to your rack. You've been dripping for some time—there's blood all over. There, got the needle back in. Willie, get another pain med." The other corpsman scurried off to fetch my shot.

"I hurt but not that bad. I'm not sure I need a shot."

"Just the same, take it as often as possible. Your system

needs to sandbag this pain med for when the real big ouchy comes, and believe me it's going to come."

I stared at the corpsman as he put the needle in. "That's just out-fucking-standing. You really know how to cheer up a guy, don't you?"

"Sorry. I really didn't mean to make it sound so bad, but your system is really fucked up now, between the shock of your injury, the loss of blood, the nerve damage, and the long hours on the cutting board, in addition to all the medication we've put in you. Hell, your body don't know shit from Shinola. Once you've settled down into some stateside hospital and they start putting you back together again, you'll really begin to feel much better."

"How long have I been out?"

"It's Tuesday, the twenty-eighth."

"Damn, I've been out for two days. Man, that morphine is some good shit. Just think of it, to sleep the Nam away . . . fan-fucking-tastic."

The corpsman laughed. "You grunts are something else. You just got blown to shit and the only thing you have to say is how happy you are to have put two days behind you by sleeping. Next thing you'll want is some chow. Don't even bother to ask. All the teeth on the left side of your mouth are gone, a piece of shrapnel went right through your tongue and lodged in the roof of your mouth, plus they had to do a tracheotomy on you so your throat is swollen. Only chow you'll get is liquid. Get some rest. The doctor will be in soon for rounds. It'll give you a chance to find out what's going on."

I began to doze off, only to be awakened by a character in a baseball cap, a loud golf shirt, and bermuda shorts.

"Good morning, son. How are you doing today?" Without waiting for a reply he continued. "Heard we had some trouble last night—your IV came out. Damn, I almost lost you in the operating room yesterday and the day before. I'm Dr. Walker, the sawbones that tied you back up the other day."

I sensed that if I were ever to get a word in edgewise I'd have to rush it. "Glad to meet you, sir—you mean I was operated on yesterday, too?"

"That's right, Eilert. It looked as if you were going to lose both legs at first, but we were able to get some circulation started and some of the damaged muscle repaired. Yesterday you began to hemorrhage and back in you went to plug the leak. I'm still not certain that you'll be able to keep your left leg. However, the right looks pretty good. We'll wait till you get stateside and let them try to save your left. There are some fine doctors back there and Great Lakes Hospital, where you'll be sent, is one of the finest facilities available for orthopedic work. . . . You're going to have to go back in the OR again today. Lots of garbage still in you. Since you were on the operating table so long the first day, we had to stop short of finishing to let you get some strength back. Just relax and get some rest." Reaching down to my left leg, he grasped my toes tightly. "Can you move your toes?"

"No, sir."

As I replied I watched the expression on the doctor's face. When he frowned I knew it was the last thing he wanted to hear. Sensing the significance of the moment I said, "Maybe I can move them a little. Please let me try again. Yes, I'm sure they're moving now."

I closed my eyes and gave out one big push. *Hell*, I thought, *it's like lifting heavy weights, maybe because of the casts. Oh, God, please let me move them just a little. God, please.* "Sir, I can feel them moving now."

I opened my eyes to look down at my foot. I could see the toes on the right foot move ever so slightly, but those on the left didn't budge. I had the sensation of movement but there was no response at all. It was as if the toes were dead.

"Please, sir, let me try again."

"Just take it easy, Eilert. You've had extensive damage to the peroneal nerve. It's probable that if the leg isn't amputated, there will be no movement of the leg at all."

I pushed my head back and took a deep breath. For some reason the idea of amputation seemed more acceptable than carrying around a dead pin forever. Damn, what a choice. Either way it was all the same—the leg was lost.

"Listen, son, it's possible that *walking* will be a blessing. Did you play any organized sports in school?"

"Yes, sir, track and football in high school and football in college. Most of all I loved to run. It was like being in another world. Whenever I got depressed I'd just start running and everything would be right with the world and me. How can I cope without my legs?"

"Look, marine. Had it not been for your legs you would be dead. The heavy muscles in your calves and thighs absorbed the blast. Just be glad you're alive. Your legs gave you years of enjoyment and now they've kept you alive to enjoy all the other pleasures life can offer."

I'd never thought of my wounds in that context. Hell, that made some sense. "Thank you, sir, I'll remember that. Thanks again for coming by."

"I'm happy we were able to help as much as we did. I'll see you a little later in the OR."

"Thank you, sir . . . later."

MR. & MRS. RICHARD L. EILERT . . .
A REPORT RECEIVED THIS HEADQUARTERS ON 30 NOV 67
REVEALS THAT THE CONDITION OF YOUR SON PFC
RICHARD E. EILERT USMC REMAINS SERIOUS AND HIS
PROGNOSIS GOOD. YOU ARE ASSURED THAT HE CONTINUES
TO RECEIVE THE BEST OF MEDICAL CARE. YOUR ANXIETY IS
REALIZED AND YOU WILL BE KEPT INFORMED OF ANY
SIGNIFICANT CHANGE IN HIS CONDITION. HIS MAILING
ADDRESS REMAINS THE SAME.
                          WALLACE M. GREENE JR. GEN. USMC
                          COMMANDANT OF THE MARINE
                          CORPS

"Eilert, can you hear me? Come on, Sleeping Beauty. You've been kissed, sucker." I looked up, my eyes unable to open. Then gradually the form of a corpsman appeared in front of my face.

"Damn you, squid, I was having one hell of a dream, and they're hard to come by in the bush. Now I have to start all over again."

The corpsman grinned. "You jarheads are really messed up."

Pain started again. I hurt in so many places it was difficult to explain where it hurt the worst. Pain shots came regularly, usually without my asking for anything. The swelling in my legs was so bad that the cast always seemed tight. I'd lost track of how many times I went to the operating room, but during each surgery the old casts had to be removed in order to get at the wounds, and new casts put on afterward. I began to lose track of time, first the hour, then the day.

Around one o'clock in the morning a hot jolt of pain ran through my body. "Please, Doc—pain med, hurry. Oh, God, hurry."

My legs were on fire, the pain so bad that perspiration and tears rolled down my face. The corpsman scurried around for the shot and was quick to drive the needle home. "There, that'll help I'm sure. Listen, Rick, you've been out for about twelve hours. It's been a long time since your last shot but rather than wake you for an injection we decided to let you sleep as long as possible. You needed that as much as anything. The medication was just wearing off. Don't worry about it. Relax. Let the shot ease the pain."

I looked over at the Oriental patient who had been moved next to me and was moaning about something. Doc said, "Oh, that's some ARVN officer. He ain't really hurt bad. He shot himself while he was cleaning his weapon and he's been telling everyone that he caught it up at the Rock Pile. Damn, that pisses me off. As if we don't have enough to do. These ARVN officers think their shit don't stink. Hell, they prance around here like so many peacocks. When, or if, they get in the field they call the marines in to get them out of the shit." I was surprised to find a corpsman who felt the way the marine grunts did.

"You're right, Doc. Every time I've been around those jerks it was always to get their asses out of trouble. Then they take credit for our work and the rear goes along with it to keep them happy."

"While you were getting carved up, our boy had his girl friend come in and she was crying like anything. Christ, what a stink. Just before she left, she put her hand under the sheet and administered the paradise stroke. Poor fellow, he's been moaning like this ever since she left. Oh, well, war is hell."

I smiled. "Yeah, but *combat* is a mother fucker." The two of us laughed, though it hurt me even to smile.

"Rick, I heard that you're leaving tomorrow for Da Nang and then back across the pond to the world."

"Hey, that's fantastic. Imagine, I'm really going to get home, just in time for Christmas. . . . Man, that's great. Say, thanks again, Doc."

A little after six in the morning, as soon as the corpsman saw me open my eyes, he came over with a pain shot.

"Got some chow for you this morning, compliments of the U.S. Navy. So it's only juice and milk—it has to taste better than that jungle breath you got. When was the last time you brushed your teeth?"

"About five weeks ago. The damn toothbrush fell apart on me. I've been using my finger ever since."

"Man, that's gross. Here, try to drink this down." The corpsman held the glass to my mouth, but I was so weak that he had to prop up my head as well. It was such a long time since I had drunk anything, and the juice was so cool. For the last four months it had been warm rice-paddy water, warm swamp water, warm river water; and, when the occasion arose, beer could be dropped by air, warm . . . Carling's Black Label.

"Man, that's great. Can I have some more? The cold feels so good on my throat. Man, that's some good shit."

"OK, just a little. We don't want you puking all over. If you start to heave hold on, 'cause you're going to hurt beaucoup, especially with that throat wound."

I didn't care. It had been so long since I'd had a treat this nice, and I was only interested in feeling good about something . . . anything.

"Here, Rick, got something for you to take home." He held out a Johnson & Johnson Band-Aid can filled with shrapnel and one bullet. "Just some goodies I took out of you." He smiled.

"Thanks, Doc. Man, this thing is pretty damn heavy. Hell, grenades didn't seem that heavy when I was throwing them at Charlie. There's a hell of a lot of metal in those damn things. Thanks, Doc, thanks for everything."

Moments later several corpsmen came carrying stretchers. The first to be taken out were the less severe cases, usually ambulatory, then those with single leg wounds, then everyone else. Nobody looked back as he left.

I was one of the last to board the aircraft. As they carried me across the landing strip, I recalled how I'd been brought in only four days before. *Damn*, I thought, *very efficient assembly-line processing. Sew 'em together, dope 'em up, and send 'em out . . . next!*

My stretcher went in through the rear of the aircraft. The interior was a maze of stretchers. Along the walls the wounded were stacked two high. In the center of the aircraft were two stretchers, side by side, stacked three high. The wounded were shoulder to shoulder. This made steerage on the *Titanic* look roomy. As soon as the last stretcher was in place, the rear ramp went up and the aircraft began to taxi. It was a very bumpy ride, but apart from groans it was very quiet. As the aircraft began to rise there was an immediate sense of relief. But that was short-lived.

Suddenly we heard the sound of metal hitting metal. Everyone knew instantly that some crazy son of a bitch was firing at the plane. There was no place to run, even if you could. I was lying on the bottom center, and I turned my head to the right just as the plane began a sharp right bank. I saw three tracer rounds pop through the floorboard right underneath one of the stretchers along the bulkhead. The rounds passed through both men stacked up on the stretchers, and as they did, both bodies rose up like dolls and dropped back down. They were dead instantly. Blood from the top rack drained through the bullet hole beneath the body to the rack below, and the blood from the bottom rack spilled onto the deck of the aircraft. I watched as the little rivers of blood and goo splashed from side to side each time the plane maneuvered. Some of the other wounded had been hit again and the corpsmen did all they could. Sounds of men cursing filled the air; someone from an upper berth asked one of the ambulatory patients to have the pilot radio back to Phu Bai—"Have security find that mother fucker and cut his nuts off"—and to request a reply. The pilot radioed the message.

In the middle of it all, I felt something warm and wet running down the side of my head. Since both of my forearms had been broken I couldn't reach up to locate the source of this new sensation. "Corpsman up!" I yelled. I had company instantly, a ten-foot-tall helper. "What's the problem?" I'd seen some big boys but this guy was the biggest of them, though the fact that I was on the bottom stretcher may have made him look somewhat larger than life. For a moment I forgot why I'd summoned this devil, but I figured my memory had better return quickly. Mr. Too Tall didn't look like the kind of a guy that likes wasting time.

"Doc, I'm feeling warm, wet stuff running down the other side of my head. I think maybe some stitches got torn out during all that commotion." Too Tall examined. "Hold on a minute. I can't see much. There's blood all over your head. I'll get something to wipe it off. Be right back."

The corpsman washed away the blood and the stitches became visible, but no blood came out. It was dark down near the floor and the corpsman was having difficulty locating the source of the blood flow. He got down on his hands and knees and reached over my stretcher looking for another possible wound. "Tell you what, I can't find any wound open—maybe you got hit by some metal fragments when those rounds came crashing through the deck before. There's blood all over you and your stretcher." He called over another corpsman with a flashlight. "Hold that light up here."

"Hey, Gary, I found your marine's wound. This guy up here has half his face gone."

"No shit, Jack. Let's see." He rose to his feet to check it out. "You're right. He must have caught the round when we banked to avoid all that gunfire. Damn, it just doesn't seem fair. Get a body bag and help to get this rack down. We better check every rack again."

I stared up at the rack above me. *Oh, hell,* I thought. *This guy's poor parents are all excited about their son coming home. All the happiness of knowing he's still alive. Hell, they probably called all the relatives, his girl, and his friends to tell them the good news. Imagine the poor slob that has to go and tell the family that their son is dead. What a lousy job that is. I wonder what his name is, what he liked or disliked. Why is it that you come all this way, all you've been through, only to be killed going back home. What a crummy world.*

The plane began its descent into Da Nang. The pilot directed the corpsmen to secure everything and added on the intercom, "Just received message from Phu Bai. Mr. C has been located near end of runway. He now has dick in mouth. That's the end of transmission." A quiet cheer went up, along with some applause. I had some trouble, but I managed a half a smile. Payback is hell.

After landing, the aircraft was quick to unload its cargo, in case some unfriendly forces started to rocket the base, as was often the case. The ramp went down and corpsmen poured into the craft, removing the stretchers to the proper wards. This was the Navy hospital in Da Nang. The wounded arrived here from all field hospitals in I Corps, Vietnam. This hospital was a staging area for the transport of the wounded back to the States.

I went to an orthopedic ward, as did most of the others. This time, not only did I have a warm, dry rack with clean sheets, but also a TV. As I was put in my rack, another corpsman came up, checked my wrist ID, and administered a pain shot.

"Hey, Doc, what's on the tube now?"

"Probably your favorite program, *Combat.*" A roar of laughter went up. We watched the show and our laughter continued. I was laughing so hard I was crying from tearing the stitches in the side of my mouth. "This is the funniest show I've ever seen. Can you see a squad walking down a trail like that? Hell, one blasting cap would kill the whole bunch of them. Look at that point man walking down that road like he was going shopping down State Street in Chicago." Someone from two racks down yelled, "Of course he's bopping around like that. He has a script and the script says no bad guys in the area and no boom-booms to hurt Mr. C. Stunning. Don't you marines understand—we should have been issued scripts, too." The laughter continued until the chow cart came in. As quickly as the conversation had started, it ended. I hoped that maybe I could get some real food. No such luck. I saw a corpsman walking toward me with a tray of juices.

"Eilert?"

I had straws in my glasses so that once the bed was raised, all I'd need do would be to tilt my head forward on a straw and suck. *Damn it, I thought, I feel like a mummy. Casts on each leg up to my crotch, and Ace wraps on both arms up past the elbow. Man, would I be a fun date, especially at the passion pit. Hell, they'd use me to hang the speaker on. Oh well, looks like I'll win the Monk-of-the-Month award. Can't get in trouble lying in bed surrounded by plaster and elastic.*

After the evening meal, things in the ward settled down considerably. A melancholy atmosphere took over. To me it appeared that until this very moment hardly anyone had thought about his own ability to cope with his injuries.

At first the idea seemed too difficult to comprehend. Back on the line, whenever there was time to relax, people would gather around from all over the perimeter to discuss everything from praying to pussy. Talk of how you'd rather lose a leg or an arm, just as long as you got home alive. No one really thought that would be hard to deal with. I looked down at my legs then scanned the room. For the first time, it dawned on me that I was a gimp now and forever. *Hell, I thought, even if they don't cut off my leg it's just going to hang there and be an ornament.* It wasn't a question of how *I* would get by, but rather how the people back home would adjust. *Damn, three days ago I was humping eighty pounds of gear around, plus my weapon and ten pounds of sweat. Now I can't even scratch my ass.*

"Did you say something? Hey, you with the long legs—did

you say something?" I turned my head to my right. The guy in the rack next to me was staring at me. "Did you say something?" the young marine asked again.

"No, I'm sorry," I said. "I guess I'm just talking to myself out loud. Hi. My name's Eilert. My friends call me Rick."

"My name is Graham, Dave Graham. Glad to meet you. I hope everything's all right."

"Yeah, everything is five by five. I'm just feeling sorry for myself."

"I know exactly what you're talking about." Dave pulled back the sheets that were covering him to his waist. Both his legs were gone above the knees. "You know, Rick, I never realized how much I loved to run until I woke up to find my legs gone. Hell, my dick's longer than my legs now."

"Don't keep that a secret, Dave—you'll get more dates than you can handle." The two of us laughed.

"Never thought of it that way. Thanks, Rick, I'll remember that. What hospital are they sending you to?"

"Great Lakes Naval Hospital near Chicago."

"Damn, that's a shame. I'm getting sent off to Philly for some new pins. I wish you were going there, too. Being in the hospital can be boring as hell."

"I know, I remember when I got my tonsils out. I was probably in for two or three days, but what a drag. The women didn't even turn me on . . . of course I was only six then, but children are impressionable."

"Rick, you're nuts. They're going to lock you up. How the hell did you ever get in the Crotch?"

"That was easy. When I was standing in line after taking my physical, they asked everyone who could prove they passed college math to step forward. Then they asked for everyone that could stand up in a bathtub filled with water while standing on two bars of soap. Then they asked for all those who could play piano. Then this huge marine gunney walked in the room. 'OK, listen up, people,' he said with a bunch of rocks in his mouth. 'Those of you who stepped forward that passed college math, go to room A. You're in the Air Force. Those of you who can stand up in a bathtub filled with water with a bar of soap under each foot, go to room B. You're in the Navy. Those people who claim they can play piano, go to room C. You're in the Army. The rest of you people get in the shit house. You're now in the Marine Corps.'"

36

"Shit, Rick, they should have made you an officer, either in intelligence or as an artillery spotter. You know them, don't you. They have you set up an ambush against your own people, or have you call in a strike on your position."

Now it seemed everyone, including the corpsmen, was laughing. A nurse walked in. "All you people settle down. Get back to your racks. I don't want any more noise in here. Go to sleep."

As she walked away, a voice from the far end said, "She looks much better without that moustache." Laughter broke out again.

Next morning, we were all moved from our racks to stretchers laid on top of gurneys. Nurses and corpsmen passed through administering pain meds, and a second group checked each patient's personal gear as it was secured for the journey home. Shortly thereafter they began taking the wounded out to four waiting aircraft. As before, I was one of the last to go aboard. The stretcher arrangement was similar to that on the flight from Phu Bai to Da Nang.

The engines of the C-141 began to roar. The ramp in the rear of the plane slowly began to rise. The craft started to taxi toward the runway. I craned my neck to watch the ramp close. Monkey Mountain was in view, as were some blue-green tracer rounds from an AK-47. *Goddamn, Charlie is doing it again— firing at the plane.* I began to break out in a cold sweat. My body felt numb. It was like those dreams where someone's chasing you. You're moving in slow motion and the pursuer is traveling at the speed of sound. For me the plane wasn't moving fast enough. The ramp was closed now and I could feel the airspeed increase. We were airborne. I closed my eyes and murmured, "Sweet Jesus, thank you."

It was as if a terrific weight had been lifted from my body. Even though I'd been told I was going back to the world, I couldn't believe it would happen. Like when I was a child and my parents continually told me they would take me to Disneyland. It wasn't really happening until we were in the car and on our way.

MR. & MRS. RICHARD L. EILERT
YOUR SON, PRIVATE FIRST CLASS, RICHARD E. EILERT,
U.S.M.C. WAS SCHEDULED TO BE MEDICALLY AIR
EVACUATED TO THE UNITED STATES AND ASSIGNED TO

THE U.S. NAVAL HOSPITAL, GREAT LAKES, ILL., FOR
FURTHER TREATMENT. THE COMMANDING OFFICER OF
THAT HOSPITAL WILL NOTIFY YOU UPON HIS ARRIVAL. IT IS
RECOMMENDED THAT YOU DO NOT PROCEED TO THE
HOSPITAL UNTIL ADVISED OF HIS ARRIVAL BY THE
COMMANDING OFFICER.

> WALLACE M. GREENE, JR.
> GENERAL U. S. M. C.
> COMMANDANT OF MARINE CORPS.

The plane's route took us first to Yokosuka, Japan, then to Anchorage, Alaska, Scott Air Force Base, St. Louis, and Glenview, Illinois. The first leg of the flight went fairly quickly. I was so doped up that sleep seemed to be all I could do. When conscious I could see legs moving back and forth down the aisle. There was a canvas partition in the center of the aircraft, probably for privacy, separating the stretchers that were side by side. I could hear moans occasionally, but for the most part the men stayed extremely calm and quiet. The drone of the engines muffled all conversation. Yelling was the only way to get attention, but since my throat was swollen and extremely sore, I bit the bullet.

In Yokosuka the plane touched down with considerable difficulty. The left tire hit the runway first and then the right banged down, jolting the fragile cargo. The nose slammed down and the pilot reversed engines immediately, causing the patients to toss about and tearing some stitches. My casts hit each other and sent white-hot shooting pains driving up from my feet through my back. A wound in the side of my head was bounced against a post next to my stretcher. The wound was already badly swollen and the stitches were digging into the flesh. Blood began to rush down my face and the side of my head. As soon as the engines shut down, the wounded began to yell and curse the pilot.

"Oh, that doesn't look too good," a nurse said. "Let me get my first-aid kit and clean some of this blood off of you." She returned quickly, gave me a pain shot, and began to wipe some of the blood off. She applied a patch of gauze against the cut on my head, then finished the job of cleaning me up.

I didn't say anything, just kept my eyes fixed on hers. *Lord*, I thought, *it's been so long since anyone has cared enough to be kind to me.* I'd almost forgotten what tenderness was. Just the touch of her soft hands seemed alien. After being on the big camp-out in the bush, not only my body but also my mind had become callous. I just wanted affection for a change.

The young nurse was a wizard with all the men aboard. It had been so long since they'd had an understanding woman to talk to they poured their hearts out to her. She reassured them about the girls waiting for them and bolstered a few egos with some devilish flattery.

After she finished tending the head wound, she read the name tag on my blanket. "R. Eilert, 2359226. What do your friends call you?"

"Most everyone calls me Rick." Now I felt butterflies in my stomach.

"Where are you from, Rick? Got a girl back home?"

"Chicago. Actually Palatine, Illinois. The family moved to the suburbs some time ago. I've got a girl I love an awful lot, and I know she's waiting for me, but how can I expect her to want me now that I'm all gimped up? Hell, she's a young, pretty girl—why would she or anyone want to be saddled with a wheelchair?"

"Come on, Rick. First of all, remember how lucky you are. You're going to live, if nothing else, to see her one more time. If marriage isn't for her now it's only because she hasn't had to grow up as fast as you. That's an important commitment for a young girl. Look at your relationship with her through *her* eyes. If you give her half a chance, maybe she'll see that your love is more important than strong legs and arms."

"The hell with my girl. Would you marry me?"

She laughed. "That's the third proposal I've had since leaving Da Nang. You marines move pretty quick."

"Yes, but I'm different than the rest of those animals. I respect you."

Again she laughed. "That's what the last guy told me. We're going to take off in just a few minutes. I have to check all the rest of those animals before we go. I'll talk to you later." She smiled as she moved away and gave me a wink. When the Coffee Brigade left the aircraft, the ramp was raised again, there was a short taxi, then the pilot put the pedal to the metal and we were off.

I was unconscious from Japan to Alaska, and after leaving Anchorage I woke up to see the legs of two nurses working on a man up one rack and down two on my side of the plane. Then they walked away and the legs of two corpsmen appeared in the same area. As soon as they laid a plastic bag on the floor I knew someone had died. Sure enough, they laid a dead man on it, zipped it up, and carried it back to where the other body bags were stacked. One of the corpsmen passed by and I asked, "Hey, Doc, would you please ask the nurse to come back here? I feel really warm."

"Sure thing . . . count it done." Within a few minutes she was kneeling next to me.

"The corpsman said you're complaining of feeling warm. Let me take your vital signs and temperature." While she held my hand, taking my pulse, I could feel my heart jumping. *Damn, she's so beautiful*, I thought.

"You're right, your pulse is a little fast." Then she pulled the thermometer from my mouth. Holding it next to the flashlight, she checked and rechecked the reading. "Rick, your temperature is very high. We have to bring it down." She turned. "Corpsman, listen, we need to pack Rick here in ice. His temp is almost one hundred five. Hurry."

"Yes, ma'am. Did you want to rub him down with alcohol as well?"

"That's right, all nine yards. The works." I started getting somewhat concerned. I did feel warm, but this seemed like lots of unnecessary work. Never having been sick before, other than with childhood diseases, I decided that maybe this was how being really sick felt. *Hell, this isn't so bad*, I thought. The nurse returned quickly with bags of ice, packing them all around my body. After that she rubbed me down with alcohol. She pulled the blanket down to my casts, exposing my privates. "Wait one," I bellowed. "I'm very modest. You're not going to rub me down there. That's the only thing that still works."

"Don't worry, Rick, I'll just rub alcohol on your belly and abdomen. You know, I've done this before."

"That's fine, but I haven't been rubbed there in seven, count 'em seven, months. Anyway she said she loved me. I wanted this time to be special." She laughed so hard that she started coughing.

"Rick, you must stay awake all night making up all these stories. Someday a smart young lady will feed you just that much bull and you'll end up marrying her."

"Good God, don't say that. I have enough trouble living with myself, let alone someone like me. I have to tell you this—

when I heard you tell the corpsman to pack me in ice I thought you had me moving into a dead bag, just like that poor marine that just bought the farm."

"Yes, what a waste. To have come this far only to die going home. He still would have a lot of trouble if he had lived. Both of his legs were blown off. He was a real sweetheart."

"What was his name?"

"David Graham."

"Oh, damn. Jesus H. Christ. Him and I stayed up half the night before we left. We were joking and laughing. He looked real good, and what a dynamite personality. Shit, when is all this hurting and dying going to stop? Five days ago I'd never have befriended a guy like him because out in the bush nothing lasts, except the hell of it all. As soon as I let my guard down, this crazy world spits out a little more of the good around me."

"I'm sorry, I didn't realize he was a friend of yours. I've been flying this trip for the last two months and each trip I get a little bit harder, a little more callous. Most of the other girls feel the same way. When I started flying these med-i-vacs, I'd talk with all the men and watch them suffering. I wanted to protect them from everything bad. But they'd die like Graham, and my heart would break. Now I can't cry anymore."

"Why not do something else?"

"I'm finishing up this month and that's it. I just can't take the pain. I know that sounds crazy coming from someone physically well like me. But after a while your pain becomes mine. That's the way it works with me."

"Are you positive you don't want to get married?"

She gave me a huge smile. "Thank you, Rick. It's nice to talk to someone instead of talking at them. I'm supposed to be getting married this spring. I just hope I can get everything sorted out beforehand."

"Your intended is one lucky man. I wish you well."

"Thanks. I've got to do my rounds. I'll talk to you later. Get some rest."

"Good-bye. How long will I have to lay in this ice?"

"Not too long, just until we can get your temp down to a safer range. See you in a little while."

I looked back at the body bags. *How come Graham died and I didn't? Come on, Lord, help me out. Why do I have to be the one with a shattered body?* I couldn't help but think, *I haven't committed any great sins in my life. Why am I being punished now?* Of course I knew there would be no answers.

The corpsman came by after about forty-five minutes to reclaim the ice packs and administer another pain shot. He walked away without a word. *Hell, he didn't even check to see if his patient was awake. He must be a union man,* I thought to myself.

A clicking sound came over a loudspeaker: "Be advised we have just crossed the Canadian-U.S. border. *Welcome home.*" Everyone that could clapped his hands and cheered. *"We're home, back in the world, across the pond."* Talking and laughing filled the plane. I couldn't yell or clap, but I could feel the butterflies moving around in my stomach and tears welling up. *Oh, my God . . . it's all really happening. I'm home at last. Lord, I'm home.*

# 3

WHEN I REGAINED consciousness the plane was already on the ground, at the ramp. We were loaded on a bus. It was a very short ride, but the sight of neon lights in the distance and the music on the radio next to the driver were confirmations that I was back in a secure area. Still, I couldn't escape the feeling that an ambush was about to be sprung.

The bus pulled up in front of some old 1940s-era barracks. One by one we were carried inside and I was put at the end of the ward, next to the nurses' station. After all the patients had been assigned racks, a nurse moved to the center of the ward and waved her hands over her head to get everyone's attention.

"May I have your attention, please. Listen up. We have five phones here so that you can call home. We will start two phones at each end of the ward and one in the solarium. You will each have three minutes on the phone, so get an idea of what you're going to say. There are a lot of people here, so give everybody a chance to make their calls. Be brief. You're at Scott Air Force Base—just outside St. Louis. You must make these calls collect."

I felt lucky. My rack was the first one in front of the nurses' desk. The nurse handed me the phone, then realized I couldn't bend my arm to hold the receiver. She did the dialing and got the call through. She placed the receiver down between my head and a pillow. I could hear the phone ringing. Suddenly there was a voice at the other end. What should I say!

"Hello." It was my sister Linda's voice.

"I have a collect call for anyone from Richard Eilert. Will you accept the charges?" I could hear a commotion in the background. Then my father's voice: "Hello, operator. You have a collect call from whom?"

"The call is from Mr. Richard Eilert. Will you accept the charges?"

"Oh, good God, of course."

"Hello, Dad. This is I, me. Christ, it's great to hear your voice. How is everybody? Listen, I can only talk for three minutes."

"God, son, we all have been so worried. How are you, Rick?"

"I'm fine, just busted up some. Dad, I'm at Scott Air Force Base near St. Louis. We'll spend the night here, then tomorrow we fly into Glenview, then bus it up to Great Lakes. So if you've got any questions, phone them tomorrow. They have visiting hours and all."

"It's so good to hear your voice, to know you're home. Listen, your mother wants to talk to you. I'll talk to you tomorrow. Boy, how we've missed you. Bye, son."

"Hello, Rick. Oh, God. How we've been worrying. How are you? Does it hurt a lot? It's so good to hear your voice." I could hear my sisters yelling in the background.

"Mom, listen, I'm fine. . . ." I was sure my mother wasn't listening to a word I said. She was just so happy I was on the other end of the line. Each time she asked a question, she started another before I could reply. Still, just to hear her voice was all I wanted. Then, in order of age, my sisters got on to say welcome home.

"Rick, this is Jan. We're so glad you're home safe."

"It's great to hear your voice, too. Listen, I'm running out of time. Please call Cheryl. Tell her where I am. I'll try to call her later, and if I can phone it has to be collect and for only three minutes."

"I'll take care of it as soon as we hang up. See you soon, good-bye. . . . Here's Linda."

"Yes, it's really me, Linda. I'm alive."

"You're alive. I know you missed me the most so you'll want to talk to me the longest. . . . JoAnn was standing here to say hello but she got so excited she started to pee in her pants, so she went to the bathroom." I could hear a door slam in the background. I started chuckling—Linda and JoAnn always made me laugh.

My brother Bobby was only five years old. After sharing a bedroom with him for the first four years of his life I felt almost like a father to him.

"Hello, Ricky. Are you all done being in the war?"

"Yes, Bobby, I'm all done being in the war."

"Will you come home now and play with me?"

"Yes, Bobby, I'll be coming home soon to play with you. Let me talk to Dad now. Good-bye, Bobby.

"Dad, listen, I've got to hang up now. I'll talk with you all tomorrow when I see you."

"Sure, son. It's great to have you back home. Good-bye, Rick."

The nurse standing right next to my rack took the phone to the next man. I pushed my head back into the pillow. There was a huge lump in my throat that just wouldn't go away. I

began to rehash the conversation in my mind, just like the letters I'd received in Vietnam that I read and reread over and over again. Gosh, it was wonderful just to hear their voices. I felt so warm inside saying their names: Mom, Dad, Janet, Linda, JoAnn, Bobby. And Mary, who was born while I was away. *I wonder if they'll ever know how much I loved and missed them. They seemed so surprised to hear my voice. Am I hurt worse than I think? If only I could talk to them a little longer. I couldn't have talked for three minutes. Three minutes never went by that fast before.* I'd hidden my emotions for so long that I'd forgotten what they felt like. And then I began to think of all the friends I'd watched die. Why had they all been denied this wonderfully simple moment? *Why do I feel like it's wrong for me to be happy? Why do I feel it should be one of them here instead of me? I know I should feel sad, but I don't. I'm happy to be here. What a lousy friend I must be. I hate myself for being alive.*

The phone went from bed to bed, each man trying to make the most of his three precious minutes. Once their calls were completed they lay staring at the ceiling in a daze. I flagged down one of the Red Cross workers helping with the phones.

"May I please use the phone again after everyone's completed their calls? I'd like to phone my girl." She nodded her head and gave me a wink.

*How am I going to talk to her when she gets on the line? Hell, I could hardly think of the right words to say when I spoke with my parents. She may be out, probably on a date. What if her father answers and won't accept the charges?* I started to panic and considered not placing the call.

The Red Cross worker came to my bedside, plugged the phone into the wall jack, got the operator on the line, and placed the call. She jammed the receiver in between my head and the pillow. "Just three minutes now, no more. We have to turn the lights off. All of you have a big day tomorrow." I just nodded.

The phone was ringing now. The lump in my throat fell down to my stomach. Suddenly she answered.

"Rick, is that you? Rick, are you there?"

All I could say was "God, how I've missed you." I heard her crying, and thought I would, too.

"Cheryl, please stop crying. I only have three minutes."

She laughed, "Rick, I can't believe you're really home. Is the pain bad? When will you be home?" The questions flowed without time for any answers.

"Listen, Cheryl, I'm fine, just a little banged up. I'll be home soon. They're sending me to Great Lakes. My folks have all that information so phone them later. Forget all that now. All I want is to hear your voice." She continued with questions, but I couldn't make out what she was saying. But oh, God, just to hear her voice.

"Damn, my time is up. . . . I love you very much, I've missed you so."

"Oh, Rick, I've missed you, too, and I love you. I'm just so happy you're finally home. Good-bye, Rick."

As the Red Cross worker took away the receiver, I could hear her crying. "Thank you, ma'am, for those great three minutes."

I closed my eyes, my heart filled with contentment, and fell asleep quickly.

There were knife-sharp pains in my left leg, and pressure. It felt as if my leg was swelling inside that case. I rang the buzzer for the nurse, biting my lip to keep from screaming. "Hurry nurse, please," I kept saying under my breath. I felt something warm under the left cheek of my ass. *Oh, great, the catheter must have fallen out and now I've got piss all over my rack.* The nurse arrived quickly.

"Nurse, may I have a pain shot? My leg is killing me."

"Sure, I'll be right back." Since her desk was next to my rack behind a glass partition, she was able to check the narcotics log quickly. "Here you are. This should help pretty soon. Where does it hurt?"

"My left leg. It feels as if the cast is on too tight. I'm embarrassed to tell you this, but I think my catheter fell out. It feels as if I urinated all over my rack." She just smiled and pulled the sheets back to investigate. She put her hand against my butt and quickly pulled it away. "It's definitely wet. Let me get my flashlight." Returning to my bed she turned on the flashlight and saw a puddle on the floor beneath my bed. Slowly she raised the light up along the side of the bed to the cast. It was blood. I was hemorrhaging.

First the nurse phoned the hospital, then the doctor on call. She woke the medics and got help from another ward. I was still oblivious as to why some blood was so important. *After all*, I thought, *bleeding is part of being shot, isn't it?*

The nurse returned and tried to find the source of the bleeding. A small army of people gathered around. They brought in a large light to hold as they worked on me from all directions. One medic, who was pushing down on my chest so that I wouldn't try getting up, asked if I felt all right.

"Sure, Doc, I feel great. Now I know how Humpty-Dumpty felt."

The medic smiled. Then the ward doors swung open as the ambulance attendants charged in with their little portable stretcher. I was amazed that this many people could be so quiet. Nobody in the ward woke up as the four medics moved me onto the stretcher.

The hospital was only a few blocks away and I was rushed into the emergency room. Doctors began to cut off the cast on my left leg. I heard the whine of a mini-saw and looked down to see somebody putting it to my leg. One of the nurses said, "Don't worry, the blade won't cut the skin. It just cuts the plaster." Another nurse gave me a shot while a medic standing over my head was setting all the IV bottles on a pole. Finally the cast had been cut in half down both sides and they started prying the two halves apart with cast separators. But the dried pus, blood, and flesh stuck to the cast. The pain became unbearable as they tore the top half away from the leg. My body heaved and I banged my right arm down on the table. Although it was broken it wasn't in a cast, and the pain from the arm shot up through my neck.

"Please knock me out. Damn you all, please knock me out."

The pain was so terrible I could hardly breathe, let alone scream. Once the top of the cast was off completely, a new problem was revealed. The leg itself was bound mummylike in gauze and pieces of cotton. The mass was brown, red, and yellow, like giant scabs over scabs, soaked in blood and pus. The gauze had become part of the leg. It was almost impossible to get a handle on anything, to distinguish gauze from flesh, and when chunks of gauze were ripped away the pain was excruciating. The medics and nurses tried to be as gentle as possible but it didn't matter. I prayed either to die or to pass out; I didn't care which as long as it was right now. They gave me more shots but without any luck. I was hyperventilating and couldn't settle down. Mercifully, they finished pulling away the bandages on the top part of my leg. I looked at the clock and noticed that it had taken thirty-five minutes. Now that they'd stopped the pain subsided. I felt if I had to go through that again I would rather die. Once I'd caught my breath I asked the medic to hold me up so I could see the leg. The medic obliged, lifting me up under my arms.

It was the first time I'd really seen my leg since I was wounded, and then the wounds had been covered by torn clothing and dirt. This . . . this was different. There was no flesh, only torn-up muscle, exposed bone, maggots, and blood. I screamed, "That's not my leg, that's nothing but a piece of mush. . . . This isn't my leg!"

A doctor walked into the room, looked at my leg, and turned to the charge nurse. "Where are the X rays on this man?"

"Here, sir." She hung the X rays up on clips over the fluorescent light.

I heard the doctor speaking in a low voice. "Look at this break here, and here, and here. Good God, the bones have been shattered in about forty places." He turned and held me by my shoulders. "Son, you're banged up pretty badly besides your hemorrhaging. I'll have to take you into the OR now. We have to cut away some of that dead flesh and plug that leak. We'll knock you out before we remove the rest of your cast."

"Thanks, Doc. This pain is driving me crazy." The doctor left the room to scrub for the operating room. One of the nurses wiped the sweat off my face. "Take it easy now, marine. I know it's been tough but it'll be over shortly."

"Thanks much. God, that was terrible. Worse than when I was hit. I never want to go through that again."

"Just relax. The medic here will take you into the OR now. Good-bye and the best of everything to you."

I was pushed into the operating room, where the anesthesiologist was waiting. The medics moved me from gurney to operating table, put me in fetal position, and administered a spinal. Almost instantly I went numb below my waist. "Thank God. At last the pain is gone. Thanks, Doc." A mask was placed over my face and gas administered. I was out for the count.

As soon as I came to the next morning, a medic came in carrying a shot and rammed it home. After a cold drink and a wash I started getting drowsy, when the door of my room swung open and in walked two big medics. "Come on, let's catch an airplane." They moved me gently but with terrific ease, laid me on the gurney, and carted me off down the corridors to an ambulance. Again, with the same agility, they swung me into the meat cart and gunned it to a waiting plane, where they laid my stretcher next to a group of windows. The plane was a DC-3, with regular seats in it, so that the stretcher was on top of the seat backs. As I lay watching the cars and roads below growing smaller and smaller, I felt a tap on my shoulder. It was the nurse from the flight that had brought me home from Nam. "Hi, marine. How are you doing?"

"God Almighty, I thought you had finished your flight in St. Louis. Isn't today your day off?"

"Yes, it is. But I heard that you and one of the other marines on board my flight had to have emergency surgery, so I decided to make sure you got home safely." I could see her eyes filling up with tears, and I thought I would start to cry, too.

"That was terrific of you. It means a lot that you cared that much. You looked like an angel when I first saw you and now I know I was right. I'll never forget this. You are one fantastic lady."

She blushed. Then the tears began to fall. Huge tears that dropped on my blanket. "Listen, you had better stop that. People will see my wet blanket and think I messed myself."

Laughing, she wiped her eyes and blew her nose. "You're impossible, absolutely certified nuts. I hope the Navy nurses will be able to handle you. I think the blast from that hand grenade fried your brains. Listen, I have to pass out medication to the rest of the guys. I'll be back after I've done my chores."

I smiled and nodded my head. I just couldn't get over her staying with the wounded all the way. What a wonderful lady. I rolled my head back toward the window, watching all the patchwork fields below. After all the time that I'd spent flying over nothing but jungle, forest, and mountains, it was good to see land that produced life instead of the decayed soil of life lost. I marveled at the beautiful geography, void of bomb craters and speckled with cars instead of tanks and gun emplacements.

As I gazed at the blue sky above and the green below, I recalled the last line of a poem called "Flight": "I have soared where eagles dare not roam. I have reached out my hand and touched the face of GOD." *Maybe the world is beautiful if you only look for it,* I thought. I nodded off to sleep and woke to the sound of the landing gear locking into place. I could see the racetrack and shopping plazas I'd played near ever since my family moved to the suburbs, and as the plane continued its descent I recognized more and more landmarks. Finally the wheels touched down and the plane taxied to a halt, shutting down its engines. I turned my head to look for the nurse but she was busy opening the door and moving the wounded down the steps to a waiting bus. First the ambulatory patients moved off. Then the stretchers. I was first of them. I could only halt at the doorway long enough to say good-bye. She reached over, cupping my head in her hands, and kissed me.

"Good-bye, Eilert, and the best of everything to you." The stretcher bearers continued down the stairs to the bus.

Inside the bus the stretchers were stacked two high and three long on each side, with the ambulatory patients standing in the center, holding on to the grab rails. As the bus doors closed I looked back to see my lovely lady standing in the doorway, waving. Then I thought, *Someday I'm going to see her again. Shit, I forgot to get her name and address.*

The bus began its trip to Great Lakes Hospital. I knew right away that I wasn't going to enjoy the ride. The bus driver slammed on his brakes at the stop sign as we left the base area. All the stretchers slid forward. My casts banged together, and one of the ambulatory patients fell on his arm. Then the bus driver gunned the engine, causing the same effect in reverse. The men were yelling and cursing at him to slow down and take it easy but he didn't pay them any mind. Suddenly the bus jumped as it passed over a railroad crossing, shaking everyone up again. Those on stretchers were tossed up in the air about two inches and slammed back down. The pain I felt was similar to the night before in the emergency room. I thought I was going to go crazy. "Slow this son of a bitch down!" I yelled.

The driver continued speeding down the highway, making no effort to avoid the potholes or ruts. Once, after slamming on the brakes at a stop light and causing screams of pain from almost everyone, he deliberately floored the accelerator from a dead stop, hitting a center-island curb with both the front and rear left tires. This caused one of the stretcher cases to fall off his rack onto the floor of the bus. The driver refused to stop to let the ambulatory patients help the man back into his stretcher.

I put my arm up against a rail in an effort to avoid slipping off myself, only to have the entire weight of the stretcher and my body banged into my arm, pinning it against the rail. At the next light, the driver hit the brakes. Again my stretcher slid forward. This time it freed my arm. I rolled my head to look out the window, hoping to find a landmark I could recognize. A station wagon filled with Mommy, Daddy, and the kids was just below my open window. I smiled at the little boy in the front seat between his parents. The sweet little boy just flipped me the bird. His parents thought it was pretty funny. I spat out the window, hitting the windshield. That made Daddy mad. I laughed. Even small victories had to do now.

Someone from the center of the bus yelled at the bus driver, "Hey, mother fucker, slow down!"

That was all the abuse the driver was going to take. He slammed the bus into park and stood up very slowly. "Who's the tough guy with the big mouth?"

I took one look at the guy and was glad I was in the back of the bus. This was the biggest, meanest black man I had ever seen. There, in the middle of the bus, was a lean, almost skinny patient with his arm in a cast up over his elbow, held close against his side by a sling wrapped around his neck. "I'm the one with the big mouth. I told you to slow down and drive nice. Was that sentence too long for you to understand?"

Hearing that remark the driver rushed at the marine, but was tripped by one of the other ambulatory patients. The driver hit the floor with a crash. When he started to pick himself up, he received a jungle boot in his face from Mr. Mean Lean, who then proceeded to pound the back of the big fellow's head with his cast until the plaster started to crumble. The driver was out, a small pool of blood forming around his mouth and nose. The men were cheering and cursing, and a chant went up to kill him. The ambulatory patients pulled the driver off the bus, his head bouncing off each of the passing stairs. They laid him in a ditch and removed his pants and shoes, while the bus was sitting in the middle of an intersection. It was a mini-coup, just fantastic, and we all were in hysterics. The ambulatory patients began driving the bus away. A patient with a good left arm drove and one with a good right shifted.

"Say, anybody know where this hospital is?"

I yelled, "Yeah, just keep going straight here about ten miles, then at One Seventy-six take a right all the way in."

Off we went slowly and easily, but no complaints. It was doubtful anyone would have complained anyway. It felt so good getting rid of the driver. Besides, it was funny as hell watching two wounded people driving a bus down the highway, grinding gears and having a ball doing it.

I was able to guide the bus, now known as the Gray Goose, all the way to the front gate, where I thought we might have some trouble. But the guard just waved us through. He'd probably done this a hundred times before. I'd been at the hospital several times, visiting a neighbor who'd been wounded in Vietnam. On many of those occasions I'd seen the buses being unloaded by the emergency room doors so my directions were perfect.

After the bus stopped outside the emergency room door, it was filled with corpsmen dressed in white. They took the stretchers off very carefully. The men were still in a lot of pain and even gentleness seemed cruel. Out of the corner of my eye I saw a massive wall of white standing next to my stretcher. It was one of the biggest men I'd ever seen. He was only six foot five or six, but wide, with huge arms and hands.

The enormous corpsman smiled at me as he gingerly picked up the foot of the stretcher. Another corpsman lifted the head and they carried me into the receiving room, where they gently transferred me from stretcher to gurney. The first one pulled out a large metal chart that had come with me and started writing in it. "Looks like you got pretty messed up. I see on your chart that they performed emergency surgery down at Scott."

I just nodded yes. "Say, Doc, can you get me something for the pain? I hurt bad enough but that damn bus driver really did a number on us."

"Was the driver a big black son of a bitch with a scar under his left eye?"

"That's him!"

"I'm surprised someone ain't killed him yet." He grinned.

A call came from across the room. "Hey, Chief, give me a hand, will you?" I laughed to myself. *Chief . . . he looks like a chief, but with his size I'd better watch out what I call him.* "Listen, I'll find out about getting you a shot after I'm done over there. Be right back."

Chief returned carrying a shot. I was really glad to see I wasn't forgotten. The horrible pain was starting again.

A doctor appeared. He was very serious and said nothing while he pulled out the chart and read all its contents. He wore dark-rimmed glasses and was balding but I paid no attention to him. Instead I watched Chief give me a small injection of Demerol.

"Well, Eilert, looks like you've been in a world of shit.

You're busted up pretty well, but hell, I've seen worse skiing accidents. We'll have you out of here in no time. I'm Dr. Boone. You'll be up on Three South. That's my ward. Keep your chin up. I know it hurts, but you'll be better soon." He went on to another gurney.

I was impressed by the doctor's manner and confidence. As he walked away he shouted orders to his big corpsman: "Chief, put Eilert here in the cast tex room on Three South. Cut that cast off his left leg and get a superstructure on his rack."

Chief immediately got in back of the gurney and began to wheel me out. He weaved the gurney through the first-floor hallways, cluttered with wheelchair patients and walking wounded using every imaginable type of prosthetic device. We stopped in front of one of the service elevators and waited, watching the floor numbers light up as the elevator came down. The doors opened and Chief shoved the gurney against one wall. The operator was a marine minus one arm. The corps had a job for everyone.

The elevator stopped at the second floor and picked up a patient on a gurney out of the operating room. He was bandaged like a mummy. Every extremity was covered and he was mumbling something as he tossed from side to side. No one spoke as we waited for the elevator to reach the third floor.

The elevator doors opened, and with just a twist of his wrist Chief pointed the meat wagon down the long gray corridor toward the ward. Gurneys lined the walls on both sides and patients sped by in their wheelchairs chasing one another.

"Chief, how long you been up here?"

"Just about a year," he stuttered, with a short pause between words.

"What's your real name, Chief?"

The big man smiled. "Emanuel Dioso. Do you know why they call me Chief?" he stammered.

I smiled. "Let me guess. Mexicans are called Poncho and guys with some Indian in them are called Tonto or Chief. Right?"

Chief laughed. "You marines are really something, always making jokes."

Later, I learned that Chief came from a small town in New Mexico. Of eleven children he was his mother's favorite. But he was so big and awkward the other children made fun of him and refused to include him in their games. He grew up alone and sought companionship in books, especially poetry. He shunned sports, not because he didn't have the talent, but to avoid the teasing that his size and awkwardness provoked.

Being poor, all the boys in his family worked after school. Emanuel was given hard labor because of his size and because it paid better than other jobs. It provided well for his family, but it convinced him that he'd rather use his brain than his back.

Upon graduation from high school he enlisted in the Navy. He chose Medical Corps school. He proved to be a natural and picked up everything quickly. Now his size drew no taunts. Instead, his comrades befriended him and made every effort to be with him, especially in bars.

The patients adored him. He was sensitive and gentle. He went out of his way to make his charges comfortable. His free time was spent running errands for the patients or writing letters for them. Wounded marines could make fun of him and joke with him. But no one else.

He was called Chief because of his Indian blood and looks. He felt great empathy for his marine brothers and wanted more than anything to join them in the jungles where he could help save lives the moment they were wounded.

"Say, Chief, call me Rick, will you? Calling me by my last name sounds too military."

"Sure. Fine by me, Rick. You're really going to like our ward. There's always lots of laughs and we got some really pretty nurses."

"Yeah, Chief, I can tell this is going to be fun and games. I thought that ass-wipe driving the truck was big . . . Chief, you make him look like Tom Thumb."

A wheelchair winged by the gurney, followed by another. "Holy shit, those people are going to crash and re-injure themselves. They're crazy!"

"Once you're on the ward a while you see things differently. Getting well is boring. Some guys have been up here eighteen months or more. . . . Well, here we are. This is home. Ward Three South. Hang loose a minute, I have to check you in."

A tall, very thin nurse walked up to the gurney. "Hello. I'm Miss Noland, the head nurse up here on the farm. How are you feeling?"

"Pretty good, but my legs are killing me. I mean really killing me."

Miss Noland looked at my chart. "You received a small dose of Demerol a little while ago. I'll call the doctor and see if we can't get another soon."

I felt relieved. "Say, Miss Noland. What's Doc Boone like?"

"He's the best here. Maybe even in the whole Navy. He may not seem very enthusiastic at first. He's hard to peg. He has a terrific memory. He can associate wounds with patients' names. Trouble is he doesn't match faces with names. Sometimes he may forget a face or a name, but never a wound."

She smiled and patted my arm. "I'll see if I can get the doctor and get some more pain medication."

I learned on my own that Dr. Boone was the best orthopedic surgeon in the Navy. He had magic fingers and an understanding of the marines he tended. If he'd been a company commander, we'd have followed him into hell itself. Doc Bone, as he was called, would bend over backward to save a badly wounded man's limb. Other doctors loved to cut, but not Doc Bone. Thus he also had a reputation in the hospital as a doctor who'd set a precedent rather than follow procedure.

He'd start his operations at five in the morning and work in the operating room all day and through the night and the next morning. In between operations he'd make his rounds and work the Orthopedic Clinic.

He didn't need to be announced on his ward. The grunts and groans of the patients he inspected let everyone know Dr. Boone was around. The good doctor had a viselike grip that brought tears to the eyes of the strongest among us, yet for him the men lay still. They knew it would hurt like hell, but if anyone could make things right, he could.

Patients from other wards with similar injuries would compare treatments. We were envied.

He wasted no time removing dressings and the pain was indescribable. Yet no one could convince us that our doctor wasn't the best in town. It was the "old-timers" that bore witness to his magic.

He was thirty-four years old. His looks made him out to be an average man, five foot ten, round-faced and full-bellied. He wore dark-rimmed glasses and his ears stood out from his head. He had a mild Texas drawl and an easy manner. His voice was always steady. He was honest and straightforward with everyone. He let them know the seriousness of their injuries and then laid out his plan for mending and recovery.

He had a sense of humor, dry and quick, but most of all he respected his men. He knew of their suffering and admired courage. He had no time for the weak. Courage should be as important on the ward as it was on the battlefield. The horror of the war zone was only the start of the wounded men's agony.

If a ward's doctor was looked up to it was because as long as their heads and asses were wired together the men had a real chance of living with their disabilities. It was the doctor who really made the difference.

I started to realize this when I first looked out past the long desk. Just above the entrance to the ward was a sign: NO PAIN, NO GAIN.

*You have got to be kidding*, I thought. It reminded me of all those jerk signs in football locker rooms and even in boot camp.

Standing around the desk were several corpsmen, with three nurses behind the desk preparing medications and organizing work details. Everyone was talking. Phones rang constantly. Out on the ward I heard TVs and radios blaring, all of them on different channels. The ward was packed with people, civilian and military. It was visiting hours. The racks were shoved very close together with just enough space in between for bedside lockers. There were metal structures over the beds supporting legs and arms in traction, with weights hanging over the end of the racks. Among all these people were Red Cross workers passing out cookies and punch. It was like a bazaar. The room was filled with cigarette smoke. It was stuffy and very warm, with a strong odor. A six-foot-high partition extended down the middle of the ward, forming two parallel aisles. Besides containing electrical and oxygen outlets for patients away from the side walls, the partition provided a small amount of privacy.

Chief walked back to the gurney and pushed it into a room marked CAST TEX.

"The nurse will be in shortly with your pain medication. In the meantime, we'll start cutting your cast off. What's the matter, Rick? You look a little pale."

"Chief, you got to be kidding me. I just had my old cast cut off last night. This is a new one. Please knock me out. For God's sake, please put me to sleep. I can't take it—the pain is horrible."

"Just take it easy, we have to take it off. The doctor didn't say anything about giving you gas, just to remove the cast. I'll get the nurse. Maybe she can call the doctor and get verbal approval for you."

Another corpsman walked into the room. "Rick, this is Crawford."

"Hi, Doc, glad to meet you." Crawford said nothing, just walked past the gurney, blowing plaster dust off the cast saw. I had a feeling that he and I were not going to be the best of friends. Crawford positioned himself at the foot of the rack, plugged the saw in, and hit the trigger—just to hear the scream of the engine. Then he began cutting the cast on the inside of my left foot.

"Wait, Doc, the nurse is supposed to phone the doctor and see if I can be put to sleep before you start cutting." Crawford smiled as he saw the terrified look in my eyes.

"Don't be a cracker ass. You think you're so damn tough. As soon as you get a little cut, you end up wanting gas to knock you out. Well, I don't buy it. I was told to cut this cast off and that's just what I'm going to do."

Chief held his hand up in Crawford's face, a hand so big that he could have picked him up by his head. "Let me ask the nurse first."

"OK, Chief, but hurry it up." Chief left quickly. Meanwhile, Crawford's face was turning red.

"You goddamn crybaby." I said nothing. I knew all I needed to do was piss this guy off and he would make sure it hurt. But my fear of the horrible pain outweighed the threat of Crawford's anger.

Chief came back into the room carrying a pain shot. "Here's the shot the doctor ordered for you. The nurse couldn't contact the doctor. She said the shot will have to do, and for us to get that cast off now."

My heart sank. "That's impossible. I can't stand that pain again. Please wait until the doctor gets back."

"I'm sorry, Rick, we have to go by the doctor's last order." Chief then held my shoulders down with a paralyzing pressure. Crawford smiled and gunned the saw once more. Without hesitation he commenced to cut from foot to crotch on the inside and outside of the cast on my left leg. Crawford refused to stop long enough to let Chief give me the shot. Chief put his arm across my chest to hold me down, then gave me the shot with his free hand.

The pain seemed even worse than the night before, maybe

58

because I knew what was coming next. Even though the cast had not yet been torn off, I could sense the agony of the corpsman pulling the blood- and pus-filled gauze away, tearing the flesh. I remembered seeing the little nerve endings wiggle after the gauze had been removed.

I kept hoping I'd pass out, but I didn't. Suddenly the saw's whining motor fell silent. "Oh, God, this is it. Chief, help me."

Chief saw the look of terror on my face. "Hold on, Rick. It'll be over in a few minutes."

I could feel the pressure caused by the cast separator as Crawford began to pull the two halves apart. Part of the leg was stuck to the top of the cast by scabs, dried blood, and pus. The bottom half was held in the same manner. When the cast began to come apart so did the tattered flesh. I was too weak and too tired to fight Chief's iron grip. Sweat and tears washed down my cheeks, my screams became whimpers, and my faith in a merciful God was gone forever. I'd heard men plead for mercy on the battlefield without response. Now I did the same thing without being heard.

The top of the cast was removed and Crawford began to pull at the leg resting in the bottom half of the cast. He slid one hand in under the ankle, and the other under the mid-calf. As he lifted the leg up, it sagged between his hands. It was like a mass of jello, as if there were no bone whatsoever.

Crawford laid the mass back in the cast shell. "Chief, get another corpsman. It'll take four hands to pull that leg out, and someone has to hold him down." Chief opened the door and yelled for someone to help. Another corpsman entered. "Smith, get some gloves on and help me pull this leg out of here." The new corpsman pulled his plastic surgical gloves on and moved into position to help.

I was getting sick to my stomach from the pain. The two corpsmen began lifting again, though the leg still fell between their hands. The cast still stuck to the bottom of my leg in places, and again they had to lay it back down. I was twisting in agony, my fingertips bleeding from the death grip I had on the side of the bed. One fingernail broke in two and stuck in my hand. Chief was mad as hell.

"Man, we're torturing this guy. Don't do anything else until I get a nurse." Smith and Crawford agreed and stepped back for a cigarette. Chief went to fetch a nurse. I was able to relax for a few moments until they returned.

The nurse surveyed the bloody mess, then came over and held my hand. "It's been pretty bad, hasn't it?"

"Yes, ma'am. Please knock me out. I can't stand this anymore."

"I've called the doctor. He's on his way up. We'll hold it until he gets here. How does that sound?"

"Great, thank you so much." I took a deep breath, then I looked at Chief.

"Is it like this every day? I'll kill myself if it is."

"No, Rick. There's pain all day, but that's healing pain and not anything like this. I doubt you'll have to go through this again."

The door opened and in walked Dr. Boone. He stood next to my rack looking at the leg and at me covered in sweat. "Been having a hard time of it?"

"Yes, sir. Please knock me out before you pull at my leg anymore." The doctor reached down and held my forearm.

"Sure. Chief, get the gas tank over here and get a new mask. Crawford, get me a scissors, Betadine, Dakin's solution, hydrogen peroxide, and some four-by-fours. Smith, start getting some plaster ready for a new cast. Miss Carter, get me a Coke. I'm thirsty." He looked down at me and winked and smiled.

The room was buzzing, everyone going every which way, but in an orderly fashion as if they'd done this many times before. "The gas is all ready to go, sir," said Chief, holding the mask next to my head. The doctor took it and held it over my nose and mouth.

"Take deep breaths, very deep breaths. You'll start to feel it working in just a few seconds." I sucked in the gas as hard as I could, fearing that the doctor would change his mind and make me stay awake. Then I was out.

I awoke on the ward and immediately looked down at my legs. There were two new casts. The blood-spattered sheets had been replaced and my pajama tops were soaked from perspiration. The room around me reminded me of a gym after the home team had won a big game. There were people everywhere. The noise was deafening. Right next to my rack a television was on full volume. Friends, relatives, Red Cross workers, or USO entertainers were at almost every bedside. The patients without visitors had radios blaring or were talking with each other.

Hanging over the noise was a putrid smell of pus and dried

blood, the same odor that hangs over a battlefield after days of killing and dying, as well as the smell of rubbing alcohol and antiseptics. The room was stuffy, almost like a greenhouse, and I found it hard to breathe. The floor was a pale gray, the walls a pale green, the ceiling a dirty white. The patients all wore light blue pajamas. The only lively colors were those on the visitors.

I felt embarrassed, for I knew I'd done some screaming in the cast tex room without thinking that I might be heard by the other men on the ward. And now that I could see all these other injuries, my wounds seemed minor. I was also puzzled that they all seemed to be having such a good time. How could someone with his arms or legs blown off be laughing and joking around?

Suddenly a mass of white moved in front of my eyes. It was Chief.

"How are you doing, Rick? I brought you a clean pajama top. You worked up a good sweat. You got visitors coming up here so we'd better get you looking human."

"Thanks, Chief. Visitors. I forgot all about that. I wish they could wait until I looked a little better."

"Don't worry. They'll be so glad to have you home that the way you look won't matter. I've got to get back to the nurses' station. If you need anything, just ring the buzzer tied to your rack."

Chief smiled and walked away. As he moved, the patient behind him became visible. I nodded. "Hi, my name is Rick Eilert."

"Glad to meet you, Rick. My name is Smitty. My first name I can't stand, so just call me Smitty. I'm not lying here on my side just so I can stare at you. I got shot in the ass so I've got to lay on my side or face down. If I lay face down during visiting hours, I can't look at these pretty ladies. How are you doing?"

"Like a bag of worms. I hurt all over."

"Did Crawford change your dressing?"

I nodded. "He sure did. What's wrong with him? I got better treatment from the asshole that blew me up than from that idiot."

"He takes care of everyone like that. I think he just gets his rocks off watching us hurting. After he finishes his tour here he goes to the Nam. Damn near everyone on the ward has written their old unit about Crawford. When he gets there, he'll be assigned to a grunt unit and he'll have a terrible accident." We both laughed.

"Smitty, where did you get hit? I mean what TAOR?"

"I caught it up near the Rock Pile. I was the door gunner in a CH-53A. A round came up through the floor right in my bung hole."

"Damn, that must hurt."

"Sure did, it ruined my whole day." Smitty smiled. "Hell, it's going to get me out of the Crotch. I'll be shitting out the side of my belly from now on and I'll probably have to eat Preparation H, but no more white sidewalls, no more lines, and most of all no more getting fucked with."

"Sounds good to me, Smitty. How long have you been up here?"

"Four and a half months."

"Four months, Christ. What are they doing, bronzing your butt or making you a new asshole?"

"Neither. I think they're going to make me morale officer for our floor. You should see me walk. Some say I move like an old whore." Smitty moved around restlessly.

"I got to get up and walk around for a while. I'm getting cramps. Must be my period. My asshole bleeds every other day." I laughed as Smitty swung his body around, throwing his feet out onto the floor. "You must be a gymnast." Smitty grunted, "Nope, I was a Baptist." Then he turned, smiled, and began to walk away. I couldn't help but smile. He did walk like an old whore. He just slid from foot to foot, never lifting them, just kind of dragging one up even with the other.

The pain was getting bad again and I was so tired, but with all the noise, sleep was out of the question. I rolled slightly to my right to ring for a pain shot when I spotted my father next to the nurses' station. Chief was pointing down toward my rack. I felt a chill run through my body and my heart sank. Tears began to well up. All the days and nights I'd lain thinking about just this moment, and all the things I'd wanted to say now seemed lost. Then I could see my mother and my sisters Janet and Linda, then at last my girl. I watched them as they moved in a silent procession down the aisle, scanning the ward for me. But every five feet they saw the body of another young lad torn apart. I could see the pain in their eyes, hoping their son was not hurt so badly. They kept inching toward me. By the time they reached my rack it was obvious that either the smell of the room or the sight of me had overwhelmed them. Mother ran over to my side and put her arms around me, crying. Dad looked down, smiled, and grabbed my hand. "Welcome home, we missed you, we're glad you're safe." My sisters and my girl were standing in the aisle, smiling, crying, and talking, all at the same time. I still couldn't say anything. The words were stuck. Then Cheryl leaned over and kissed me.

She was a little embarrassed because my parents were there. I could only stare at her. *God,* I thought, *I'd love to pull you down into this rack,* but I suddenly realized what I must look like. It had been a month since I'd taken a bath, and that was in a river. I hadn't washed my hair since I was wounded, so it was filled with dirt, rock chips, dried blood, grass, and bamboo chips. On top of that were the wire stitches hanging out of my face, hands, and arms, and casts on both legs all the way up to my crotch. All the time I'd thought of this moment, the things I would say to her, the romantic place we would be in. Instead, here I was lying on a hospital bed, smelling like a goat.

Now they stood back from the bed a little way, either to be polite so everyone could see or because they were so grossed out that they wanted to leave. For just a moment things seemed a little tense, nobody knowing what to say. Then Linda broke the ice.

"You don't look as bad as they said you did." Everyone's eyes went up to the ceiling as my other sister, Janet, elbowed Linda in the side.

"How bad did they say I was hurt?" I asked. "Look, I feel fine. Most important thing is that I'm alive and I'm home." Then they all began to jabber, asking questions and crying.

Linda continued her train of thought. "They said your face was blown up. I thought your nose or lips were gone."

"Sorry to disappoint you, but all I lost were some teeth." Though the questions continued to flow, my eyes were fixed on Cheryl.

"What happened?" asked my father. "The telegrams we received were sketchy. How did you get wounded?"

I didn't want to talk about the patrol. I tried to make light of the whole incident. It was over and the details seemed unimportant.

"Not much, Dad. We were on patrol, supposed to find a company of NVA in the area. They found us first and ambushed us. I was teaching a new guy to walk point because I was going on

R and R. He took the wrong trail and tripped a booby-trapped grenade. I zigged when I should have zagged. They got me out pretty quick. I just got a little bent up." My father smiled.

"I'm surprised they even told you about me getting wounded. They asked us if we got wounded did we want our families notified. I signed a paper saying no. I didn't want to worry anyone. Maybe they thought I was pretty bad off."

My mother pulled a batch of telegrams from her purse and presented them to me, one by one.

I shook my head. The messages were so vague. "It says I was wounded by a 'hostile explosive device.' That could mean a cherry bomb or an H bomb. It doesn't say if I lost my limbs or eyesight." I laughed. I could imagine the hell my family and friends had gone through. My mother described the situation while I read.

"We tried desperately to get more information on your condition. When I called the Red Cross they told me to contact Western Union. The Marine Corps and Navy could only give us the information we were already given. The Marine Corps sent someone out right after you were wounded. I opened the door and saw a man in dress blues. I thought you were dead. I know now that a chaplain would have been with him had you been killed, but the shock nearly gave me a stroke.

"He showed me a casualty work sheet. It contained all the basic information we got in these telegrams. By the time he left I felt sorry for him. What a terrible job, telling families their sons are dead or seriously wounded.

"We tried to get in touch with you directly. I phoned Western Union, who said they couldn't get a telegram to you. Red Cross just said they couldn't help. Finally, Glenview Naval Air Station said they'd try to radio a message. We decided to send you a message through them." My father handed me the scratch paper he'd written the message on: "All of us and Cheryl hope you keep pitching and recover quickly. Our prayers and love. We need you. Your gang."

"They wouldn't allow the message to be sent in this form, and made us rewrite it until it read, 'Received wire, General Greene, Washington, advising of your very serious wounds. All of us and Cheryl pray and hope for best. We need you. Dad and family.'"

"I never received anything," I laughed.

I noticed that Janet and my mother were both looking pale,

probably from the stink and the stuffy, warm room. "Jan, why don't you and Mom go get some fresh air? It's kind of stuffy in here. . . . It's great to be home, Dad. I missed all of you so much. Cheryl, want to go dancing tonight?"

It was as if it all got to her at once. She began crying, with big tears dropping from her cheeks. "Rick, I never thought I'd see you again. I can't help it. I'm so happy to see you. I was so scared when they told me you got hurt." I reached up with my bandaged arms and put them around her neck. "It's all over now. I'm home forever. I won't ever leave again."

Just then the nurse came around. "I'm sorry, visiting hours are over. You'll have to leave now. Visiting hours are from one to three-thirty in the afternoon, and from seven to nine in the evening."

She smiled and walked over to some of the other visitors with the same tale. Over the loudspeaker a voice blurted out, "Now hear this. Now hear this. Visiting hours are now over. All visitors are requested to leave the hospital at this time."

# 4

CHERYL STAYED JUST a minute after my family had gone, and before she left she leaned over and kissed me as I'd dreamed about for so long.

As she walked out Smitty came charging back with a friend. "Hey, Rick, want you to meet someone. This is Toby. He was a corpsman with One Nine, got his arm all fucked up with an AK-47." I reached out my bandaged hand to shake Toby's. "Glad to meet you, Toby." Then I saw that his right arm hung dead at his side.

"Welcome aboard. Smitty and I are the only two ambulatory patients on the ward, so if you need anything just let us know. Say, was that your woman up here with the mini-skirt on? Next time she comes up here I'll stand behind her so nobody takes any more cheap peeks."

"Thanks, Toby. That's nice of you to volunteer."

"Say, Rick, are you from around here?"

"Yeah. I live about thirty miles away."

"That's really great. Everybody else around here is from all over the country. The closest is Michigan, where Smitty and Manning come from. So our visitors have to be imported. I'm going to lay down for a while. I'll talk to you later."

Smitty leaned over the edge of my rack, his arms resting on the overhead superstructure. "That your family?" I nodded. "Sure are nice people. You know, when my parents first came up here, I thought I was going to cry. I'd been gone so long I'd forgotten how much they meant to me. In my whole life I never won anything. Now I feel so lucky to be alive, it's like I've won a lottery. I wonder why I was the one who got so lucky. There were a thousand other guys that deserved to be home more than I do. Yet they're dead. It just doesn't seem right."

"Maybe we're dead and this is just a dream."

"Yeah. I once got a letter from this guy's mother. He was killed one night on an LP. Anyway, she wrote asking me stuff like how did he die, and what he said before he died. I never answered her. It was as if she was wondering why he died and I didn't."

"Yeah, that's it. Say, Smitty, what time do we get chow up here?"

"Any time now. They had you on liquids all this time?"

"Yeah. I'm starting to gnaw on my lip just to feel something hard between my teeth."

"One thing for sure, Rick, it's hot and it's stateside. No more John Wayne key and a can. A knife, a fork, and a spoon, even get a napkin. Not that any of these jarheads know what to do with them." Smitty rolled over to his other side and began to talk with the patient in that rack. I felt a tap on my shoulder.

"Hi, I'm Wilson. Did you just get in?"

"Yeah, today. Man, you look like you're doing OK. I thought Smitty and Toby were the only ambulatory patients on the ward."

"That's right. They *are* the only ambulatory patients." He threw his stump up on the side of my rack. "I just got my leg blown off. Pretty soon I'm going to Philly for a new leg."

"God, I'm sorry. I couldn't see."

"It doesn't bother me so it shouldn't bother you. Are they going to chop off any of your pins?"

"I hope not. It's possible. After I first got hit they were going to take both of them. Now just the left leg's in doubt."

"Don't worry about it then. Doc Bone is great. He only takes it if all else fails. He's the best damn doctor anywhere. I don't mean just the military, I mean anywhere. That doesn't mean he's easy. It can smart at times, but he'll make you well. Unless gangrene sets in, then you're up shit creek. When did you get hit?"

"What's the date today?"

"Sunday, the third of December."

"I was hit on the twenty-sixth of November. About six or seven days ago."

"You got here pretty quick. Most people spend time in Japan or on one of the hospital ships. See you later, the chow cart is on the way. I can hear those wheels calling me."

"OK, Wilson. Nice to have met you."

By this time the shot I'd received in the cast tex room was wearing off and the spasms of pain had returned. I pressed the buzzer for the corpsman, and Chief was there in an instant. "What can I do for you, Rick?"

"Chief, my legs are killing me. Please get me a shot."

A nurse appeared a few minutes later. "Are you Eilert?" she demanded.

"Yes, ma'am. I just arrived today."

"I have your pain shot. Your chart shows that you were taking morphine before. The doctor has put you on Demerol. This might make you drowsy, maybe even put you to sleep, but the dinner trays are on the way up and if you take the shot now you may fall asleep before you can eat. How about you eat, then I'll give you the shot?"

"Sounds fine. The pain's bad but I'm so hungry."

"Fine. I'll be back after you've finished. Just ring."

The nurse left and I noticed everyone scurrying around. The patients that could get out of their racks were pulling themselves into wheelchairs and rushing toward the nurses' station.

"Smitty, what's happening?"

"It's chow time. I've got to get up there. Anyone able to get out of their rack, including wheelchairs, has to help the corpsmen pass out trays. Lay back. I'll roll up your rack so you can see your food." Smitty waddled over to my rack and stooped down to turn the lever. This was the first time I'd been in a sitting position since I was wounded, and it felt very good. Then Smitty started toward the nurses' station.

From a sitting position I was able to see most everything and everyone around me. The trays were brought up in a large stainless steel cupboard on wheels. The corpsmen would pass a tray to one of the wheelchair patients and he'd go speeding down the aisles to a bedridden patient.

When Chief brought my tray I sat there looking at the food as if it were a picture.

"The doctor said I could unwrap the Ace bandage on your right arm," Chief said, "down below the elbow. The arm was cracked at the wrist and they wrapped it this way to keep you from moving around in transit. Now you can feed and shave yourself."

"That's outstanding. Chief, look at this. Lasagna, garlic bread, corn, white bread with real butter, chocolate milk, coffee, and would you look at this—ice cream." Chief and Smitty laughed. I realized later that they'd seen this ritual time after time. Some poor grunt, tired, racked with pain, getting his first stateside meal. It was like Christmas every time. It was amazing that something so insignificant could produce such happiness. I dug in but I'd forgotten that the teeth were gone on the left side of my mouth. The simple motion of chewing caused considerable pain, and the place on my tongue where the shrapnel had passed through was on fire. The pain in my mouth must have triggered something because suddenly all the pain in my body hit at the same time. It was horrible.

"Chief, get me some pain med, please." My leg was throbbing in quick spasms. There was white-hot pain in both legs and that started to frighten me. Chief returned quickly with the shot and administered the medication. I could feel the pain disappearing, first in my legs, then slowly upward. The nurse had been right about the drowsiness. I passed out with the fork in my hand.

I slept until eleven-thirty that evening, and was awakened by the odd sensation of having to urinate. Ever since I'd been wounded I'd had a catheter in me, but when I reached down to check for the line it was gone. I rang for some help and luckily Chief was still there.

"What's wrong, Rick?"

"Chief, my catheter is gone and I have to piss bad."

"Don't worry, Rick, we took it out after you fell asleep. I'll get you a duck." He turned around and ran for the nurses' area. All the lights were out on the ward and it was completely quiet. The only thing I could see was Chief's huge frame running back and forth in the lighted nurses' station. He came romping back to my rack, puffing as he tried to get his wind back.

"It's too late, Chief. I pissed all over myself. God, I feel terrible. I just couldn't hold it. I'm really sorry." Chief shook his head and smiled, then began to strip the bed of the sheets and blanket.

"Don't worry. It happens to a lot of guys. I'll be back in a minute. I need clean sheets. Use the duck if you still feel that you got to piss.

"Here we are, Rick. Pull yourself up on that handle above you. I can slide the sheets under your body." I reached up with my right hand, and the pain was sharp and hot. A one-arm pull-up was a lot more difficult than I'd imagined.

Chief saw the trouble and he moved his right hand under my butt, lifting. I was amazed. Chief's hand engulfed my rear end and his strength was incredible. He was able to complete the bed making without any trouble.

"That's great, Chief. I'm really sorry you had to get such a lousy job." Chief smiled. Nothing seemed to bother him at all. What really amazed me was that anyone his size, and with his strength, could be so gentle.

"Chief, why are you still on duty? You've been here as long as I have—that's about ten hours."

"The night corpsman is late so I volunteered to wait until he gets here. No sweat. I like my job. I feel good when I help someone, especially you marines. Pretty soon I'll be sent overseas and I want to be a good corpsman. I learn from you guys. Besides, if things stay as bad as they are over there, I'll probably end up back here on my back just like you, if I'm lucky."

"Listen, Chief, marines in combat treat you corpsmen like kings. After all, your job is to keep us alive. As big as you are, ain't nobody going to give you any shit. Say, Chief, can you get me another shot? My leg is starting to ache again."

"Sure thing. I'll call the nurse. It'll take about five minutes. She's up on Five now." Chief walked away carrying the wet sheets under his arm. There weren't any sounds at all. It seemed strange since not four hours ago the ward had been a madhouse. Then Smitty rolled up on his side from his belly.

"Need anything, Rick?"

"No, thanks. Chief was just here. Say, Smitty, it seems like a lot of these guys are still awake. Isn't it odd that it's so quiet?"

"Odd, maybe, but did you talk at night when you were in the Nam?"

"No. As a matter of fact, almost never."

"Well, after a while, even though you're safe and far away, you still get the feeling that you're back in the bush. It's the strangest thing. Besides, if you fall asleep you just have nightmares anyway."

"Nobody even snores out there. It gives away your position."

"That's right, Rick, and if you hear any snoring in here it's not a grunt. It's probably an office-poggy or a wing-wiper."

"Chief's coming with my shot so I'll say good night now." Smitty nodded and rolled back onto his stomach.

I was awakened by the noise of radios blasting and a tapping on my shoulder. I opened my eyes to find a short, skinny corpsman in black-rimmed glasses, with a badge on his chest that read, "Student Corpsman."

"Good morning, Eilert. My name is Smith. I'm going to help you wash up and shave."

"Why, student corpsman, is this an experiment?" The corpsman went to the foot of my rack and began cranking the bed up. After removing my pajama top and pulling the sheets away, he reached into a bucket on the floor, rinsed out a sponge, and began to wash my body. I was embarrassed to have someone washing my privates, especially another man. It just didn't seem natural. Then he shaved me, which took some time because of the small wounds on my face. At least I was able to brush my own teeth. Another corpsman was summoned to help Smith change my rack and he bellied up to it.

"Good morning, Eilert. I'm Sam Blass, senior corpsman on the ward. I understand you had some trouble last night. How do you feel now? Is the pain still bad?"

"Yes, it is. The casts feel tight and the pain is persistent. It never goes away."

"It'll be like that for some time, especially with most of the smaller wounds healing up. Now all the pain is channeled into your legs. Some of that is just in your mind, but you grow accustomed to that soon enough. Here's a list of the rules of the hospital. Read them. Then when you're finished, hand them back to one of the corpsmen. If you have any questions, just ask. Dr. Boone will begin rounds shortly, so if you have any questions to ask him, think of them now. Once he starts rounds he moves very fast, and once he's gone it's hard to get in touch with him. He's always in the operating room, the clinic, or in Receiving—drumming up new customers." I noticed the rows of ribbons on Blass's chest. It was obvious that he'd seen a lot of combat.

"What unit were you with in the Nam, Doc?"

"Two Twenty-six, Whiskey Company."

"I was with Three Twenty-six, Mike and Lima companies."

"Aren't you the unit that got the shit kicked out of them up at Con Tien?"

"Yep. Sixty percent casualties in five hours." Blass smiled. No war stories were necessary. He knew I'd been in the shit.

"Talk to you later, Eilert. I've got to get ready for the doctor."

"Thanks, Doc . . . later." Smitty rolled slowly back up on his side. "Don't pay any attention to those damn rules. They're all broken anyway. If you've got any questions about anything just ask for the ward NCO. He's the senior man on the ward. We call him Gramps."

"Why Gramps? Is he one of the Korean War gunneys?"

"Nope. He's the oldest man on the ward, twenty-two. And he's been up here for eight months. Gramps has both age and tenure. He has one arm gone and one hell of a scar over the left cheek. He's back in the solarium, just there around the corner. Usually the most senior men on the ward move in there. There's only room for three racks, but once you go south, as they say up here, you've got it licked. Since they have a door to the room and because they've been up here so long, they get their own TV and can keep it on all night if they want to. They can also have girl friends in there with some privacy, if you catch my drift. If you get in good with them, you can go south at night and watch the tube. Anyway, if you do need anything, just ask for Gramps."

"Thanks, Smitty. I'll keep it in mind. What time do we have to turn the lights off in the ward?"

"Twenty-two hundred. I mean, ten o'clock."

Now that the baths were over and racks had been changed, the TVs were turned on and the radios were turned up against their noise. I was amazed at the number of songs I didn't recognize. The TV programs seemed alien. It was so weird to watch the news from Vietnam, and see units I had friends in getting shot up and places I'd been at that were now leveled by bombing and gunfire.

Pain started to bother me again, so I rang for another shot. When the corpsman reached my rack I signaled him for an injection, but he shook his head.

"The doctor is on the floor. He's just about to start rounds. You'll have to wait until after he's gone, probably another thirty minutes."

I looked up at the nurses' station and caught a glimpse of the doctor. The radios and TVs were turned off and the ward fell silent. With the doctor were the senior corpsman and head nurse, both carrying clipboards and taking notes. In back of them walked a student corpsman pushing a trash cart, into which the doctor threw the bloody dressings he had just removed. Starting at the first rack the doctor moved quickly, asking each patient several questions and occasionally joking as he worked. The doctor wasn't exactly gentle when pulling the bandages off, and I noticed that each patient in line braced himself for the coming pain. But once the doctor started removing the dressings, pain was not expressed unless it was really horrible, and then only in grunts and groans. No one wanted to break down and cry, especially when those with much more severe injuries had been able to remain silent. I was worried that he'd have my cast pulled off again, and that, more than anything, scared the living hell out of me.

When the entourage reached Smitty's rack he'd already pulled part of the dressing off himself, and pulled his drawers down to his knees. That was a bright spot in everybody's day. The doctor laughed. "So this is my half-ass patient. How are you doing, Smitty?"

"Yes, sir, I'm the asshole you deal with every day." The doctor began to pull the bandages from the area around his tailbone. I saw Smitty grasp the frame on the side of his rack. He held on so tight that his knuckles turned white. It looked as if he'd crush the metal. He didn't groan or scream. He just closed his eyes and buried his head in the mattress. Then I saw the wound. My first thought was *How could anyone with a hole that deep and so close to his bunghole keep from having shit all over himself?* I couldn't help but stare at it. It was about two inches in diameter and three inches deep, leaving part of the tailbone exposed. The doctor was investigating the wound with a long Q-Tip, poking it deep and rubbing it all around. When he pulled it out pus and blood dripped from the end. Smitty kept trying not to move, which would only drive the Q-Tip deeper. The doctor took tweezers and began pulling foot after foot of packing out of the wound, it, too, dripping pus and blood. This was the entry hole. The exit hole over on his abdomen had obviously healed, as the doctor only worked from the back. I wondered how Smitty could stand the pain, remembering when I'd fallen on my tailbone once and how it had taken my breath away. I saw perspiration dripping from Smitty's brow, down to the mattress and the floor. Even his hands were wringing wet.

The doctor took a four-by-four-inch piece of gauze, inserted it into the wound with a tweezers, reaming out the inside, then pulled it out, dripping with more blood.

"Sorry, Smitty. I have to get that area to granulate, for new tissue. Blass, I want this changed twice a day, and have the corpsman cause the wound to bleed. If that pus doesn't clear up we may have to operate again." Then he slapped Smitty's butt and said, "OK, partner, it's all over. Relax. Blass, don't forget to have this wound tripped with Dakin's solution, hydrogen peroxide, and Betadine, then packed again."

"Yes, sir." Blass noted the instructions on his clipboard.

"Smitty, after you get out of the service you should join the rodeo."

"No way, Doc. I'm going to get a nice cushy job like yours, and just go around all day shoving my fist up people's assholes." The doctor, nurse, and corpsman all laughed as they moved toward my rack.

"Good morning, son. How do you feel this morning? I understand you had some trouble last night."

"Yes, sir. My legs are killing me and the casts seem awfully tight."

"That tightness is from swelling. That will soon be reduced. We're going into the OR tomorrow morning. I have to debride that left leg. It's also possible that we might have to take it. If there's a chance of saving it, I'll have to put a pin through your heel and attach a weight to it. This will pull the leg straight, so we can leave the cast off and tend all the wounds on the leg. The right leg will also be cleaned up. Afterward we'll cut windows in the cast so that while your leg is setting we can also tend the wounds. We won't leave it open like the left leg, which has so much tissue damage over so much of its surface."

"Thank you, sir. When can you take these Ace wraps off my arms?"

"I'll have the nurse take them off in a few weeks. The arms weren't fractured, just cracked. They'll heal very fast. You can use them as long as you're not lifting anything heavy. Take it easy. I'll see you in the operating room tomorrow morning."

"Thanks, Doc."

I looked back toward Smitty, whose head was still buried deep in his pillow.

"Smitty, are you all right? . . . Smitty?"

74

Smitty turned his head just enough to be heard. "Fuck, no. I'm not all right." Then pushed his head back into the pillow.

I felt stupid. *Of course he doesn't feel good. How could anyone feel good after that?*

Across the aisle I heard the doctor tell a patient, "You're getting out of here in a few days. Your PEB has been typed and signed." He moved to the next patient without a word and began pulling the bandages off, then the gauze packed deep in the poor guy's hip. The doctor stuck his entire fist past his wrist up into the wound.

"Please, Doc, please stop. Please hurry and finish," the patient murmured to himself.

"Easy, Dennis, take it easy. . . . I'm almost done. . . . There, finished."

I could see sweat rolling down Dennis's face. Or was it tears? I heard the doctor instruct the nurse and corpsman to change his dressings three times a day and trip the wound. *Dear God,* I thought, *I never realized how much pain and suffering you have to go through to get well. This sure isn't like the movies.*

It had taken the doctor forty-five minutes to go through the ward. When he left, the corpsmen returned with their dressing carts and began to apply new bandages. This was just as painful, in some cases even more so, as each wound had to be scrubbed, packed, washed with Betadine, reamed to promote tissue growth, and finally covered. This was an agonizing ordeal and the patients were far more vocal than they'd been with the doctor present. For the most part the corpsmen took it in stride, though it caused some of them to press and scrub even harder and longer.

Awaiting the second half of the process, Smitty rolled on his side to face me and said, "Rick, ain't this the shits?"

"No kidding. The damn enlistment posters never said nothing about pain. It sounds naïve, but I never thought that getting wounded involved so much agony."

"Up here wounds are the one thing we all have in common. They're great topics of conversation. There are people on the other side of the partition that I've never met and I don't know their names, but I know who they are by their wounds. The more messed up you are the more prestige you have. One thing, Rick, if you get Crawford or Cole changing your dressings, stand the fuck by. They love to inflict pain. The more you show them it hurts the more they'll try to make it worse. I've got to lay on the other side. I'll talk to you later."

"Are you Eilert?" I looked up to find a tall, beautiful nurse with fantastic blond hair rolled up on her head and the most terrific blue eyes I'd ever seen. Her body, or what I could see of it, was a miracle of construction.

"Are you Eilert? . . . Are you dead or deaf?" I was searching for a word, any word.

"Yes, I am, yes. I mean, yes, ma'am."

"You ordered your pain medication? I have a shot of Demerol for you."

"Yes, ma'am . . . er . . . Miss Altman." I'd taken my eyes off hers long enough to read her name plate, which was pinned over her left breast. I thought, *Oh God . . . did she have to hang her name* there!

She caught me staring at her chest and broke into a smile. And as she drove the needle home, asked, "How long have you been in the jungle, marine?"

"F-four months, ma'am."

"I thought as much. It looks like you've got a lot of metal stitches in you. When the doctor says they have to come out, let me know. I'm good at pulling stitches."

I blushed. "Maybe the doctor should take them out."

"That's not necessary. Besides, the doctor won't take the time to pull stitches. Where else do you have them?"

"Well, ma'am, I've got a few on my hip, and a few more on my . . . ah . . . ass . . . and a few more on my personals."

"Your what?"

"You know, my privates. All right, my penis." My face had turned beet-red, and all the other men in the area were laughing.

"Sorry, Eilert, I didn't mean to embarrass you. I really do take most of the stitches out of the guys on this ward. If you'd rather have Crawford do it, that's fine, too."

"No, ma'am, no way do I want that gravedigger touching me. Please, would you do it? Please?"

"Sure . . . no trouble. Is that shot helping at all?"

"Yes, ma'am, a lot. I feel like I'm going to drop off any time now."

"That's fine. I'll come by later. Bye."

"Good-bye. Thanks for everything." I looked over at Smitty's rack, only to see him staring back at me with a big shit-eating grin on his face. For that matter, everyone was grinning at me, even Johnson, and he hardly ever smiled.

"Now what are you going to do, slit your dick with a razor blade? I guess it's probably worth it," Smitty laughed.

"No, really, I do have stitches in my dick. Do you really think I'd stoop that low?"

"You bet your sweet ass I do."

"Hell, you're the one that's the pervert. How many stitches has she pulled out of your ass?"

"None yet, but the next time I go to the OR I'm going to ask the doc to put a few in."

"OK, you two, break it up." Chief walked in between us. Smitty mumbled, "This is a total eclipse."

"Let's go, Smitty, back on your stomach. I've got to pack your butt again."

"That's right, Chief, just another pretty face. You corpsmen are all alike. Just pack my ass and leave with not so much as a how-do-you-do."

"You marines are all alike. You're just plain crazy. You don't even appreciate the three hours of first aid I took before I came on the ward."

Chief pulled on a pair of sterile gloves and laid out his tools before he set about cleaning Smitty's wound. Watching the gauze scraping across the raw flesh sent chills through my body. Smitty said nothing, didn't even moan, but his fingers were locked on his bed frame. The expression on Chief's face was just as telling. His lips quivered with each thrust of the Q-Tip, and every time Smitty's body heaved in pain Chief would plead, "I'm sorry, Smitty."

It was obvious how exhausting these dressing changes were for the wounded, but for someone as sensitive as Chief the mental fatigue had to be almost as awful.

"There you go, Smitty." Chief tossed the old dressings into a garbage bag and crossed the aisle to Dennis's rack. When I looked at Dennis, I saw the face of terror again as Chief pulled away the doctor's temporary dressings and began to scrape the tattered flesh. Dennis was just a skeleton covered with skin, yet in the midst of his dressing change his entire body, with Chief leaning on it, would lift at least an inch off the mattress in spasms of pain.

Chief's fingers disappeared into Dennis's hip as yards of

gauze and packing were shoved into the beet-red folds of bone and muscle. Betadine solution was then poured over the whole job until it filled and dripped out of the wound. Dennis's dressing change was harder to watch than Smitty's. Maybe because it was so massive or maybe because Dennis lay face up. His eyes were wide open. The look on his face was wild with pain, but he didn't make a sound. Chief put the final bandage over the wound, cleaned away the dirty dressings, and pulled off his plastic gloves. "OK, Dennis, it's over. See you after lunch."

Dennis was able to relax and wait for the next round.

Chief went on to Toby and down the line. All pretty much the same, rarely a sound. Watching it all, waiting for my shot to take effect, gave me cause to wonder whether my experiences at Scott and the cast tex room were only a sample of what was to come. I didn't know how I could put up with that pain. *Maybe they don't hurt as bad as me,* I thought. But I knew that wasn't true. All those times I'd wished to get wounded so I could be sent home, and now that it had happened it just seemed too high a price to pay.

# 5

"EILERT . . . EILERT, WAKE up. . . . Come on, you've got a phone call."

I opened my eyes, still groggy. "Yeah, OK. I'm awake. What do I have?" The corpsman cranked up the head of my rack so I could hold the receiver, and set the phone on the bedside stand.

"Hello?" I'd almost forgotten how to talk on a regular telephone. I'd started to say, "Over."

"Rick, this is Mom. How do you feel this morning? I can't believe you're home, so close and safe. How did you sleep last night?"

"I slept just fine, Mom, except I wet the bed. Sound familiar? Otherwise I was feeling really good. I've met a few more guys up here. It's not such a bad place. Are you coming up today?"

"Yes. Dad and I'll be up this evening after dinner. Cheryl and Janet are coming up this afternoon. What do you mean you wet the bed?"

"It's nothing, Mom, just an accident. Don't worry, they don't send the dirty sheets home to be cleaned. If I don't make any sense it's because of these pain shots. They make me feel really groggy, almost drunk. I'd forgotten just where I was . . . I mean I forgot I was home. There's been so many mornings that I wanted to be home . . . now that I'm here I feel so far away."

"I know what you mean. When Dad left for work he said, 'Let's go up to see Rick this evening.' It sounded so strange. We used to sit home and watch the TV for news of your unit. Now we don't have to worry anymore. Did the doctor come by this morning?"

"He sure did. I'm not too sure I'm going to like this wounded stuff. It hurts. Anyway, he said I'm going to the operating room tomorrow morning. They're going to take some more crud out of me and put me in traction. He said I still might lose the leg, but first he wants to try everything to save it. From what the rest of the guys have said, Dr. Boone is tops."

"Oh, Rick, does it hurt very much?"

"Listen, Mom, after some of the wounds I saw this morning I feel like a piker. You know, I always wanted to find out what I was made of . . . that's kind of why I went into the corps. But I've got a feeling that the battlefield was only step one in the guts course. I guess I'm scared."

"You know everyone is praying for you, don't you?"

"Yeah, and I'd be a fool not to think it might help, but when I prayed that Happy and Clayton and Madison, Petrouski, Peterson, Young, and all the rest of my friends wouldn't die . . . they all died anyway. I'm not too sure the Lord has me on radar yet."

"Well, I'll never be able to feel what you've been through, but you have to take one miracle at a time."

"Forever the optimist, Mom. I can't wait to see you and Dad tonight, and bring me some pictures of Bobby and Mary. I'm starting to fall asleep. I can hardly keep my eyes open. There's so much I want to ask you but maybe it can wait."

"Sure, Rick, that's fine. Your grandfather called me last night. He's worried about you. He said he didn't phone you because he didn't want to bother you."

"Hell, Mom, that's foolish. I can't think of anyone I'd rather talk to. Tell him to phone me in a few days. Better still, why don't you and he drive up here sometime this week?"

"He'd love that. Are you sure you're up to having visitors?"

"Gramps isn't a visitor, he's my family. I got to get off now. Talk to you later."

"That sounds fine. I'll tell Gramps. See you tonight."

"Eilert . . . Eilert, wake up. You've got another call."

"Oh . . . ah, thanks."

"Hello, Rick. This is Cheryl. How do you feel this morning?"

"Just fine, especially now. God, I've missed you. I love you so much. I meant to tell you that yesterday, but it was awkward with everybody up here. Are you crying again?"

"Yes. Just because I'm happy. You know, I read your letters over and over."

"Your letters meant a lot to me, too. I even looked forward to your chocolate chip cookies, though they gave me the shits. The rest of the guys in the squad hated to walk behind me after I ate them. I'd have to stop every half hour. They'd have to walk by my droppings all day."

"Rick, you're terrible. Come on, my cookies weren't that bad."

"They were good, all right. They just went through me like shit through a goose. Are· you coming up this afternoon with Janet?"

"Yeah, I told my boss that you'd come home and he said I could have the day off to come to see you."

"That's terrific. God, it's great to hear your voice and know you're only an hour away."

A corpsman came back to my rack and signaled me to get off the phone. "Eilert, you have to hang up. One of the other patients has a call."

"Cheryl, I have to get off now. I'll see you this afternoon."

"OK, see you later. I love you."

"I love you, too. Bye." I lay there staring at the ceiling, unable to believe that less than a week earlier I'd been sleeping with leeches and waiting for some unfriendly son of a bitch to try to kill me, when a new face appeared over my rack.

"Rick, I'm from the Ortho Clinic. You're going to surgery tomorrow, right? I have to prep you."

"You're going to do what to me? Are you from California?"

The corpsman laughed. "I have to prep you. Shave your legs, et cetera."

I watched as he began to lather up with his little can of foam. Then he pulled back the sheets to find both legs in casts.

"That's just outstanding. I'm told to prep you for surgery and the only place to prep is your groin. This man's Navy sucks." Infuriated, he started applying the shaving cream.

Once the corpsman left I reached up to the trapeze hanging over me so I could inspect his work. There was a thin coat of plastic around the metal bar and as I grasped it I realized there were fingerprints embedded in it. They felt even deeper than the plastic and I knew just how they got there.

I closed my eyes and listened to the music blaring out of several radios. They were all songs and bands I'd never heard of. I was excited about being home, but somehow it wasn't anything like what I'd envisioned. Maybe it was all the shots, or remembering the friends that would never feel the love of their families again. For some reason, as happy as I was to see Cheryl, it seemed flat. Maybe my innocence was gone, that blind affection. In Vietnam I felt that all these emotions had died, but now at home I felt overwhelmed by them. *God*, I thought, *have I changed that much or is it everyone else that's so different?*

"Eilert, I'm from the lab. I have to take some blood and get you to furnish some urine."

I'd had my eyes shut and was startled by the lab technician. "Yeah, sure, whatever's customary."

"Here, fill the duck so I can get out of here."

I obliged him and then let my mind drift again. I was so tired, but I had too much to think about.

"Eilert, telephone for you. It must be your stockbroker. Everyone else has called."

"Hello, Rick here."

"Hey, buddysuck. It's Mike. How are you doing? Man, you've

had everyone worried. The whole gang has really missed you, and rather than all of us calling you separately, they chose me to do the honors." I felt choked up. Mike and the buddysucks were all the guys I'd gone through school with. They were the kind of friends I thought would stay together forever, like brothers.

"Mike, it's great to hear your voice. I'm fine. Just a little bent out of shape. How's everyone doing?"

"Well, Tuna got bounced out of school. Ed's still going to Northern and taking out Sharon. Brian's in the middle of the basketball season, and I'm going to college over in Evanston. Nothing's changed one way or the other."

"How about Bobby? Isn't he going to college? He never bothered to write to me the whole time I was over there."

"Bob said he didn't write you because he didn't agree with you being over there, and he wouldn't be up to see you for pretty much the same reason. I think maybe he's more embarrassed than anything."

"Jesus H. Christ, that's stupid. Why would my fighting in Vietnam have anything to do with me wanting to hear from him? You mean he doesn't want to see me anymore?"

"I have no idea. I've only seen him once since you left. Anyway, do you want some company? I really want to see you. How about I come by with Tuna later this week? By that time everyone would have phoned you and come by to see you. You aren't going to want to see us if Cheryl's there, anyway."

"That sounds terrific. I've got to get off. We can only have the phone for three minutes. Thanks for calling. Squeeze it easy, Mike."

"Play nice and share your toys, buddy. See you soon and take care."

After hanging up I couldn't help thinking about Bobby. The two of us had been so close and it hurt to think that I'd lost *another* friend because of that fucking war. I'd always thought that a person is a little bit of everyone he has ever known or talked to . . . and that friends are even a bigger part of your personality. When a friend is lost, so is a big part of you. Knowing that Bobby felt that way really crushed me. I wondered if Vietnam would ever be over.


Nurse Noland stood next to me, holding out some papers. "What are these for?"

"We have to get your written authorization for surgery tomorrow. The doctor has already explained the procedure, and that it's possible that you might lose your leg if it looks like he won't be able to save it."

"Yes, ma'am, he explained all that."

"OK, fine. You don't have to sign if you can't move your hand. I can sign for you with someone else as a witness."

"No, that's all right. I think I can scratch my name out." She held the papers while I slowly wrote my name on three different forms.

"That's great. The anesthesiologist will stop by later to tell you what you're going to get to knock you out, and ask you some medical background. Also, you'll be NPO for surgery after midnight. That means nothing is to be taken by mouth. No food or drink and it's better that you not smoke as well. They don't want you to toss your cookies on the operating table."

"I understand. Thank you, ma'am."

"Fine. And good luck tomorrow." As the nurse walked away, Smitty rolled out of bed onto his feet.

"Rick, don't worry at all about tomorrow. If the doctor was going to take your leg he would damn well let you know. Bone is one hell of a doctor."

"Yeah, that's all well and good, but I saw those dressing changes today, and Bone said that he was going to put the left leg in traction, in some kind of a contraption so they could change the dressing. He said the right leg would have a cast with windows cut in it so they could change those dressings, too. I don't know that I can put up with that kind of pain."

"The secret is to make believe the legs are gone, that they're someone else's you're looking at. Then when they work on you, fix your eyes on an object and just concentrate on that thing until it's all over. Most everyone does it, and it does help some. Fighting the pain is a lot like fighting Charlie. You can close your eyes and dream him away, but when you open them he's still there. Same thing with pain. Besides, you'll be off pain med soon, so you have to come up with some gimmick. OK, now if you believe all that . . . do you want to buy some swamp land in Florida?"

"I know there's logic somewhere in there, but when the hurting starts I've got an idea I'll forget it all. I'll tell you, I doubt I'll be getting a whole lot of dates when I'm three feet tall instead of six two."

I'd resigned myself to losing my leg right after I was wounded, so the fact that I might have it chopped off now didn't particularly bother me. I just wished it was done with instead of still being a threat. A "to be" seemed much worse than a "was" at this stage of the game.

The noise level began to build as the food cart was wheeled onto the floor. When I got my tray I went at it like gang busters but, like the night before, I found I was unable to do justice to all that chow. And the trolls came in droves for the leavings. People I hadn't even *seen* before called me by name, asking for a little of this and a little of that. In no time at all the food was gone except for two cartons of chocolate milk, one of which I was going to try to get down. Then out of nowhere I heard mumbling. "Can I have your milk?"

"What do you want?"

"I want your fucking milk."

I looked over at Smitty. "Did you say something?" Smitty shook his head.

"Can I or can't I have your goddamn milk?"

"It's Stumps," said Smitty.

I looked over the end of the table and saw a hand reaching up for my milk. So I put the carton in the hand and watched it disappear.

"What was that all about?"

"That was Stumps," said Smitty. "He's in rack sixteen. He got both his legs blown off above the knees. When the Red Cross people came up a few weeks ago they gave everyone a pair of slippers. Stumps taped his to the bottom of his stumps and walked around the whole ward like a chimpanzee. Every once in a while you can see him swinging around in the superstructure over his rack."

"He sounds like one of those things that live under bridges. I don't know what he looks like. All I saw was his hand."

After lunch the whole ward took a nap. All the TVs and radios were turned off and there was no talking. It seemed crazy. I hadn't seen anything like this since kindergarten. But a corpsman came by and gave me a pain shot and I, too, dropped off to another dreamless sleep.

I was awakened by a warm kiss on the cheek, and when I looked up I saw Cheryl and my sister Janet. "Hello, brother. Brought you some junk food and magazines."

"Cheryl, why are you standing back there? Come here. What's the matter—you look so sad. You look like you're going to cry. Everything is going to be just fine. You'll see. This is just a temporary setback."

"You had such nice legs," she said. "Are they going to have to cut one off?"

"Maybe not. The doctor said that if it looks like he can save it, and it'll still be functional, then I can keep it."

"That's great. Then you can still dance and all that when you get better."

"I hope so, I really hope so." I could tell that Cheryl was very uneasy. I knew it wasn't any fun for her looking at all these mutilated bodies. Besides, the smell of the place was horrible.

Just then two marines in the uniform of the day came limping down the aisle with a movie screen, which they set up right next to my rack.

"Hey, what's going on? I got visitors."

"You get movies twice a week. One day this side of the partition, the next in the other aisle. If you don't like it, write your congressman. I've got to do this crap until I get out of the Crotch."

"What's the movie?" I asked, hoping it would be a quiet love story.

"*The Dirty Dozen.* Must be about some old bakery or something."

"I've heard of that. It's just my luck to have the screen right at the foot of my rack. Hell, Cheryl, if I want to kiss you everyone in the room will be looking in this direction."

"Janet, where are you going?"

"Just downstairs to get you that carton of cigarettes." She winked and walked away. Janet is one terrific sister.

"Rick, do you realize this is the first time we've been together in almost eight months?" Cheryl took my hand and tears began to fall again. When she finally got herself composed and ready to try talking again, the movie came on. The lights went down and the whole room was dark except my rack. The sound was turned on full so the patients on the other side could hear the story even if they couldn't see it.

Talking was impossible. Cheryl could see me, but I was blinded by the projector light. Completely frustrated, I pulled her hand across my chest to kiss her. The hell with everybody watching.

86

"Cheryl, I love you."

"What?"

*"Cheryl, I love you."*

"What Rick, I can't hear you." I gave it all I had. I'd waited a long time to tell her my feelings. But it was just then they cut the sound to change the reel. The room was silent.

"CHERYL, I LOVE YOU . . ." The lights came on with a roar of applause and whistles. Then laughter. Cheryl sat down in the chair next to my rack and put her head in her hands.

"I heard you, Rick."

"I'm sorry. You shouldn't feel so bad. You can sneak out of here but I've got to stay and get razzed the rest of the day. My timing was perfect."

The sound track got louder and louder as the movie neared its conclusion. The only thing for us to do was to sit it out. The lights came on when the movie ended and Janet reappeared.

"Now hear this. Now hear this. Visiting hours are now over. Will all visitors please leave the hospital."

"I don't believe this. Ten minutes of talking and an hour of movie. . . . Thanks a lot for bringing Cheryl up, Jan."

"No trouble, bro. I'm sorry it had to be lousy."

"At least we got to be together," said Cheryl. "That's a lot more than we've had for a long time. I'll call you tomorrow afternoon to find out how the operation went. If you're feeling OK maybe I can get the car tomorrow night. We'll see you later. Good-bye." She leaned over and gave me one hell of a kiss. Then Janet moved over and kissed my cheek and began to walk away. Tears welled up in her eyes. "Good-bye, little brother. I'm so glad you're home."


No sooner had the visitors gone than the dressing cart was pulled out on to the ward. I glanced at Smitty. He'd seen the cart, too. Crawford was manning it. Most of the conversation on my side of the ward stopped when Crawford was spotted. Smitty lay on his belly and turned his head toward me.

"This is the shits. After that fine movie and your wonderful performance with Cheryl, the day has to be ruined by Captain Pain. Some days I wish I'd never woke up."

"Can't you complain to the doctor about Crawford?"

"Nope, not really. You see, Crawford's changing the dressings as ordered. The fact that his hands are just heavier than everyone else's makes it really hard to discipline him. Payback is hell and someday he'll get his."

Crawford moved down the row of beds. The patients were far more vocal than during the doctor's rounds.

"... *aah ... shiiit ... you son of a bitch ... I'm going to kill you ...*" But these comments seemed only to fuel Crawford's vengeance.

"Rick, watch him now. He's going to change Johnson's dressings and Johnson never makes a sound no matter how hard Crawford tries. I think Johnson has more guts than brains. I've been in this rack next to him for over two months and I have yet to hear him say anything to anybody. He's never had a visitor or a phone call that I've seen. He doesn't even ask for pain meds. They just bring them to him every five or six hours after he has surgery."

Crawford jumped square into Johnson's shit. He peeled the dressing away, often with pieces of flesh attached, and rather than cleaning out the inside of the wound with a Q-Tip, Crawford wrapped a piece of gauze around his finger and twisted his finger around the walls of the wound until blood filled it and began to run over Johnson's body and into the rack. The corpsmen were supposed to get the wounds to bleed as that promotes new tissue growth, but there were less painful techniques.

Johnson never gritted his teeth or bit his lip or moaned. The only sign of pain was the perspiration rolling in streams down his face.

Smitty was next. Crawford laid out a sterile field consisting of a large sterile pad a foot wide and a foot and a half long, with several packages of four-by-four-inch pads open and laid out on it. Next came a package of Q-Tips, a pack of tweezers, and a pair of scissors. These things were laid out so that once the corpsman started he wouldn't have to contaminate his sterile gloves by grabbing any unsterilized packages. Crawford was good at his job. He followed procedure to the letter.

I watched as Smitty prepared himself. His hands were gripping the bed frame. His face was buried in the pillow and he held his body stiff. Crawford grabbed the packing and with one swift jerk pulled it from the wound. Some of the gauze had dried and stuck to the flesh so that when Crawford pulled he lifted Smitty's body until the flesh tore away.

Smitty's scream was muffled, but when he turned his head

for air I saw tears flowing down the side of his face. I wanted to kill Crawford.

"You dumb mother fucker!" I could feel blood rush to my head and the veins on my neck swell. I was filled with hate.

Crawford couldn't have cared less. He reamed that wound out. Smitty's body was rigid and his hands were white as he held the frame in a death grip.

"Crawford, you son of a bitch. You're going to die slow . . . real slow. When you get your orders reading WESTPAC you're going to curse your mother for giving you birth."

"Blow it out your ass. All you crybabies make me sick. Big tough marines. First off, ain't no way I'm getting sent overseas. I've got a critical MOS so even if I was sent over it wouldn't be to a grunt outfit."

The dressing change over, Crawford moved to his favorite victim, Dennis. As he swung the cart around he turned to me. "I'll get you in a few days." Then he stood at the end of Dennis's rack.

"Good afternoon, Dennis. We're going to have a little fun."

"Come on, Crawford. Take it easy, will you please?" There was terror in his eyes. "Just this once, take it easy . . . please." Crawford smiled as he laid out the sterile field. Dennis grabbed the bar over his head and held his breath. Crawford deliberately stopped short of pulling off the cover bandage until Dennis had relaxed enough to pull in another breath. Then he yanked the bandage away.

Dennis threw his head back and his body heaved in a spasm of pain. Crawford continued pulling out foot after foot of blood- and pus-soaked gauze.

Smitty had gotten up and was standing next to my rack. His pajamas were soaked. "Crawford is a real asshole, but in some ways his method isn't so bad. He gets in there and does what has to be done fast. There's a lot to be said for speed. Chief and Cox and a lot of the other corpsmen go slower and a lot gentler but the pain is just as severe. It's just that you have more time to psych yourself up. Hell, if one of the other corpsmen were working on my dressing, he'd still be inside me."

"That might be true, Smitty, but Crawford isn't doing it that way to get it over fast—he does it to inflict pain."

"Hell, yes, he does, but if you want to keep your head screwed on straight just keep it in your mind that it's for your benefit. See old Dennis over their squirming just like Crawford wants . . . well, that's what I avoid."

"Smitty, do you think there is really any difference in pain thresholds?"

"Sure, but like in Dennis's case, there are a whole slew of exposed nerves around the opening of his wound. Just the air hitting those nerve endings would be enough to drive you nuts."

"Yeah, I know. I've got a few of those, too. When you touch them they pull back like little worms. Damn, that hurts."

"No shit, Sherlock. Well, that's just what Dennis is going through right now," he said, then added, "Only three times a day." Smitty looked firmly into my eyes. "Don't let Crawford beat you, not once, not ever."

Sometime later Smitty said he had a terrible fear that his wound would never heal and that dressing changes would be part of his day until he died.

"Man, that's a hell of a nightmare," I said. "If I knew that was my fate, I'd start sucking the end of the gun barrel right now."

"Rick, when you're well enough to get into a wheelchair, you go out by the elevators. If you look out over the tops of all the buildings you can see a red light flashing on a tower. That's the VA hospital. In there you'll find guys from both the big wars. Some of 'em got gassed back in the first. Can you imagine suffering for all these years and ain't nobody gives a damn? Let some other mother's son go die for me and mine from now on. I don't owe this country jack shit and it owes me everything that I want. This fucking country probably paid hundreds of thousands of dollars to kill a single slope, but ten thousand to my family if I died. I'm only sorry it took so long for me to see what America is."

I couldn't say I agreed, but I understood all of it. We'd been betrayed by our country and deserted by our friends. This was one hell of a world we lived in.

"Hot damn, Rick, there's the dinner cart." Off went Smitty, straining like a racehorse to get to the cart before all the trays had been passed out. He couldn't spread his legs apart without tearing away at his wound, so he walked as if someone had tied his knees together. The wheelchair brigade sped past him, carrying their precious cargo of chow. Smitty arrived at the cart last again and was handed his tray.

Crawford brought my tray. I thought I should check it for poison. Maybe he put broken glass in the potatoes. But instead of acting like a complete asshole, Crawford was now the opposite.

"Here you go, Rick. Want some coffee?" I nodded and off he went to fill the cup. When he got back he set the cup down gently.

"Want any cream or sugar?"

"Ah . . . yes, thank you." I didn't understand what was going on. Crawford opened the sugar and cream, then stirred it for me.

"Thanks, Doc. My fingers are swollen and my wrist's still sore. It's hard for me to open those little creamers."

"No trouble. Enjoy your meal." He turned and walked back to the nurses' station.

"Smitty, did you see that? What gives with him, anyway?"

"Don't try to figure that guy out. When he isn't changing dressings he's as nice a guy as you'd want to meet. Something happens to him when he sees blood. That's why when you bitch to the nurses about him they don't believe you."

"Sounds like he should see a shrink, or a minister, or a whore."

It was strange. I'd been hungry when I filled out the menu, but as soon as I started to eat, I felt bloated. "Hey, Eilert. I understand you've been handing out food. Mind if I'm first in line? Bill Adams."

"Bill, glad to meet you. Here, take whatever you want . . . except the milk. There's a little guy somewhere that's helping me drink all I can get." Adams pulled the pot roast onto a piece of paper in his lap. Then he turned and sped away.

"Say, Smitty, what rack is Adams in?"

"The first rack."

"The first rack. I thought the guy in the first rack was black."

"That's right, he is black. Adams is from the fifth floor, two decks up. The word moves fast up here."

"I'll say it does. My first day and they know my name and location already. Hell, he had to know what I was having for dinner, too. This is a hell of a medicine show."

"You're catching on, Rick."

I spotted a hand coming up over the tray, reaching for the chocolate milk.

"Hey, Stumps, is that you?"

"It's me. Can I have the milk? We can't order more than three, and I love chocolate milk."

"Sure, go ahead." Stumps took it and disappeared. I still hadn't seen his face.

Suddenly a hot pain moved up my left leg into my ass. I knew enough about anatomy to know it was my sciatic nerve, and I flagged down Crawford.

"Doc, I'm really hurting. Can you get me a pain shot?"

"Will do." Off he went.

I lay back trying to think of something, anything, other than the terrible pain. Crawford was back almost instantly. "Here we go, Rick. You lucked out. The med nurse was getting someone else a shot, ergo . . . no waiting." Crawford whipped the speck of blood away with a soaked cotton ball.

"'Ergo'? What the hell is 'ergo'?" Crawford winked and walked away.

I tried to fall asleep. I hadn't slept at all that day. Whenever people phoned they would say, "Get some rest." But how could I rest if I was on the phone with them?

"Rick . . . Rick . . . it's Mom."

"Oh, Mom. Sorry . . . I haven't gotten much sleep today and I just got a shot about an hour ago. I feel like the frog prince, awakened by a kiss. Hi, Dad. I'm glad you could come up here. What is it, about twenty-five miles from home?"

"Yeah, not much more than that. You look a little better than yesterday. What time do you go to the operating room?"

"Probably about six in the morning. I'm third on the schedule. Dad, I want you to meet Smitty. Hey, Smitty, these are my folks."

Smitty smiled. "How do you do. Very nice to meet you."

"My mother brought some sandwiches for later."

"That's great, Mrs. Eilert. There are plenty of people up here to help him eat what he can't finish." Smitty then had to roll over to his other side.

Dad pulled up two chairs. "How are you feeling today?" I could see the agony in his eyes as he surveyed my wounds.

"I'm OK. As long as they keep giving me pain shots it's not

so bad." I felt my stomach tighten and the tears welling in my eyes. "God, I don't know, Dad. I've lost so many friends . . . I'm twenty years old and I feel like eighty." My father laid his hand on my head. He'd never shown much affection for anyone, so I was surprised to see him this way.

"It's all right, son. It's the one thing all young men in all wars have gone through. It's a bond that'll always hold you close to the ones you shared that nightmare with. You've had to grow up too fast but you've handled it like a man, and for that you have all my respect. No father ever wants to have a son go through that."

When he saw Mom was in tears, Dad changed the subject. "When you get out of surgery give us a call, if you feel up to it. Otherwise just get some rest. We won't call and Mom will ask the aunts not to call either. That's the last thing you want after surgery. You'll be groggy and will want to sleep all day. Listen, we'll get out of here now and let you get some shut-eye."

Mom stood up and kissed me on the cheek. "I'm sorry. I'm not much fun. I'm so glad you're home. Give us a call, and keep your chin up."

I took a deep breath as they left. I was so happy to see them but I felt uneasy when they were around. For that matter, when anybody was around. I didn't know what to say. I knew I'd changed, and I didn't want to be different. When I'd asked Cheryl what was new, I knew what she would say. To her nothing had changed. Her routine was still the same, but to me nothing was. Still, I *wanted* to hear that nothing back home had changed. I'd dreamed of home as it used to be, and I longed for it.

When I opened my eyes the lights on the ward were being turned off. Smitty was already asleep and the corpsman was moving down the aisle passing out medications. My leg was throbbing so I rang for a pain med. A new corpsman appeared.

"Doc, could I have my pain shot?" The corpsman looked at the end of the rack for my name.

"Sure, Eilert. Do you want your sleeper, too?"

"You mean I get a sleeping pill, too? Yeah, I'll take whatever I can get."

"OK. You're NPO for surgery. The doctor probably ordered it to make sure you get some sleep. Some guys can't sleep the night before surgery."

After the shot I lay back waiting for it to take effect. I felt the pain med moving up from my feet and the sleeper moving down from my head. When the two waves met at my belly button, I passed out.

I was awakened at five. The lights were still off on the ward and the only rays were from the nurses' station. I opened my eyes to see a man in a cape, with white fangs. I thought I was still dreaming or that the drugs I'd been taking were causing me to hallucinate.

"What the hell is going on? Who the heck are you?" The figure said nothing but I felt the sting of a needle in my arm. Whoever it was had been taking a blood sample.

Finally he said, "I need a urine sample. Fill the cup." I obeyed, pouring the contents of the duck into his little cup. The stranger grabbed the cup and left in the darkness, his cape flapping behind him.

Later I learned he was from the blood lab. He took blood samples just before surgery to crossmatch blood and get a white blood cell count.

Just as I started to doze off I was awakened again.

"Eilert . . . got to get you ready for the OR. I've got some needles for you. First a little something to help you relax, then something to dry up your mouth, and finally a saucy little item to make you soar with the birdies."

"Christ, Doc, you make it sound like a French menu. When are they going to take me down?"

"Soon. The doctor's already finished with one patient and there's only one in front of you."

"Eilert . . . wake up . . . meat wagon's here." I had a hard time opening my eyes and an even harder time talking. The drugs had paralyzed me. It took three corpsmen to get me from my rack onto the gurney. I was stripped naked and a sheet was pulled over me, then we were off to the races. It wasn't until I was wheeled into the hallway outside the operating room that I was able to open my eyes. There was a large light overhead, and a woman's face.

"Eilert, I'm the anesthesiologist. I'm going to start your IV now so we won't have to wait when you get inside." I couldn't say anything, just nodded. The only sensation was that of the cold needle being pushed up the vein in my arm, then the cool fluid itself.

Directly across from me, lying on another gurney, was someone with a sheet covering his head. At my feet lay another corpse. In every direction there were men on gurneys waiting to go into the operating rooms. The corridor was cold and I was shivering. I tried to pull the sheet up to my chin.

At one point I heard some commotion in a nearby operating room. A corpsman in a green gown ran past my gurney, then came charging past me again carrying two plastic sacks of blood, and nearly ran into a gurney being pushed out into the corridor. Someone said, "Too late." Then there were three bodies stacked against the wall. The man carrying the blood leaned against the wall, then slid down it to his butt. The only thing I heard him say was *"Damn."*

The door to my OR opened and out came a gurney bearing a survivor of the meat market. His legs were up and bent, one knee had a pin through it with a weight attached, and there was a cast on one arm, holding it up at a forty-five-degree angle.

Within moments I was wheeled into the inner sanctum. One corpsman was mopping the floor, another was laying out some instruments, another was adjusting the overhead lights, and still another was helping the anesthesiologist. I heard someone say, "Count backward from one hundred," and felt a cold sensation running through my arm. I never saw the doctor enter.

"Eilert, can you hear me? . . . Eilert, wake up, come on now. . . . Open your eyes. . . . You're in the recovery room." I couldn't open my eyes but I was able to ask for water. The nurse brought me some, not in a glass but in a soaked rag.

"Suck on this. You'll get a glass of water when you're back on the ward."

When I opened my eyes a nurse was standing next to me and I was surrounded on all sides by gurneys holding wounded marines. There must have been thirty-five, all sucking on rags. Then I noticed I wasn't on a gurney but in my bed. My left leg was elevated at a ninety-degree angle in a hammocklike contraption. There was a metal pin sticking through both sides of the heel on my left foot. A line tied to the pin hung over the end of the bed, where some weights were attached to it. The leg itself was bandaged, and not in a cast as it had been. My right leg, in a cast up to my crotch, had four bandages of various sizes taped over it.

There was a clock that read three o'clock. It didn't seem as though that much time had elapsed. The pain in my legs was terrible and I asked the nurse for some medication. I was obliged. After the shot, the nurse said that one of the corpsmen from the ward was on the way down to fetch me. Before she had finished a tall, redheaded corpsman came up from behind her. "Got someone for Three South, ma'am?"

"Sure do, right here . . . Eilert. Here's his chart. Take care of yourself," she said to me. "I hope I won't see you down here much more."

The corpsman maneuvered my huge rack with terrific speed. It was obvious that he was no novice to the course. The elevator, which was already waiting for us, was operated by a wounded marine in uniform. "We're only expendable on the battlefield."

The operator laughed. "It beats the hell out of burning shitters."

"No screaming eagle feathers. Say, Doc, what's your name?"

"Cox. I room with Chief. Have you met him yet?"

"Yeah. He's an all-right dude. But he's a big son of a bitch."

"He sure as hell is. We make a lot of money off him. Have you seen him tear up any books yet? He can tear a Chicago phone book in half. That's damn near impossible so a lot of other people on the wards bet against him, but he always wins. Only trouble is that you can't find a Chicago phone book anywhere on base."

I couldn't believe it, but knowing how big Chief's hands were, I wasn't going to bet against him.

As I was pushed into the hallway I saw a lot of racks lining the walls. "Doc, what are all these racks doing out here?"

"We've run out of room on the wards. Until space becomes available the less serious patients have to bunk out here. It's this way on most of the wards."

Another corpsman was taking my vital signs again while Smitty lay there watching me like a mother hen. The corpsman left and several guys in wheelchairs came up to my rack. Smitty was the first to say anything.

"How did it go, Rick? Does it hurt much?"

"No, I'm OK. They just gave me a shot a little while ago."

"A little while ago . . . you've been asleep ever since you got back. It's nine-thirty. Visiting hours are already over. Your girl was here but I didn't want to wake you. She just sat there reading a magazine. She left about eight-thirty."

"Thanks, Smitty, but I wish you'd have gotten me up. The sicker I am, the hornier I get." Smitty laughed.

"Say, Rick, I want you to meet a few of the ward cripples, Bridger, Doyle, and Collins. They're from the other side. They all have wounds pretty much like yours."

Bridger was the first to speak. "I understand you've got some pretty neat holes. When they start changing your dressings, let me know. New wounds around here are something to talk about. Besides, you're the new kid on the block, and that way you've got more people to talk with. Talking about sex up here after six in the evening can be kind of bad 'cause who wants to wait in line to get into the head?" Everyone cracked up but Cox came over and broke up the gathering.

"We still have to change a few dressings so get back to your racks. Meds are also coming so stay put. Lights off in twenty minutes. Eilert, you're on some new antibiotics. You get this shot six times a day."

"You mean I'm going to get stuck six times a day in addition to my pain shots? Man, I'm going to have calluses on my rump."

"Not to worry, Eilert. We can give them to you in your thigh."

"A shot there is unnatural, Doc."

Cox patted the area he was about to strike, then jammed the needle home. "Whatever you say, but sooner or later you'll beg us to change the injection area. Here's your sleeper. If you're not out by the time I'm done with passing out meds, I'll ask the nurse to get you a shot."

I fell asleep fast. The sleeper had really done its job and this was the first time I'd been able to fall asleep without a pain shot. And for the first time I had dreams. It had been so long since I'd dreamed that for a moment I felt as if I weren't asleep. Unfortunately, with the ability to dream came the ability to have nightmares.

On this occasion, Crawford had the night duties for the ward. The night corpsman's rounds were made about once an hour. Any unusual problems were registered in a log, along with any medications administered during that watch.

I fell asleep thinking of Cheryl, but in no time I was back in the jungle on ambush. My friend Nick and I shared the same fighting hole. It was only about eight inches deep but was as long as we were. We lay on our stomachs. The only things that stuck up out of the hole were our helmets, our weapons, and possibly our butts. It was dead quiet and pitch-black. There were only the sounds of mosquitoes buzzing and our own hearts pounding. Suddenly a figure appeared in the darkness, and from my angle it looked ten feet tall. Afraid to fire my weapon and allow the muzzle flash to give our position away, I unsheathed my K-bar. I hoped the figure would pass by and let someone else take him down so I lay there as still as possible. The dark figure started to walk around me, but at the last minute cut back, walked straight into my position, and stepped on my right leg. I flew up out of my hole, plunging my knife into the enemy's throat.

I sat up in bed with my eyes wide open. Crawford was on the floor clutching his throat. I lay back into my pillow, my body dripping with sweat and pain pounding through my legs.

Smitty had heard the commotion and rolled out of his rack, almost stepping on Crawford's hand. Dennis, Toby, and Johnson all sat up too. Then like dominoes every man in the ward woke up, one after the other.

"What the fuck's going on down there?" came a yell from the other end of the ward. Some more yelling from the other side of the room: "Why'd you have to wake me now, you son of a bitch? I was in bed with my girl." Laughter went up. The night nurse came in from the other ward, saw the commotion, and ran toward us.

Sensing what had happened, Smitty came over to calm me down. "Easy, Rick. What happened, did you have a nightmare?" By now I was starting to wake up and was really embarrassed by the whole thing.

"God, Smitty, I'm sorry I woke you all. Charlie stood on my leg and I jumped up and put a knife in his throat." The nurse had just noticed Crawford lying on the floor holding his throat.

"What the hell is going on here?" she asked as she knelt to help him.

Luckily for me I had an attorney. I was still pretty shook up. "It's OK, ma'am," said Smitty. "Eilert here had a bad nightmare and Crawford was in on it, that's all. Everything's fine except that Eilert needs his pain shot."

"Everything is not OK. Hitting a corpsman can get you court-martialed, no matter what the excuse is."

Crawford stood up, but when he started to speak the words wouldn't come out. After a few deep breaths and a drink of water he was finally able to say, "Smitty's right, Miss Hogan. I saw Eilert tossing in his rack. I thought he was in pain so I reached over and grabbed his leg to see if I could help him. The next thing I knew I was laying on the deck with the world's worst sore throat."

"That's still no excuse to attack you or any other corpsman."

"Yes, ma'am, it is. One of the first things they tell us in corps school is to approach patients by shaking their feet first to get their attention. These guys are still in the jungle when they're asleep. It was just a conditioned reflex. Next time I make rounds in the middle of the night I'll stay in the aisle like I'm supposed to." Crawford's attitude surprised everyone.

The nurse was still upset. "Well, if that's the attitude you're going to take, then so be it. I'm still going to put this on my report."

My leg was throbbing as I waited for my shot. "Miss Hogan, can I have my pain med now?"

"Just a moment," she snapped, and stormed back to the nurses' station.

"Say, Crawford, I'm really sorry for all this."

"That's all right. But you know, I'm still not convinced you were asleep when you hit me. I'll go and get your shot." As he walked away some of the patients applauded.

"Rick, you were really asleep, weren't you?" Smitty asked.

"Say, Smitty, what's wrong with that nurse, anyway? Does she got a burr up her ass or what?"

"You son of a bitch, you did hit him on purpose, didn't you? Don't try and change the subject. You really smacked him on purpose, didn't you?"

"Honest, Smitty, I didn't."

"Eilert, you asshole. Now I'm going to be up all night wondering if you did or you didn't."

"Hey, Smitty," from down the aisle, "will you and that corpsman killer be quiet? Besides, I was dreaming about Eilert's girl friend. She's got such nice long legs." Everyone started to laugh.

"Come on, Smitty," I whispered, "what's wrong with that nurse? Why is she on my case? I've never even seen her before tonight."

"It's not you. It's the Navy she's all pissed off at. She hates it so damn much she's been trying to get pregnant to get out, but something's wrong with her. She can't even get pregnant."

"That's too bad. Do you know what's wrong with her?"

"Yeah. She's such a bitch nobody will screw her." I broke up laughing.

"Smitty, you're insane."

Crawford returned with the shot, walking carefully as he neared my rack. "Eilert, are you awake?"

"Yeah, Doc. I'm up."

"I'm staying clear of you for the rest of the night so you'd best sleep away."

Reveille came at six in the morning. The lights all came on, and the ward filled with student corpsmen preparing their patients for washing and changing racks. On came the radios and televisions. Cartoons were the favorites that early.

Somehow I wasn't awakened by all the noise that morning. I found out later that word of the previous night's activities had gotten around. The student corpsman in charge of my morning routine was scared stiff. The student corpsmen had usually been in the service only six months before they pulled duty on the wards. On-the-job training. They'd heard about all the battles in the Nam and had been led to believe that their patients were hardened killers. And some of the patients just liked to scare the hell out of the kids. No matter how well briefed they were by the older corpsmen the students were easily intimidated.

I woke up only after Blass, the head corpsman, shook the end of my rack, and then I shot up just like the night before.

"Easy, Eilert. Are you all right? Maybe you should see the shrink."

"No, Doc. I'm all right. I just can't get this dream out of my mind. I'll be all right." Blass called the student corpsman over.

"OK, Edwards, the corpsman killer is all yours."

Across the ward Wilson was yelling at some poor student. "I'm going to bite your nose off if my rack's not made up when I get back from the head." Of course everyone knew that any patients who could get up were responsible for making their own beds. The student corpsmen were especially aware of this.

"Come on, Doc, let's get this over with," I yelled. Edwards waved over another student and the two of them changed my sheets. Once this was accomplished a pan of water and soap were presented to me.

By the time personal hygiene was completed the breakfast trays had rolled in at the nurses' station. Watching Smitty make the long trek for his tray made me crack up—his slow, deliberate steps, his body stiff as a board and bent forward at the waist. He walked as if he were a hundred years old. Still, I could see how much guts it took for him to move at all, let alone walk. The pain had to be terrible. By the time Smitty got back to his rack almost everyone else was finished eating.

I was getting used to real food. What a luxury it was to chew on anything solid. Still, it killed me when I bit down the wrong way or got a piece of food stuck in one of the cuts in my mouth. If hot coffee hit one of them it would send me into a fit of agony. But it was so long since I'd had hot meals the pain seemed worthwhile.

When the trays were taken away I tried to get some sleep but couldn't. Hot, pulsating pain was shooting up and down both legs. I rang the wall button several times without any reply. I asked Smitty to ring his button, in case mine wasn't working. Then I saw Doc Bone starting his rounds. My heart sank. Perspiration started to bead up on my hands and forehead. My time was at hand. *This is going to hurt. Please let me pass out if I start to scream*, I thought.

The doctor moved closer and closer. It seemed to me that the rounds were going much faster than before. For some reason the men weren't moaning and groaning as they had the other day. Now he was at Johnson's rack. *Johnson never says anything, anyway*, I thought. *Maybe I can be as quiet as he is.* Then he was at Smitty's rack. I lay there watching as Smitty clenched the bed frame. I turned, not wanting to feel Smitty's agony.

Suddenly the doctor was standing over me.

"How are we doing today, son?" As he spoke he began removing the dressings on the left leg.

"Just terrific, sir. Do we have to go through this today? How about after Christmas?"

The doctor chuckled. "No, now's the time. I'll try not to hurt you. Now let's see what we've got."

I tried to keep my head down but couldn't help staring at the doctor's hands as he worked. Instead of just tearing away as they had at Scott and in the cast tex room, he sprayed a clear, watery fluid all over the bandage so that some of the gauze just fell away. The cool sensation of the fluid in the wounds hurt like hell but I was able to keep silent. Then the doctor started peeling away the layers of bandages. I could feel the flesh pulling from the gauze that had dried to it. I just kept watching. The closer he got to the leg, the redder the gauze was and the more it pulled. As more of the leg was exposed, I saw that almost all the flesh that should have been covering the bones and muscles was gone. The first part I saw was my knee. Although the gauze stuck there the pain was really no worse than getting it skinned on the street. But when more of the bandage was lifted my heart sank. My kneecap, bone and flesh, was almost completely gone. There was just a huge gash about an inch wide. The doctor continued unraveling. The pain became excruciating. The blood and pus had dried as much as a quarter inch over the top of the gauze, so that when the doctor pulled at the bandage my leg was literally lifted into the air. You could *hear* the tearing and it was a ghastly sound. My leg was repeatedly pulled up, only to tear away by its own weight, leaving bits of skin and muscle hanging on the gauze. My body heaved in spasms of pain again and again. The doctor ordered a shot but even that didn't deaden the pain. I prayed to God to let me pass out. Tears ran down my face, but at least I hadn't cried out. Blood ran down my chin, for I'd bitten my lip. The doctor finished the left leg. I looked up and for the first time saw my leg as it really was. I had to hold back the urge to barf up my breakfast. My leg lay in a bedlike contraption with the top and sides exposed. The back wasn't as badly damaged. The leg was mush. There was nothing that resembled a leg from the knee to the ankle. Nothing but a mass of red, raw, bloody muscle, bone, tendon, and an occasional nerve ending, pulsating. There was no skin at all to my ankle, and there the top of my foot lay open, the bone split and all but two of my toes broken from the force of the blast. Then I noticed the large chunks of flesh dug out of my thighs. Chunks so large it was impossible to sew the spaces shut. These, too, would have to heal from the inside out. I lay breathing deep, heavy breaths, with perspiration rolling down my face and arms and chest. The doctor moved around to my right side.

"It's a real mess, isn't it? Charlie didn't leave much for us to work with. But as long as it hurts it's yours, and anything that's yours is better than a piece of lumber hanging from a stump." He turned to Blass and the nurse to explain what he wanted done with dressing changes.

"I want this leg tripped three times a day, and the wound scrubbed down with Betadine solution. Then when you bandage up the area, soak down the whole site with Dakin's solution so the gauze won't stick so much. Now let's look at the right leg."

I'd forgotten all about the other leg. The blood rushed out of my head. I felt as if I were going to pass out, but I didn't.

There were four large wounds on the right calf from ankle to knee, all too large to sew shut. The leg was in a cast to the crotch, with windows cut around the wounds. The doctor took these bandages away much faster than those on the left leg, but as before the bandages stuck and had to be ripped away. One of the mid-calf wounds went almost all the way through and the gauze there stuck not only to the flesh but to the bone as well. The doctor used tweezers, poking them deep inside the wound to pull loose the last threads.

"Doc Bone, are wounds like this any different from car accident injuries?" He chuckled and looked up from my leg.

"Well, in a car wreck or even in wounds from civilian-type weapons, the foreign objects move at low velocity. They hit the flesh moving in a straight line and often go right through the arm or leg. The skin and nerve damage usually is restricted to a small area around the wound so it can often be stitched shut. Grenades and high-velocity military weapons are different. When shrapnel hits the body there's a shock wave that explodes outward, destroying huge areas of flesh and nerves. I once plucked a piece of shrapnel the size of your little-finger nail out of a hip. It had shattered the pelvis. In addition, shrapnel is red-hot when it enters the body and it burns much of the surrounding flesh. This can be good because it cauterizes the blood vessels it's just severed, but stones, dirt, and pieces of trees and plants also get blown into the wound. All this garbage, plus the damage done, makes it necessary to remove the dead tissue around the wound. Then the wound must be left open to manage any infection and allow the healing to start inside . . . and that's the name of the tune."

He probed the tweezers back into the leg to pull out the last threads, smiled, then ripped off his surgical gloves.

"There we go. All over. You can relax now."

# 6

I WENT LIMP, completely drained of strength. The doctor gave the dressing-change instructions, then moved across the aisle to Dennis.

"It kind of hurts, don't it?" Smitty smiled. "Feels kind of like you just got raped by a lion, don't it? Well, stand the fuck by, 'cause they still got to dress the wound. Welcome to Three South."

I had forgotten about the dressing changes. It was like falling off a cliff and just after hitting the ground getting shot in the nuts. Not only would I have to handle it after the doctor left, but after lunch, and again after dinner.

"Goddamn, Smitty, how am I going to stand this three times a day? It takes all the energy and concentration I can muster just to have them ripped off. The only reason I don't scream is that I can barely breathe."

"It's not going to make it easier anticipating the pain. There's plenty of time to hurt, so enjoy every hour you have that isn't full of pain. Now you get pain shots when they change the dressings, but the time will come when you have no pain meds and you have to handle the pain on your own."

"I know you're right. I know I have to handle it. Now I know how JC felt waiting to go up on the cross. No way to pass the pain off on someone else."

"Well, one thing we've got to be thankful for is that we're not dead. That could be a lot worse."

"Yeah, but for just a few minutes a while ago, I wished I was dead, and I meant it."

"You're lucky we've got Smith doing dressing changes today. He's nothing to brag about when it comes to quality work but at least he isn't heartless."

"I'm glad to hear that. Believe me, a few months of these dressing changes and my brain will be jelly."

"Rick, sooner or later you're going to get well. The sooner the pain starts, the sooner it will stop. That's why they got that sign hanging up by the nurses' station. No pain, no gain. Sounds stupid, but it's true."

"Yeah, I guess you're right. Here comes the dressing cart." My heart started throbbing. The pain shot had helped me relax since the doctor had gone. I hoped it would work long enough to keep the pain away a little longer. With the doctor gone the moans and cursing started all over again. The corpsman moved closer and closer. It seemed he was skipping patients en route to my rack. He was at Young's now. I hadn't met Young yet, but I found out who he was from his scream.

"Goddamn you, Smith, you duffus ass-wipe."

"Young, you've got one of the sweetest wounds on the ward yet you bitch more than Dennis. Will you just shut the fuck up?" That was my introduction to Young.

Now Smith was at Johnson's rack. As usual Johnson said nothing, just broke out in a heavy sweat. He moved on to Smitty. I tried to concentrate on something else without success. Smitty never made any noise but just to look into his eyes during a dressing change was enough to send chills up and down your spine. It seemed impossible that anyone with wounds where Smitty had them could keep from passing out.

I was finding out that other people's injuries often look much worse than your own. But it's because you've only started to cope with your own wounds, and you can't understand how others can cope with theirs. At least that's what Smitty had told me.

Corpsman Smith finished cleaning up the bloodied bandages from around Smitty's rack, then pulled off the plastic gloves and tossed them into the garbage bag.

"Well, Eilert, ready for your first hold-your-breath contest?"

"Not particularly. Come on, Doc, let's get this over with."

Smith laid out the sterile field and pulled away the dressing the doctor had left to cover the wounds. Now with the leg completely exposed, Smith pulled on a clean pair of gloves, grabbed the Dakin's solution, and began to squirt it all over the wounds. The cold sensation felt quite good at first, then within seconds the pain hit. I threw my head back deep into the pillow, pulling myself into the mattress by the frame around the bed. It was like pouring cold water over the exposed nerve of a tooth . . . only this was over an area one thousand times the size. Then, wrapping the gauze around his index and middle fingers, Smith began to rub my leg in all directions. My body heaved involuntarily. I wanted to ask the corpsman to stop for a moment, just to let me catch my wind, but my breath was gone. I watched as he rubbed the raw, exposed muscle. It looked like he was rubbing very gently but it felt like he was using a red-hot iron. Tears and perspiration rolled down my face. I wanted to scream but the pain was too intense. Breathing was hard enough.

He repeated the cycle, this time with hydrogen peroxide, which had the same effect because it, too, was cold. But it also began to foam up wherever there was an open area. At first it foamed white, then quickly went yellow-brown, then reddish brown. The visual effects didn't help at all for it was obvious that this, too, would have to be wiped off. Out came the gauze wrapped around the fingers, then the rubbing began again. I remembered that when as a kid I'd cut myself the iodine had hurt the same way, but over such a wide area it was torture. Next came the Betadine solution, with a deep red color and about as thick as blood, but cold as ice water. It foamed, too, but reddish brown. By now I was grabbing hold of the trapeze over my head. With each swipe of the gauze across the raw skin I grabbed for a new hold somewhere else around the bed. Lastly, after the Betadine rub was completed, the wound was washed with Dakin's again. Large slabs of gauze soaked in Betadine solution were laid over the wound in strips three layers high and covered with a large cotton pad.

After that came the wounds on my thigh and knee. The same process was repeated there. The pain was bad but somehow it wasn't as severe as in the lower leg. These wounds were deep but not as massive. The corpsman moved to the lower left leg. Each wound was soaked just as the others had been. Only this time, instead of wiping it clean with gauze around his fingers, Smith wrapped the gauze around tweezers, thrust them into the wound, and reamed with a circular motion. The touch of the cold metal around the bone was so bad I felt I was going to vomit.

Each solution was applied in order, and each time the tweezers were poked into the wound the metal would ram the bone with a dull thud. After the wound was cleaned it had to be packed, which required several feet of thin gauze and the handy tweezers. It was like filling an overnight suitcase with two weeks' worth of clothes.

Smith thrust layer upon layer of gauze deep into the wound. Each time he pressed in the dressing he pushed so hard the leg was driven into the mattress. Then when he pulled the tweezers out, the bed springs propelled the leg up so quickly it bounced on the mattress. This went on until the packing was level with the top of the wound. This was repeated on all four wounds on the lower part of my right leg. One was particularly sensitive, as several small nerve endings were exposed. Whenever they were even lightly touched my whole leg would jump.

For some reason this was the wound that took the longest to pack. And there was just no way to avoid hitting those sensitive little strands. The pain shot up my spine, pulsating as it went, right to the base of the skull. I wanted to pass out so badly that I even tried to hold my breath, but each time the packing was pushed into the leg the breath was knocked out of me as if I'd been hit in the stomach with a bat.

Finally it was over. I lay motionless. The dressing changes at Scott and in the cast tex room had been nothing by comparison. The whole process had taken forty minutes, without any letup, and I was exhausted.

"All done for now, Eilert. Your next change will be at about twelve-thirty, just before nap time."

"Thanks a whole bunch, Doc." I hadn't even looked to either side. If I had, I would have seen several wheelchair cases watching the show.

"Damn, Rick, you is fucked up. Those are some of the nicest holes I've ever seen, bar none. Looks like you got hit by a Claymore or a beehive round."

"Gee, thanks, Smitty. Just what I wanted to hear." Toby walked up shaking his head.

"Rick, we should sell tickets to your dressing changes. I'm not kidding. Man, forty minutes for a dressing change. That's three times longer than a short feature at the movies."

"No thanks, Toby. Hell, if I had known I was being watched now I'd have tried to smother myself with my pillow."

The people in the wheelchairs turned to wheel away, some shaking their heads. One backed up to my rack. "Say, thanks a lot, really nice to look at. I'm glad I didn't order spaghetti tonight." I couldn't believe it.

"Smitty, this is like a freak show. Who are these people?"

"They're from Three East. Every once in a while we make wagers with the people on that ward. You know, stuff like which ward has the most fucked-up body, or who's got the worst dressing changes. We also have wheelchair races, and pin the tail on the donkey games with the blind guys on some of the wards."

"You're kidding. Pin the tail on the donkey with the blind guys?"

"No, it's true. We haven't gotten any blind guys for a while. But we have the corpsmen keep a lookout for draft choices as they come in. We're due now. Fifth floor got the last two. We don't get them down here unless they got bones screwed up."

"You people are sick."

"You guessed it, Rick. That's why we're here."

"You mean those guys from Three East came to watch me get my dressings changed?"

"We had a hundred bucks of the ward benevolent fund riding on your dressing changes. We knew you wouldn't let us down," said Toby.

"You mean you bet money on my wounds? How were you so sure they were bad enough?"

"Sure we bet on you, and we won. Crawford and Chief see almost all the wounds that come on to the ward first. They told us yours were very interesting, and a sure bet."

"I can't believe you people. What if they had someone with worse wounds? You'd have lost all your money."

"Listen, Rick, there are plenty of guys with worse wounds than yours. Just not with as many ugly ones as yours. Face facts, man. A dog would piss on a tree trunk covered in shit before he'd go near your leg."

"Thanks, Smitty. Thanks a lot. You really brighten up my day."

"Look, you've won ten bucks, so don't bitch about it. We bet five bucks of your money, but either way we won."

"And if I had lost? What if I had lost? Suppose they had someone more fucked up. What then?"

"The guy they got was hit with an RPG while he was sleeping in a tank. Man, was he a humm. But he's only got twenty-nine holes. You've got thirty-three. Chief counted them the first day you went into cast tex."

"I'm glad you warned me. From now on I'll try not to show the pain so much. I don't want to embarrass myself."

"No, no, don't change a thing. Those little fits of anguish enhance the whole thing. Keep up the good work."

With that most of the men returned to their own beds to have their dressing changes or watch cartoons. "I tell you what, Smitty. It's easy to see why they don't put officers on the same ward with the enlisted men. At least officers got a little class."

"Hey, there isn't an officer that's a patient who can give us any shit. That happened about four months ago. Some second lieutenant tried it out on old Wilson."

"So what did you do?"

"Wilson couldn't give a shit. He's getting out anyway so it mattered not if he left as an E-5 or a PFC. Anyway, Gramps got some of our corpsmen to find out what day he was going to OR."

"What was he going to OR for?"

"He was getting married and he wanted to get circumcized."
We started laughing wildly.

"You got to be kidding, Smitty. Nobody gets their dick pricked when they're that old."

"It's the truth. Ask Chief and Thomas. They're the corpsmen that handled the job for us. Anyway, they find out what time this clown gets into recovery, then they have the corpsman on phone watch in the officers' ward call them when he's to be picked up. The two of them go down to fetch him. When they get down there this guy is wide awake, so they tell the nurse that the guy's in pain. She gets him a shot of Demerol and out he goes. Then they wheel him into the morgue. Nobody ever goes there, so they take a bunch of obscene pictures of this guy and a chicken. I mean a real live chicken. There he is, the son of a bitch, dead to the world, his pecker all bandaged from this dickotomy, and this ugly chicken. Anyway, they take him up to the ward and then get the pictures from the Polaroid and give them to Wilson and Gramps."

"You mean they didn't get caught?"

"Well, the guy wasn't supposed to get any pain shots, just this thing you break open and sniff. It gives you one hell of a rush. Anyway, they just chalked up the pain shot to a mistake and that was it."

"So how come this guy didn't bring charges?"

"Well, it wasn't from the pictures so much as from Wilson's ability to get someone to go through all that elaborate planning. Let alone pull it off. He figured he was lucky he wasn't dead. So he just didn't press any charges."

"Remind me never to mess with Wilson. He's nuts."

"He's not as bad as O'Hara and McCarthy. They are a little past strange. They hover around bizarre. I got to roll over Rick—my ass is killing me. Talk to you later."

"Sure, Smitty. Thanks for the horror story. Smitty . . . they didn't really pull that off, did they?"

The corpsman was finishing up with Dennis's dressing, and now it was easy for me to sympathize with him. *He may be a screamer,* I thought, *but I would have done some yelling, too, if I had been able to catch my breath.* I wondered how anyone could explain real pain to someone who'd never been injured.

I started to light a cigarette when I noticed skin hanging from the palms of my hands. I had pulled so hard at the frame of the bed that I'd torn off strips of skin. Then I looked at the trapeze bar over my rack and there was blood smeared all over it. I rang the buzzer to get some wrapping for my hands, and then noticed the blood all over my pillow case. I'd forgotten how I'd bitten my lip during my ordeal. The student corpsman who'd been charged with my care that morning came to my aid. My lip had stopped bleeding but my hands still hadn't completely clotted.

The young student grabbed some Ace wraps and gauze from the dressing table, along with some Dakin's solution.

"How the hell did you do this?"

"Easy, Doc. I got a big boom-boom. Instead of screaming, I like to inflict pain on myself."

"Man, it must have hurt something awful for you to do this to yourself. Can't they give you something?"

"The doctor gave me a shot when he took the dressings off, but it didn't really help then. It helps now, to settle me down."

The corpsman washed the blood off my hands, wrapped them in gauze, then wrapped some Ace bandages around them.

"I just never knew it was possible to hurt that much. I've heard of people in so much pain that they pass out. But I was never around anyone hurt like you guys."

"Your time will come soon enough. You're going to be assigned to a grunt unit, aren't you?"

"Yeah. At first I was looking forward to it. Now I'm not so sure. It scares the hell out of me to think I'll end up like you people up here. I sure hope I just get stationed at Pendleton or Okinawa."

"There ain't no way I would be a corpsman. If you're in an outfit that gets in the shit, chances are excellent that you'll get killed."

"Just what I wanted to hear. Listen, I've got to finish charting all the morning activities. I'll stop back in a little while in case you need anything."

"Sure, Doc, thanks. Later."

The sounds of radios and televisions on different channels and all the conversations, the moaning and groaning and swearing, made sleeping impossible. Closing my eyes and daydreaming was the next best thing.

The morning passed quickly. I wasn't bothered until the lunch trays came, and that was a welcome interruption. I'd often heard of terrible hospital chow, but the people I'd heard it from hadn't been eating C rations day and night. However, no sooner had the trays been cleared and the lunch cart towed away than the dressing cart appeared at the first rack. Dressing changes again! I rang the buzzer for a pain shot. Maybe that would help some. At least I could relax until it started.

A corpsman walked up. "You have a phone call." He plugged the phone into the wall outlet.

"Doc, would you ask the nurse to get my pain shot?" The corpsman nodded.

"Hello."

"Hi, Rick. This is Mom. How do you feel? Was the doctor up today? Have you started eating yet?"

"Hey, slow down, Mom. All those questions will just confuse me. Us marines aren't noted for our brains. Yes to all three. I prefer yes-or-no questions to multiple-choice anyway. Sorry if I sound grumpy. I just had my first introduction to dressing changes."

"Was it bad? I hope you're not in a lot of pain. I worry about that a lot, and I pray that you heal quickly." *Damn*, I thought, *why did she have to say that?*

"No, Mom, it wasn't that bad, really it wasn't." I could feel my tongue turn black for such a foul lie. But I knew how emotional she was and I figured she'd been through enough worrying.

"Rick, since you're not awfully uncomfortable, I'll come up with Gramps tonight, if that's all right."

"Sure, Mom, that would be fine. I've missed Gramps a lot and it'll be great seeing him. Hold on a minute. I've got to get my shot."

The corpsman held out three shots. I was baffled.

"I thought I was going to get one shot six times a day."

"Nope, two antibiotics six times a day, and this other one is your pain med. They were supposed to start these this morning. Someone screwed up. Where do you want them?"

"In my other cheek. My right one feels like a golf ball." I began talking to Mom again.

"Yeah, Mom, sorry about that. I'm getting three injections in my a . . . aaa . . . ass. . . . Damn. It's hard to talk with a needle in your butt. Anyway, for now I get twelve shots a day not including pain shots, and they change my dressings three times a day. The doctor hasn't said much. It'll probably be some time before he knows what's going to happen."

"Is Cheryl coming up today?"

"Not that I know of. She can't get off work for the afternoon visiting hours. And she can't get the car every night to come up here. Besides, she should still go out with her friends, too. It's got to be a drag coming up here all the time. I don't mind. I'm not going anywhere."

"Do you think you'll get out for Christmas?"

"Gosh, that would be nice. I haven't asked the doctor yet."

"I'll get off now so you can take a nap before you have dinner."

"Fine, Mom. I look forward to seeing you. I've got a dressing change now anyway. Talk to you later. Good-bye."

There was another new corpsman I hadn't seen doing the dressing changes before. He was moving very quickly, talking to each patient as he worked on him. It looked as if he had changed all these wounds before . . . many times before.

Smitty returned to his rack as the dressing cart neared. Once in bed he began to pull away some of the dressing himself, then he lay down on his stomach, waiting patiently for a little doom and gloom. He turned his head to talk to me.

"Hey, Rick, here comes O'Hara. Ask him if it's all true about Wilson and that second louie."

"You're not kidding, are you. You're serious. That all really happened?"

"Rick, I wouldn't shit you. You're my favorite turd."

I chuckled, "Smitty, you are outrageous."

O'Hara was at Johnson's rack now. It seemed even more impossible to me that a man could hold back pain as Johnson did. Now I knew how much it had to hurt him. Yet perspiration and an occasional gritting of teeth were all he showed. I made a pact with myself to be another Johnson. I saw the way the others admired his strength. I wanted that respect as well.

I laughed to myself. *Imagine, all through school I was competing in grades and sports. Now I lie shredded and broken, and I'm still competing for someone's respect.*

"So you're Rick, the corpsman killer. I've heard a lot about you. Like you've earned the ward a few dollars, you're not too fond of Crawford, and your girl has a great pair of legs."

"You really keep on top of things. Say, is it true that you took some picture of some second louie with a dickotomy?"

"You mean the one with the chicken. Did Smitty tell you about this?"

"You guessed it."

"In that case, it's true. He was going to marry a nurse on this ward before that happened. Hey, how was I supposed to know the girl I was sleeping with was his fiancée? When we carried out the request I had no idea it was the same guy that met Wilson's stump." While he was talking he prepared the sterile field and set up all the extras.

"OK, Rick. . . . It is OK, right?" He didn't wait for a reply. "This may sting a little." He started ripping the dressings off, not waiting to hear an "ouch" or a "damn."

I grabbed the frame, gritting my teeth and slamming my head into the pillow. O'Hara had done that task so fast that, although it hurt very much, I was still able to get my breath. The next phase began, scrubbing the wounds. Since it hadn't been too long a time since the bandages had been changed they didn't stick to the flesh nearly as much as before.

"Come on, Rick, help me. Talk to me. It was a long night and I haven't got much to say." He sprayed the wound with hydrogen peroxide. "Come on, watch this; they say if the wound's infected it will foam up. Let's see. *Aahhh*, too bad, it's infected. Well, maybe tomorrow it will be gone." I was laughing until I was crying.

"O'Hara, you asshole, you crazy squid. . . . Damn, that hurts."

Now came the Betadine solution scrub. My rack was surrounded by onlookers and comments like:

"Look at them holes."

"Oh, what a lovely pattern."

"That looks like my stool after I got hit in the gut."

I heard a small gruff voice coming up from the floor: "That looks like the inside of Berker's colostomy bag."

That had to be Stumps. It sounded like someone with a mouth full of marbles.

Smitty picked Stumps up off the floor and sat him on his lap. He looked just like a Charlie McCarthy doll. I smiled hello but the spasms of pain were shooting through my body. Even the crowd of onlookers couldn't help keep me from crying. I tried so hard to put on a show of strength, but the pain was too great.

O'Hara finished the lower left leg and moved up to the thigh. I didn't have to pretend that the pain wasn't bad. All those watching this marathon dressing change knew just what I was going through. It always helped them when they could watch. It reassured them that they weren't alone in their suffering. But I still had to find that out.

O'Hara was oblivious to the crowd around him. He continued chattering while working. It was all part of his technique. The words he threw out were just something for the patient to direct his anger and pain at until the change was over.

I was twisting in every direction, looking for some comfortable position. My hands were changing position with the same frequency, groping for that one place on the bed that would make the pain go away. O'Hara finished with the left leg and moved quickly to the right.

"OK, Rick, only one leg left and we're out of here. You know something, you ought to tell your girl to leave us sailors alone after she's been up here to see you. That's just not very nice."

I sat up cursing a blue streak. "You son of a bitch, O'Hara." Just as I reached out to grab his throat, O'Hara yanked the dressings out of two of the holes on my leg. I threw myself back into the mattress, both of my legs tight with pain. The packing was soaked with blood and pus and some of it splattered, hitting a few of the spectators, who voiced their disapproval. "O'Hara, you animal, that's not sanitary."

"O'Hara, you asshole, pus on his holes is one thing, but pus in my mouth is another."

The corpsman worked as quickly as he could. Finally it was over. I was left exhausted, but content that the torture was over.

"O'Hara, that was one hell of a ride. I don't know whether to thank you or swear at you."

"Hey, don't complain, thirty-three minutes. You won't get a better time anywhere. I'm quick but clean. How long did it take this morning?"

"Forty minutes."

"So what's the bitch? I've already shaved seven minutes off your pain time. Once I know the wounds a little better, we'll get down to thirty on the head. I bet you're starting to feel better already."

"As a matter of fact, I am." I was beat, completely used. But it was over and for that I was grateful.

"Rick, you've got a phone call." A student corpsman plugged it into the wall then handed me the receiver.

"Hi, Rick. This is Aunt Mary. How are you doing, really? Listen, do you want any visitors this afternoon? I've got all the aunts here. We're going to leave right now. We can't stay long. See you soon. Bye-bye."

I hung up wondering how, just a few minutes after the dressing change, I could feel so good about the thought of having visitors. My aunts, my mother's sisters, had all been like mothers to me at one time or another. They had written me often while I was in the Nam and their letters were very special, for they carried all the news of my many cousins, who were like brothers and sisters, and the latest on all the little things. I was so happy I forgot about pain for the moment. When it started in again I wondered if I dared take medication. By the time my aunts arrived I would be chasing the white rabbit. I decided to wait.

The time passed quickly for me. The corpsman got me a clean pajama top and I gave myself a GI shower with a little can of deodorant. I even tried to comb my hair. Strange, I thought, that I hadn't worried about my hair until now. I tried to pull the comb through it and couldn't. It was tangled and filled with pieces of bamboo, dirt, dried blood, and a few stitches. I had forgotten all about the wound up there.

The corpsman returned with the phone. "You got another one, Rick."

"Rick, this is Cheryl. How do you feel today?"

"Fine, just fine. Are you coming up?"

"No. I can't get the car this evening, and I can't leave work early enough to get there for afternoon visiting hours."

"That's all right. My aunts are coming up this afternoon and Mom's coming up this evening with Gramps. I'd rather see you, though. Can't you get a ride up here with one of your girl friends?"

"No, I can't."

I recognized a shortness in her voice. I could sense what was happening, but I had resigned myself long ago to how this relationship would end.

"OK, fine. Well, maybe tomorrow, if you can get the car."

"Tomorrow is Saturday, and my brother uses the car on the weekend, so there's no way I can get up there."

"No problem, my folks are coming up this weekend. You could come with them."

"No, I can't talk to you when they're there. I'd rather come up by myself."

"Sure, whatever you want. Say, I've got to get off. I'll talk to you later."

"OK, Rick. I'll call you tomorrow afternoon."

I hung up. I knew where this was headed. I might be in this hospital a long time. I might never get better. What right did I have to expect her to want to spend her life with a cripple? Christ, she was only nineteen. There was no way she should have to be put on the spot. It hurt—it hurt a lot—but I shouldn't push. Besides, if I really loved her as much as I said I did, then what she wanted should come first. I wasn't being noble, just logical.

It was hard to believe that two years before I'd been a freshman at Northern Illinois University, struggling through my first mid-term exams. My roommate, Larry, hardly studied and pulled outstanding grades. I studied hard and just got by, only to be placed on academic probation. Of course, important time was devoted to our pet boa constrictor and flushing cherry bombs down toilets, partying, pranks, nighttime visits to the stadium, and drinking. Classes were important but when I studied it was torture. So much was happening. I felt that I was missing something. Weekends I went home to see Cheryl.

Vietnam was just a place you went to after getting kicked out of school. Larry and I talked about the war more and more. We both wanted to find out what it was all about.

Larry enlisted in the corps during second semester. That left me alone in my dormitory room. Scott and Charlie lived just down the hall from me. Both were juniors carrying good grades and still they never seemed to miss a good time. They took me under their wing and vowed to oversee my education. We bought an old car without an engine and had it parked in a lot below my third-floor window. We managed to get a telescope and set up an observatory in my room. Then we charged two dollars an hour to couples who wanted to park. Privacy was hard to find on campus. Then we charged fifty cents a head to anyone who wanted to watch from my room. Profits were high but studying in my room was difficult. My ex-roommate's snake was eating three mice a week now, so we charged twenty-five cents a head to watch the feeding. When the snake escaped and ate a neighbor's kitty the jig was up. By then so was the semester. Charlie and Scott stayed up all night studying and passed. My enterprise ended my college career. I was asked to leave.

I realized the foolishness of it all, but I didn't have any idea of what I was in school for or where I was going afterward. I envied the people who knew what they wanted. So many people know they want to be doctors, lawyers, shepherds, bounty hunters, or starship commanders from early childhood. But I just wanted desperately to find a reason for being on this planet.

Cheryl had graduated from high school, and in her I found all I cared about. We were young but the next logical step seemed to be marriage. We decided to wait and get high-paying jobs to build up a nest egg.

I became a draftsman, possibly the world's worst. The money I made barely covered room and board at home and gas, dates, and taxes. Drawing a straight line lost its attraction fast. Then I heard Larry had been wounded. That was all I needed. I'd always wondered about Vietnam, but now the reason for being there seemed clear. My friend's blood was in its soil. It never dawned on me that my blood would make pretty good fertilizer, too. I enlisted. After I did, I realized Cheryl would be left alone. With her beautiful green eyes, blond hair, long legs, healthy build, and lively personality she wouldn't be alone long. That really hurt.

A year ago I'd been playing around. My biggest decision was whether to go dancing or to catch a movie. How fast it had all changed after months of just trying to stay alive . . . to find a dry piece of ground to sleep on and to kill other young men my age. My whole life had turned around, and suddenly I had nothing to say about how it would turn out.

There was a commotion down at the nurses' station. It sounded like a stampede was coming down the aisle. It was my aunts. The rules said there could be only two visitors at a time per patient, but I had three determined aunts. O'Hara, not a very military-minded person anyway, checked them in as two for me, one for Smitty.

My spirit soared at the sight of my wild, beautiful, outrageous aunts. At first they seemed a little hesitant: there was the smell, the thick warm air, and all the bodies hanging every which way from the superstructures over their beds. They must have been asking themselves, *What is this kid going to look like?*

They spotted me at the end of the ward and their pace quickened. They were probably relieved to see that my nose and eyes were in the right places. As the three of them embraced me they all had tears in their eyes and runny noses, but those disappeared with a flurry of questions, the answers to which nobody paid any attention to.

"We heard so little about your injury, and we all thought the worst. We didn't know what shape you were in. You look great." Aunt Mary was such a terrific liar. But that's what I wanted to hear. Aunt "Bercy" and Aunt "Soo-Soo," names I'd called them for as long as I could remember, stood at the foot of my rack just in line to see the pin in my heel. Their eyes and their mouths dropped open because Betadine solution was still dripping from the bandages. They thought it was blood. I quickly reassured them that I wasn't bleeding to death. They exchanged small talk about home and their families, but I couldn't concentrate on what they said—only on the sound of their voices. It was so good to hear them talking and cracking jokes and laughing that I was oblivious to most of the questions.

The pain was starting to shoot through my body, and caused me to roll from side to side. For a while, I didn't concentrate on the pain. It was more of an inconvenience than anything else. Yet I was losing the battle of will against it. I couldn't relax, but I couldn't let the pain throw me into a fit in front of my family. I rang the buzzer. Aunt Mary asked if there was something she could get. At first I joked, "Yeah, an easy girl," but quickly recanted. "Would you ask the corpsman if he'll get my pain med?"

"Sure." She scurried off.

I was embarrassed that I had to give in while they were there. I'd hoped to hold out until they left. As much as I tried to make light of it, the look in my eyes gave me away, and they knew I wished they'd leave. They offered their regrets that they had to go so soon. There was still a half an hour left to the visiting hour, but they all made up good excuses.

"Thanks for coming to see me. I missed you all so much. Thank you for your letters while I was away. They meant a lot to me. Say hi to everyone and please come back."

"Sure we will. Next time we'll make something to eat as well. After all, you're the one with the bottomless pit. We'll be back soon."

As they walked out a corpsman came with my injections for the pain and the antibiotics. "Here we go, three for the road." It took no time at all to fall into a deep sleep. Not to feel any pain was so wonderful.

"Eilert . . . come on, Rick. Time for your dressing change." Chief was on dressing changes that evening shift. I heard him trying to wake me. I didn't want another dressing change but I knew it had to be done.

"Yeah, Chief, I'm awake. Go ahead and hurt me. Everyone else has taken a cut at me."

"Rick, it's not that bad. You've just got to get used to it. I'll try not to hurt you, but don't be angry with me if it does."

"I know, Chief. Just get it over with." Chief had set up the cart already. All he needed to do was get his gloves on and start pulling the dressings off.

At first it wasn't so bad, certainly not like the previous changes. Chief moved very slowly, almost too slowly. It really didn't hurt that much at first, but as he got closer to the flesh itself, the pain increased. Then he poured the cold liquid over the leg. The shit hit the fan.

My body went rigid, and I shook in spasms. Chief continued to work without hesitation. His face showed pain, too, and every time I flinched or gritted my teeth so did Chief. Still, nothing new was happening. It was as if I knew what to expect with each movement of Chief's huge hand as he scrubbed the wound. As long as I anticipated what was going to happen I could brace against the pain. It still hurt, but it was predictable.

As Chief moved from the left to the right leg I was able to catch my breath.

"Chief, you're doing a great job. It hurts like hell but not as bad as the one this morning. Thanks for taking it so easy." Chief smiled and continued to pull the packing from the wounds. He worked inch by inch, not foot by foot like the others. It was an hour before he finished, but as far I was concerned, he could have taken longer.

Chief cleaned up the area, filling the garbage bag. Then, taking his gloves, he moved over to Dennis's rack. Dennis didn't care if it was Chief—the pain was still horrible and nothing was going to change that. "Chief, be gentle. Don't make it hurt so much. Please, take it easy. It's really bothering me today."

"Take it easy, Dennis. I'll go as slowly as I can. You know there's no way that I can stop the pain."

Chief seemed a little annoyed with Dennis. As he lowered his hands down to begin removing the bandages covering the wound, Dennis screamed.

"Chief, I asked you to take it easy. Now I mean it—go slow."

"I haven't even touched the bandages yet. You can't get it any easier than that."

Still, whatever speed he moved at, Dennis bitched. He knew he could get away with it as long as Chief was working on him.

My mom and grandfather arrived just at seven P.M. Some dressing changes were still in progress. Visitors were allowed in as long as the patient they were visiting had been taken care of. The patients still getting worked on had a screen set up around their racks to give them some privacy.

"Hey, Rick, isn't that your mom? I hope she brought some sandwiches. Chow really sucked this evening." I smiled and shook my head.

"Hi, Mom. Gramps . . . God, how I've missed you and your

cooking." I sat up as well as I could, putting my arms around Gramps.

"I got that last package you sent me. You must have read my mind when you made that one up—all those nuts and popcorn and crackers. I had to hide the bourbon in the bushes just to get a couple of swallows before the rest of the squad got the scent. We really enjoyed that. I especially enjoyed your letters—they meant a lot to me. Thank you."

"Is the pain bad?"

"It's not that bad." *There I go lying again,* I thought. My legs still hadn't stopped throbbing from the dressing change and I hoped they wouldn't stay too much longer. I wanted to get a shot but knew I'd fall asleep. Then my leg really started to hurt. It was something like a muscle spasm. I'd never felt the pain like this before. It wasn't intolerable, just very uncomfortable.

"Mom, my leg is really starting to hurt. I'm going to have to get a pain shot, but it will make me fall asleep." I rang the call button. "I'm really sorry, Gramps."

"Don't be sorry, Rick. That's why you're in the hospital, to stop the hurt and make you well."

The corpsman came to the rack as Mom and Gramps readied themselves to leave.

"What do you need, Rick?"

"Can you get me my pain med and a duck?" The corpsman nodded and went to fetch the medication.

As soon as they left I reached down and shifted my leg. I couldn't find a comfortable position and the throbbing just wouldn't stop. The corpsman gave me the injection. I lay back waiting for the medicine to take effect. I could feel the pain leaving my legs as the medication moved up my body until my eyes began to bob up and down.

My grandfather was a wonderful man. He'd left the farm and joined the Army during World War I, but he never got out of the States. After the war he went to Chicago and got a job in a machine shop, a job he held for over forty years. He was a devoted father and grandfather. He always placed his family ahead of himself. My grandmother had died two years earlier, which devastated him, but he found love and comfort enough from his children and grandchildren and friends. He was an impeccable dresser and would never be seen on a visit without a coat and tie. His appearance was unchanging. He wore a smile always. He was balding and wide in the belly but just the sight of him was reassuring. I always felt safe near him, and he always seemed to know how I felt without exchanging words. I'd lived with him for a year when I was in grade school. He was one of the world's last gentlemen. He never had anything bad to say about anyone. He was always calm and very courteous to everyone he met. He had thirty-eight grandchildren and he always had time for each of them. Whenever he was introduced to their friends he treated them as if they were part of the family, too. He performed miracles at his workbench. He could fix anything from a cut finger to a broken motor. He always had the right tool for every job.

When we fished together he'd talk to the fish. After a while I expected the damn things to jump into the boat; then his line would give a tug and he'd reel in a four-inch-long bluegill. He'd laugh and carry on as if he'd finally caught "Old Fighter." God, how I loved to hear him laugh, and how I missed him. I fell asleep thinking about him.

# 7

IT SEEMED TO me that I'd only just gone to sleep when I was awakened by Blass, the head corpsman. Doc Bone was just finishing his inspection of Smitty's wound. I didn't move, hoping that this was just another strange dream. It wasn't. The doctor moved on to my rack.

"Good morning, Rick. How are you feeling today?" He began to peel the layers of gauze pads from the leg. "I understand that you got yourself unplugged last night. You've got to watch yourself and try to fill the silver saddle once every day or two."

"Yes, sir," I replied, gritting my teeth and grabbing the bed frame.

"We go back into the OR tomorrow. I want to take some bone fragments out of the legs. Then, if that slows some of this infection along with the antibiotics, maybe we can start to skin graft in a few weeks. The sooner we do all that, the sooner you'll start feeling better."

"Yes, sir. Doctor, will I be able to go home for Christmas?"

"No way. You're in traction. They'd have to take you home in your bed. Besides you're on a strict timetable of dressing changes and medication. You won't be going anywhere until your casts come off and that skin graft takes."

"I figured that's what you'd say, but there's always a chance." I was ripped with pain as the last layer of gauze was removed. *God, that's terrible,* I thought to myself.

The doctor continued talking as he investigated my wounds. "All right, looks good. I'll see you tomorrow morning."

He held my hand firmly. "Don't let yourself get down. No one said it would be easy. Just keep up the fight."

"Yes, sir, whatever's customary." We both smiled.

I hadn't planned on going back into the operating room so soon after the last operation. I had assumed that I'd have only a few more surgeries before I'd be well enough to go home. For that matter, I was still under the impression that I'd be going back to my unit in Vietnam. I knew that I was seriously wounded, but I really believed that it would be like in the movies. The wounds would heal and I'd be as good as new.

I slept the rest of the day, with the exception of dinner and the dressing change. At nine in the evening my legs were prepped for the OR, blood and urine samples were taken, the anesthesiologist visited, and the nurse had me sign the necessary forms for the OR. Then I took a pain shot again, sleeping until I was awakened for early morning blood samples. As had been the case the first time I went to the OR, I was visited by a guy in a cape and wearing Dracula fangs. This character said nothing, just took what he needed and vanished.

Before the lights came on, the night corpsman brought the shots given to everyone before going down to the operating room.

"Eilert . . . time to go. Come on, Rick, wake up." I opened my eyes. "Is it time already? I've lost a whole day by sleeping—now I'll lose another day going to the OR." I saw the handful of injections, rolled over slightly to the right exposing my left buttock, and continued talking.

"Say, Doc, did I get any phone calls yesterday? Man, I was beat." The corpsman answered as he gave me the shots. "I have no idea. You probably had a few. You're from this area, aren't you?"

"Yeah, about thirty miles away, may as well be a thousand miles. Being so close to home is as much a curse as a blessing."

The combination of injections didn't put me to sleep. I just felt so relaxed that I could hardly move. My eyes wouldn't even close so I just stared at the ceiling. After a short wait a corpsman dressed in a green gown and wearing a green pizza hat took me down to the corridor and left me just outside the operating room. Just as before I scanned the gurneys waiting in lines against the walls. Again I was shocked by the lost, frightened expressions on the faces of those whose young minds and bodies had been torn apart. Suddenly I felt as if I'd joined a very small fraternity for which my wounds were the initiation, but it was one hell of a lousy fraternity to belong to. Other young men my age were sophomores and juniors in college now. Their fraternities had dances and parties, and they could sit around in comfort and talk about how they'd change the world.

Now here I was, my life shattered. I'd probably never be able to play sports again, to sense the taxing of my strength and the joy of competition. Then I saw the body of another young man, a sheet pulled over his face. *That could be me*, I thought. *Within the hour I could be the one lying there with someone else looking at me.* I had a bad feeling about this operation. I didn't know exactly what it was that bothered me so, but I'd had these feelings before, when I was in the bush. It was the same instinct that told me to take a different trail or to study my steps—carefully—watching for booby traps.

The anethesiologist came up to my gurney carrying all the equipment needed to hook up the IV bottles. She grabbed my arm, checking my identification bracelet and chart.

"Eilert, I'm Miss Gale. I visited you last evening about the operation today . . . remember?"

"Yes, ma'am. I was half-asleep, but I remember."

"Good. I'm going to hook you up here, then when you get inside we can start the blood without having to start another IV. I'm going to give you a general anesthetic, sodium pentothal, just like you had the last time. OK, I'll be back in just a minute, and we'll take you in."

She set up everything and walked away. Within two minutes she returned with a corpsman and wheeled me into the room, setting the bed under the lights in the center of the room. Another corpsman was mopping some blood off the floor. Doc Bone walked in.

"Are you all set, Eilert? OK, what are we going to do today, cut off your nose or arm?" He studied the X rays on the wall. I was startled.

"No, sir, you said you were going to take out some bone fragments, remember?"

*Gosh, what if he's got me confused with someone else!* I thought.

"Oh, yeah, that's right." He returned to my side, his hands shaking. "Let's get cutting." He pulled the mask over his mouth down just enough to let me see that he was smiling and kidding around. The anesthesiologist said, "Eilert, start counting backward from one hundred." I had a strange sensation of something cold coming through the IV tube. "Yes, ma'am. One hundred, ninety-ni . . ." I was out.

Someone was calling me from way off. The voice sounded so light that at first it was just a mumbling of words. Then it steadily got louder and louder.

"Eilert, wake up . . . can you hear me? Eilert, where are you . . . what ward are you from?"

"Three South . . . say, can I have some water?" I felt as if I were mumbling, for I could barely hear myself talk. When I felt a wet rag in my mouth I began to suck it dry, then I spat it out and asked for some more.

"Please, nurse . . . can I have a refill?" My mouth felt like it was filled with cotton balls.

"Eilert, do you know where you are?"

"I'm in recovery . . . I think." Then I was able to lift my head. It seemed that every minute or so I was able to do a little more, becoming more and more alert. Once my head seemed less heavy I was able to open my eyes. Then the pain started in, sharp stabbing pain. I was on a bed, not a gurney, my legs bound in thick bandages, almost hidden. I felt terrible. So weak and tired, not like the last time, and the pain was terrible.

"Nurse . . . nurse, can I have something for the pain?"

"Yes, you can. Just a moment, I'll be right back." I looked around the recovery room, packed with gurneys on which men were sucking rags and with nurses yelling at other patients to get them to wake up. *What a circus,* I thought. The nurse returned with my shot, giving it to me in my arm.

"Thank you so much. This pain is terrible. Why would it hurt worse now than when I went in?"

"Could be that they had to do a lot more work this time."

"I guess you're right. It feels like they cut me toe to crotch."

"I'll call the ward now. You can go upstairs."

"What time is it, ma'am?"

"It's eighteen hundred." I was surprised. "That means I've been out for about twelve hours. I wasn't in the OR all that time, was I?"

"I'm not sure. I just came on duty an hour ago, and you've been here all that time. Ask the doctor when you see him."

"Yes, ma'am, and thank you. I'm sure I'll see you again." I began to fall asleep from the shot. Before I closed my eyes I saw

Crawford and Cox grabbing for my bed. I didn't wake up until ten, just in time to see lights out. I was in agony. My legs were throbbing and I felt warm and terribly uncomfortable. I rang my call button, but the corpsman was already at my side taking vital signs.

"You had a pretty rough time of it today. You've got a high fever. The nurse is on the way up here. We have to pack you in ice for a while to get that temperature down."

"Doc, will you get my shot?"

"Sure will." As the corpsman hurried away for the medication, Smitty walked up to my rack.

"Hurt pretty bad, Rick? If you need anything, anything at all, just call. I'll take care of it. Don't bother with the corpsman— I'll get what you need."

"Thanks, Smitty. Damn, I feel like shit."

"Yeah, you look like shit, too. You got a few calls today. One was your mom. Didn't you tell them that you were going to surgery today?"

"No, there's nothing they could do but worry. I just figured that it would be better this way. Did Cheryl call?"

"Don't know. Is there something wrong between the two of you?"

"Not really, she's just a little mixed up right now. She wants to go out and all, but I think she feels guilty dating around while I'm in here. The thing is, I'd rather have her dating and me know about it than if she did it on the sly. Hell, if you were a woman, would you want to be saddled with a gimp the rest of your life?"

"No, Rick, I wouldn't. Makes me wish I was playing student now instead of playing wounded."

"Rick, I got your shot." I rolled to my side, and the corpsman hit the target.

"Hey, Smitty . . . Smitty, how long have I been out of my head?"

"Rick, God, you gave everyone a scare. Man, you've been in and out for over a week. I thought that you'd bought the farm."

"Good God, a week. How can I have lost a whole week?"

Smitty rang the call button to signal my rebirth. Before the corpsman reached my rack, Miss Noland stuck her head through the screen to check. She was surprised to see me talking to Smitty.

"Eilert, you're awake. That's great. Are you feeling a little better? After we get your vital signs again you'd better call your folks. They've been very worried and they've been here just sitting by your bed. So has Cheryl. She came up by herself last Friday. I think it scared her. Anyway, you've been receiving a lot of packages lately. The corpsmen put them in your locker."

I leaned over to inspect their contents. Besides a copy of *Playboy*, I'd received eleven pounds of candy.

"Smitty, want some candy? I've got pounds of it." The wheelchairs began to pull up from all sides.

"Eilert, did you say you couldn't eat your candy? Well, just pass it around. I'm sure we can find someone hungry." I didn't even know the guy asking for the chocolates, but he handed out several of the boxes to be passed around. Then the mob disappeared as fast as they had come.

"Smitty, who was that guy? I've never seen him before."

"Oh, that's Anderson. He's one of the three in the solarium. He has six toes on each foot. Really looks odd." Two corpsmen came to take my vital signs. They cleared the screen away, then took my temperature, respiration, pulse, and blood pressure. They couldn't believe how quickly I'd recovered. They'd taken my vital signs only an hour earlier and every test was cause for concern.

"Say, Rick, you are now the Miracle of Three South."

"Doc, my legs are throbbing. Could you please get my pain med? And please bring the phone? I want to call home."

Once the corpsman had left, Smitty began to question me. "Did you know what was going on while you were out?"

"Yes and no. A few times I caught some little things, but for the most part I was out."

"I heard the nurses talking. They said you was in a humm. Especially with your temperature going up so high. They gave you alcohol baths and packed you in ice twice."

"I must have really been gone not to remember that. Here comes the phone." The corpsman gave me my shot, then plugged the phone into the wall socket.

"Here you go, Rick. When the operator gets on the line, tell her that you want to place a collect call. You can't dial direct out of here."

"Thanks, Doc, will do." I directed the operator, then waited for the phone to ring at the other end.

"Hello." My mother answered the phone, accepting the charges.

"Hi, Mom. This is number one son."

"Rick, it's wonderful to hear your voice. We've been very worried about you. When did you start feeling better?"

"About an hour ago. I couldn't believe it when they said I was out so long. I feel pretty good now. Could you call Cheryl and let her know that I'm among the living again? The nurse went to call the doctor about my recovery. So maybe I'll get to talk with him today and find out what's going on. They just gave me a pain shot, so I'm going to hang up for now. I'll talk to you later. I just wanted you to know that I was all right. Bye, Mom." I laid down the receiver and closed my eyes to let the pain medication make me feel comfortable. After an hour I was shaken by Doc Bone.

"Eilert, I understand you're feeling better. You had a pretty rough time of it." I opened my eyes, anxious to find out what had happened and why I'd been out for so long.

"Yes, sir. I feel a lot better. What was wrong? I felt so lousy."

"Your whole system was infected and it took some time to get you flushed out. Now let's take a look at that left leg."

I winced as the doctor took his scissors and cut into the pile of wrappings. The blade of the scissors touched the leg, sending me into a fit of agony. Once he'd cut all the way through the gauze from the ankle to the knee, he grabbed both edges of the wrapping and peeled it back with a quick rip. I let out a hearty groan. The pain was horrible and at first I thought I'd pass out.

The leg was bare. I opened my eyes to inspect the operation. Instead of the leg's being red and bloody, it was yellowish white and covered with pus. The doctor wiped the leg with the gauze he had pulled off.

"Looks like we have to go back into the OR and clean this up. That's why you've been feeling so badly. Now that we've got an antibiotic that the infection is sensitive to, we can control it and you can start healing. Tomorrow's as good a day as any to get started. How does that sound?"

"Fine, sir, just as long as it'll help."

"OK, then, tomorrow morning first thing. I'll see you then."

"Thank you, Doc." As soon as the doctor walked away, the corpsman brought out the dressing cart and began cleaning up the wounds just as before. When he had finished I was lying exhausted in sweat-soaked sheets. The dinner cart rolled onto the floor and the ward became a whirlwind of speeding wheelchairs, amid the clanging of plates and silverware. Smitty began his pilgrimage to the cart, as usual arriving last. I tried to compose myself. I pulled the towel from my bedside locker and wiped away the perspiration and tears.

For the first time in a long time I felt hungry. I had roast beef, potatoes, vegetables, milk, and coffee. The only thing I couldn't finish was the dessert, but it felt good having a full stomach.

After dinner I had the usual visitors willing to help me eat whatever I didn't want, but they were disappointed to see the tray cleaned off. A corpsman brought the phone to my rack.

"Got a live one for you," he said as he handed me the phone. It was Cheryl.

"I'm doing just fine. I understand that you came up a few days ago. I'm sorry I missed you. Must have been a gas sitting there watching me sleep."

"No, I was glad I was there. I've been so worried about you. You were out so long that I thought that you might die."

"Come on now, it wasn't that bad. I was just a little under the weather." We talked on. "I got to go back to the OR again tomorrow." I could hear Cheryl's voice change to one of deep concern. "The doctor just wants to clean me up some. It's not all that serious. I probably won't be in that long anyway. I miss you an awful lot. That's about all that's really wrong. I just wish you were here. It's hard being this close and still not being able to see you. It'll all be over soon enough, and I'll be home good as new. You'll see. This isn't the easiest thing we've ever gone through, but if we stay together after all this is over with, nothing will ever seem hard to overcome. I know this is especially hard on you, and for that I'm sorry. I just want you to be happy, even if it means going out with someone else."

"But Rick, I don't want to date other people."

"I don't mean it that way. It's just that when your friends are all going out to shows and dancing, you don't want to stay at home. So there's no reason you can't go out with them, is there?"

"No, I guess not."

"Damn, you don't have to agree with me so fast." We both laughed, and for the first time both of us felt comfortable saying things as they were. We were both frank with each other and it felt good not having to guard every word, trying to avoid hurting each other.

"You know, I really like those mini-skirts you're wearing. It's just that if you're going to bend over to give me a kiss, I don't have the advantage of the view from the other end that the rest of the ward has. I didn't realize how much I was missing until I heard what terrific legs you have from the people at the other end of the ward." She laughed. "They're all watching you. They're shot up, not dead. I'm just a young marine that's lived in the jungle too long without the benefit of female companionship. A dirty, ugly, sweaty marine isn't much of a turn-on. Well, twice somebody took your picture for the night."

"What for? Oh, come on, you don't mean that . . . that's terrible. You must be feeling better—you're starting to sound like you did the night you got home from boot camp."

"I get horny when I'm sick."

"You get horny when you're not sick. When are you not horny?"

"That's beside the point. I've missed you very much—*very* much—and I'm awfully happy to be home."

"I've missed you, too. I was just so worried every day that you were gone, and every night on TV they talked about how many people had been killed. I always thought of you and it scared me."

"I didn't know that they had all that on TV. I saw cameramen but never when we were in the shit, only when we were coming back from a fight. I saw something on the television the other night . . . a week ago, I guess. They talked about the courage of the front-line cameramen. They didn't say a thing about the guys doing the fighting, just their cameramen. They got a lot of guts, but the only ones I ever saw were behind me."

"It doesn't matter anyway. You're home and that's all that I care about."

"Try and get up here day after tomorrow, OK?"

I hung up the phone feeling much better. I'd been so worried that she was unhappy that I'd forgotten how much I really meant to her.

Visiting hours started, and along with the visitors came waves of veterans' groups, ladies' clubs, Doughnut Dollies, and even some people on their own to offer smiles and conversation. It took me a while to realize that this was Christmas, with only five days until Santa came, and that I'd been in the hospital for almost a month.

The groups brought their gifts in large carts. They were not small gifts either: radios, stereos, televisions, cash, cartons of cigarettes, boxes of goodies from manufacturers, even fresh sandwiches. It was really nice, especially since most of the men felt outcast, even responsible for the war. Now, with all this attention, spirits were raised. Laughter and Christmas carols filled the ward.

Many grade schools sent teachers with Christmas cards and greetings that their classes had made, so that each patient would have cards and letters from someone. It was really touching. The ward was slowly being decorated with ornaments, baby Christmas trees, all the things that help get you in the spirit of the season. I heard the carolers singing "I'll Be Home for Christmas," and remembered that it was the last song that I'd heard on the armed forces radio before I got hit. I hung on each verse as I listened. For a brief moment I thought I would cry. I'd forgotten how wonderful it was to be part of the Christmas season.

Then I began to wonder how I'd do any Christmas shopping. Not only was I unable to hit the stores, but my pay record hadn't caught up with me, and what would I do for money? I wondered if I could swap some of my gifts. My sisters Linda and JoAnn could use radios, and maybe I could get enough cash to buy a few gifts.

"Hey, Smitty, did you get any radios in your packages?"

"Yeah, I got one, but I got two of those little cameras."

"How about I swap you a radio for a camera? I'm trying to fill my Christmas list."

"OK, it's a deal. Here you go. That's not a bad idea at all. I can swap with everyone on the ward for all the gifts I'd like to get. Hell, this hospital is going to be like a department store for the next few days. With all the nice things we've been getting, there's bound to be something for everyone on my shopping list, and what we can't trade for we can buy with the cash we've gotten."

"What cash?"

"Rick, at first I thought that the cards we were getting were just cards, but I've already pulled forty bucks out so far and that's just from this evening's haul."

"Smitty, this may be the answer to my prayers. I was feeling bad that I couldn't give any gifts this year, but now I'll be able to get something for everyone in my family and Cheryl. Sell my clothes—I'm going to heaven. This will be a merry Christmas after all. Now all I have to do is get my sister to pick out something for Cheryl."

Smitty's enthusiasm caught hold of him and he started on his mission to spread the word that the great Christmas gift swap was on. He stuffed the gifts he wanted to swap in a pillowcase, then went from rack to rack like a peddler. Then the ward came alive with trading and buying of presents. Just like doing our own shopping. Christmas spirit was in the air. For a moment all the horror, pain, and loneliness were gone.

Five o'clock in the morning came quickly. I slept soundly that night. To awaken to Dracula was becoming routine, and so was the night corpsman who came with the shots preparing me for the OR. I lay back, turning my head to watch the snow flying outside the window. Small pieces of ice hit the glass and built up on the pane. I could sense the cold and it felt so good to pull the blankets all the way up to my chin and enjoy the warmth.

The injections were taking hold when two corpsmen from the OR appeared, checking my ID bracelet and chart for a cross match. Bed and all, I was taken down the corridor, down in the elevator, and directly into the operating room. I was the first of the day for the doctor. The anesthesiologist wasted no time starting the IV, hanging the bottles of blood, and telling me to start to count. I was becoming an old hand at the procedure and played my part flawlessly.

This time, when I woke up there was no one else in the recovery room except for one nurse and a corpsman.

I raised my hand. The nurse spotted me and, without being asked, wetted a cloth and brought it over.

"Thirsty, marine?" she inquired, as she stuffed the rag into my mouth. I nodded my head; saying yes with a rag in my mouth was a trick that I still hadn't perfected.

Chief came to the recovery room three hours later to take me back. Normally they would have sent two corpsmen for such a task, but not when Chief was on duty.

"Come on, Rick, let's get out of this slum. You wouldn't believe the commotion up on the ward. Most of the ambulatory patients are going home today. It's like prom night. Half of the corpsmen are over at the PX picking up ribbons for the patients' uniforms, and toiletries. Hell, I didn't think that half of those people could even get out of their racks. Now they're hopping around looking for uniforms that'll fit.

"From what I hear, everyone is going today or tomorrow, except for you and two people from the other side of the ward. Even Dennis is going. His folks hired an ambulance." Chief maneuvered the bed through the halls into the elevator and began the procession into the ward.

I could hear the noise, the happy sounds of young men going home for the first time in twenty months, in some cases. But something was wrong. I wasn't pushed all the way back to the end of the ward. Instead I was slotted in rack two, right near the nurses' station.

"Hey, Chief, what's going on?"

"Your rack's been changed so they can keep their eyes on you. With everyone taking off, you'll be the only one over here."

Smitty walked up to my rack. He was half-dressed in his uniform, his fly open and shirttails hanging out.

"Say, Rick, I'm going to be leaving here toot sweet. You take care of yourself and have a nice Christmas. I'm sorry that I'm going to lose you as a bunkmate, but I'll be down to visit you three times a day when the chow cart comes. Man, am I going to get drunk."

"Smitty, who's going to change your dressings when you're home?"

"My mom or dad, whichever doesn't faint first." We both laughed.

"Take it easy, Rick. I could say that I wish you were going home instead of me, but why lie?" He smiled then and turned to shuffle away.

"Hey, Smitty, merry fucking Christmas to you, too."

# 8

I SLIPPED OFF to sleep and didn't wake up until after visiting hours were over. When I opened my eyes, damn near everyone was gone. There were only five people still on my side of the ward; the other side sounded dead quiet except for the televisions. Those patients that were still waiting to go home couldn't do so until Christmas Eve, because their dressing changes were so involved that the hospital figured the parents would never be able to rip the dressings off their kid— they'd be either too grossed out or too afraid of hurting him. I could just see Dennis's folks trying to change his dressings, with all the moaning and groaning that he went through.

The dinner cart pulled up and I ate what I could, but the effects of the surgery still left me groggy and food was the last thing that I felt like. I lay back listening to the TV news. That was usually enough to put me to sleep.

Dad called an hour later, just as the corpsman was pulling the pain shot out of my ass.

"Here you are, Rick." The receiver was handed to me.

"Hi, son, it's Dad. How are you doing?"

"Pretty good. Everyone has been leaving for home since I got back from the OR, so it's pretty quiet."

"Do you want some company tonight? Your mother and I thought that we would drive up."

"I'm feeling pretty groggy. . . . It's hard to stay awake. I doubt that I could keep from falling asleep long enough to talk. How about tomorrow night? I've been out most of the time. Most everyone has gone home for the holidays. There's only six other guys and four of them are leaving in a few days. I wish it was me going home."

"At least you're close. Isn't it better than spending your time back overseas? At least the guys back in your unit will get a little break over the holidays. They said there's going to be a cease-fire truce for Christmas and New Year's."

"I know that's what they say, but something's happening there. I can't explain exactly. That last day on patrol we found big caches of rice all over the place, like there were a lot of troops moving around out there. The unit that we ran into was really big, but rather than finish us off like they could have, they left only a few behind and bugged out to avoid any contact. They're fixing to make a stand. We could feel it. Before when we ran into any good-size units they'd always stay to get their licks in, then take off. Now they're concentrating for something big. We've been relaying all that back to the rear, but nobody's paying attention. I'm worried about the guys still there."

"That's understandable, but you know they're happy you're here. In fact, we got a letter from Gary in your fire team. He also sent a letter to you. So we'll bring that up with us tomorrow."

"Has Cheryl phoned? I told her yesterday that I was going back into the OR today."

"Yes, she called yesterday to say that she talked to you, but I haven't seen her for a while. We'll come up to see you Christmas Day and bring our gifts. You get some rest then and we'll see you tomorrow. I'm glad you got over that infection. That gave us all a scare. Take care, and I'll call Cheryl—maybe she wants to come up with us tomorrow. In any case, I'll tell her you're out of surgery and doing fine."

I began to think about the conversation. It seemed strange that Gary would have written so fast. When I'd been hit my unit was sweeping up to Khe Sanh. We weren't supposed to get up there until the end of December, but for Gary to have enough free time to write they must already be there. Khe Sanh had been a nasty place when we were there before. Something was up. It worried me.

The people in my squad and in my platoon were all very tight—like brothers in many ways. We knew each other better than anyone else could ever know us. But when someone got hit, or even killed, all the emotions would be tucked away, nobody wanting to show they cared. It was hard losing friends day after day, and it wasn't easy for me to forget them. I felt as if I belonged back there, that I was skating through the shit while my people were getting their butts shot off. It was impossible for me to shake the awful feeling that I'd let everyone down and that something was going to happen.

For the rest of the day my mind kept going back to the bush. If I closed my eyes for over a few minutes I really was there. Maybe it was the drugs, maybe just the shock of all that had happened, but it was as if my body forgot that it couldn't move in certain directions. In the middle of one of my dream periods I recalled the first man that I ever killed face to face. I had to stab him during a night attack after I ran out of ammunition. I'd intended to cut his throat, but I was so frightened that I missed and hit him in the eye. My knife stuck, and all night long I struggled to pull it out. It wasn't until I heard another intruder approaching that I stood up, put my foot over the dead man's throat, and pulled the blade out.

I awoke screaming in pain. In my daze I'd thrown my right leg over my left, twisting the left leg at the knee. A nurse was returning from Johnson's rack when it happened and she quickly lifted the right leg back over, so that I was lying flat. Fortunately, I hadn't damaged my left leg, but the agony was unbearable. I was hyperventilating and unable to ask the nurse for a pain shot. But she needed no prompting and got the medication into me as fast as possible.

"Eilert, take deep breaths. Breathe in very deep." I did as instructed, and slowly I was able to calm down.

"That's fine, Rick. Just keep it up. . . . Good. OK now, whatever made you think that you could go for a stroll? Are you crazy?"

"Just a bad dream. I'm fine now. Thank you."

"Just a bad dream, my foot. You could have thrown yourself out of the rack and onto the floor. I'm going to have to tell the doctor about this. It's possible that you could have the same dream over and over again—then what are you going to do?"

"What good is it to tell the doctor? He's not going to make the boogie man go away. Why bother him?"

"We bother him because he's the one that has to piece you back together again if you take a dive. Maybe one of the doctors up on Five North can help."

"Isn't Five North the psycho ward? That's the last kind of doctor I want to talk with."

"I'm not going to argue with you. . . . Now, feel better?"

"Yes, ma'am, much better. Thank you, and I'm still not talking to any shrink. It's just a simple bad dream. It's all over with."

"Fine. It's your body, but I still have to report it. You might have injured yourself, and if the pain persists and I'm not here, they'll need to know what happened."

The nurse turned and went back to the nurses' station and began writing on my chart.

I closed my eyes and took deep breaths until I didn't have

any shortness of breath. The face of that man stuck in my mind. I had lain looking into the face of the man I'd killed for three hours that night. Now whenever I closed my eyes that face was there. I tried so hard not to close my eyes, but the pain medication took effect and I fell asleep. Luckily I didn't dream.

The following morning and afternoon passed uneventfully. I spent most of the day watching television or sleeping. That evening my parents came up with Cheryl, and behind them came the last of the Christmas visiting groups.

"Gosh, Rick, this is fantastic! Look at all these gifts you've gotten, and they're so nice, too." My mother then opened my locker, only to find more booty.

"Mom, would you and Dad please take all this home with you? I made up this list of names and next to each name I've put what gift to give. Would you wrap these for me and make sure that everyone gets their presents?" My father took the list of names.

"Holy cow, look at all these radios." Just as he said that, two of the Christmas throng presented me with two more small packages. I didn't even have to open the gifts. I knew exactly what they were.

"Here, Dad. Two more radios." We all laughed.

"Don't you want to keep any?" Cheryl asked.

"Sure, but more than one of each is a little much." I pointed to one of the larger boxes on the floor next to my bed. "Cheryl, would you open that one for me?" She lifted the heavy box to her lap. When opened the carton revealed eight more radios of various makes. She smiled. *Is this what I'm getting for Christmas?* she thought. I could read her expression.

"No, Cheryl, I'm not giving you a radio." We both chuckled.

"Why don't we take some of this candy and drop it off at the old folks' home? I'm sure that they'd appreciate it. You're certainly not going to eat all this."

"That would be fine. Good idea."

Some Christmas carolers came into the ward and we started to sing along, happy that we could all be together. For my parents their boy was home and that was all that mattered. Cheryl almost started to cry as she held my hand.

Once the singers had left, my parents broke out a bag full of Christmas cards that had been sent to me at the house. Mom opened each one of the cards and handed them over to be read.

Cheryl excused herself, and I took the occasion to ask my parents to help me find her a special gift.

"Dad, would you ask Janet to go to the store tomorrow and find a gift for Cheryl? Tell her to use her own judgment and to get whatever she likes. Janet's got about the same taste as Cheryl. That's all I can think of right now, except thanks for bringing her with you tonight. This is the happiest day of my life next to the day I got home. . . . I just want you and Mom to know how much I love you both. . . . I'm sorry for the hard times I've given you."

Both of my parents started to cry and Cheryl returned from the ladies' room to find everyone in tears.

"What happened?" she asked.

"Nothing, we're just so happy to see you. We thought you lost your way." We all broke up laughing.

"Thanks for coming up and taking away my treasures." My parents hustled about trying to get their coats on. The corpsman brought them a large plastic garbage bag, and they were able to get almost all the gifts inside it.

"Oh, before we go, I almost forgot," Mom said. "I've got that letter from Gary and a card from your platoon. I hope I can find them. . . . Here they are." Everyone waited to hear the news, for they'd come to know all my friends in Vietnam.

I opened the card first. It wished me a merry Christmas in Vietnamese, and it was signed by everyone in the outfit. Then I opened the letter. It started out with small talk; skipping over that, I began to read excerpts aloud.

"Listen, Dad, he says that they're already up at Khe Sanh, that the spotter planes have seen lots of signs of heavy troop concentrations. Damn, they're in for something big. Oh, God, Doc Toner's dead."

I couldn't hold the letter my hands were shaking so badly. My parents knew that it was Toner who'd saved my life. My mother started to weep. I picked up the letter again and continued. "It says that he was returning from R and R. The plane he was in was on its way up to Khe Sanh when it was shot down. Everyone on board was killed. Oh, damn. He was a nice guy. He screwed up occasionally, but never when he was needed. What a Christmas present for his family."

It took a few minutes for us to gather our composure. Then Dad said, "Why don't you write back and ask for his family's address? Then you could write to his folks. It would make them happy to hear what their son did for you guys."

My parents said good-bye, then left Cheryl alone with me for a few moments.

"I'm sorry, Rick. . . ."

"Everyone is very close, maybe not the best of friends, but everyone knows almost everything about each other in the squad. It's just happened so much and I'm so tired of it all. I feel like my insides are all torn out. Sometimes I feel that I may crack up." Cheryl hugged me and gave me a kiss. She knew that there was nothing that she could say to help. She had never seen me like this and it really upset her.

"Good-bye, Rick."

"Wait, Cheryl. I need you to do something for me. Here's some money. Would you see that Janet gets it to buy something for my parents? I don't care what it is just as long as they get something from me."

Cheryl took the money, then gave me a good-bye kiss. I smiled as she left, but it was hard for me. I just couldn't justify my living and Doc's dying. The corpsman came by and gave me my antibiotic shots.

"Would you give my sleeper and pain shot again this evening? I'm not feeling too hot."

"Sure, Rick, just as soon as I pass out the rest of these meds and straighten out the ward."

"Thanks."

I lay back, feeling as if I'd been hit in the stomach.

At times like this I doubted not only the existence of a merciful God, but the presence of any God at all. God let students send aid to the NVA. Then he took the life of someone who'd saved more lives and eased more suffering than any ten other people could do in a lifetime. Nothing made sense. I wept quietly, trying not to disturb anyone.

The corpsman came around with the night meds and finally I passed out, listening to the sound of snow blowing against the window as another day died.

The next day was a real downer. I watched the departure of those going home on leave. When they'd gone, only three of us were left. It was so depressing. There was no music, no noise, just complete stillness as three men too sick to talk, im-

142

prisoned in plaster and gauze, unable to move, lay looking at the ceiling. The hours couldn't pass quickly enough.

Christmas was a repeat of the previous day. My parents came up along with two of my sisters. It was nice while they were there, but once they left it became just another day. Cheryl phoned and we talked for some time but I just couldn't get myself up for the conversation. The memories of Doc Toner were just too much.

That evening the three bodies on the ward were presented with a turkey dinner, real turkey—not the pressed kind—with all the trimmings: mashed potatoes, gravy, vegetables, desserts. Not the normal hospital food at all. It was a real feast, one that raised even my spirits. It had been a long time since I'd had a dinner like that and I savored every morsel. There were no visitors that evening. I watched a little television, then went to sleep.

The following morning the doctor made his rounds and removed my dressing for the first time since the surgery four days before. As usual the pain was unbelievable. I wasn't getting used to all the hurt, but now I knew what to expect and braced myself against it.

"Well, Rick, it's really looking much better. We're going to trip the wounds for the next four or five days. If they're still without any infection then, we'll try a skin graft. How does that sound?"

"Sounds great, Doc. Let's get on with it."

"OK. How was the holiday—have any visitors?"

"Yes, sir, my family and girl friend came up, plus loads of groups and clubs and phone calls. It's just a little lonely."

"Well, I think you can watch TV after lights-out. There aren't too many people that you can disturb. Just keep the sound down low. Keep your chin up and don't let all this get you down. You're going to get better."

"Thank you, sir."

The next four days went by without incident. Dressing changes were all that occurred to mark the passage of time. There were phone calls and an occasional visitor, but for the most part it was quiet and routine. My worrying was about Cheryl and my friends still in the bush.

The following Friday the doctor decided to attempt a skin

graft on the left leg, using skin from my stomach as the donor site.

I awoke Saturday afternoon in the recovery room feeling as if I'd been asleep in the sun, but it wasn't until I got back on the ward that I was able to see what my discomfort was all about. Suddenly I had an idea that skin grafting wasn't all that it was cracked up to be. As soon as I was back in my rack, I pulled the sheets back to see an eight-by-four-inch swatch of skin missing from my stomach, and a six-by-three-inch section missing from my left thigh. Covering both areas was a very thin gauze mesh, nothing more.

It hadn't been a very long procedure and at least I was comfortable compared to after the other surgeries. I'd been on the ward for an hour or so when the doctor came back up to check on me. "Well, Eilert, can you feel yourself healing already?" He grinned. "Everything went just fine. Now just keep your fingers crossed that the graft takes."

"What if it doesn't? Can't you just do it all over again?"

"Sure, we can do it over and over again, as long as we've got someplace to take the skin from. In your case, there's been so much soft-tissue damage that we have a limited area to work from. If this doesn't work, then we have to go to your stomach again, then your right thigh, then your can. Since you're on your back all day, taking skin from your buttocks could be uncomfortable."

"Yes, sir, then let's hope that this takes. Something about having my ass skinned worries me."

"You're going to have a new neighbor tomorrow. His name is Winston. He's been in Intensive Care for the last week and a half. You won't be lonely—he seems like a real nice kid. He caught an automatic burst all the way up his side, calf to shoulder. He's been in a lot of pain, and we're still worried about him. You would be doing me a big favor if you could keep an eye on him for us. He doesn't complain at all, but he's scared to death."

"Yes, sir, whatever I can do."

"Thanks, Eilert, I appreciate it. Take care now. We'll take that dressing off in a few days."

The doctor moved on to Winston and then to the other side of the ward. There wasn't much work for him, compared to when the ward was filled. This gave him some time to be with his family as well.

Cheryl came alone that evening. She wore a necklace that Janet had picked out for me. She really looked good. She took off her coat then gave me a kiss.

"Rick, you've got to get that hair washed. There's all kinds of things in there. Can't one of the nurses help you? Now that everyone's gone it should be easy."

"Yeah, that's a great idea. I asked the corpsmen a few times, but they're too busy. Gee, that's a hell of a greeting: 'Why don't you wash your hair.' You should be a diplomat in Paris. I bet the North Vietnamese would love someone like you there."

"You really look good, Rick. You've got color in your cheeks and you seem a lot more with it than before. You've got to be feeling better."

"I really am. This skin grafting wasn't that bad."

"Rick, thank you for the necklace. It's really pretty. I feel badly about not getting you anything."

"We've already discussed that. What good would it do for you to buy me clothes or something like that, when my size will have changed because of all this weight loss? Just give me a gift when I get out of here. . . . What's up? You seem uneasy."

"I've got a date for tomorrow night, Rick, New Year's." I rolled my eyes. "Now wait, Rick. My girl friend is throwing a party and I can't go by myself and there's no way I'm going to sit at home on New Year's Eve. You really don't mind, do you?"

"Of course not. It would be great for my ego to think that you'd want to pine away at home all night. But then you'd just feel bad all night. Then you'd hold that against me one way or another."

"I'm not going out because I don't love you. The guy is just a friend from high school. I've just got to get out of the house."

"I understand. Now let's talk about something else, like sex or even dirty sex. How about it?" She smiled.

"You're crazy. Here you are all torn up and all you want to do is talk about sex. I'm going to have to watch out when you get out of here. You've been in the jungle too long."

"Yeah, I guess I have been at that. I sure did miss you, though. There were times I never thought I'd see you again. I wanted so much just to let you know how much I loved you. I was so afraid of dying before I could say it to you again." Cheryl leaned over and put her head on my chest. Then she kissed me.

"At first after you left I wasn't frightened," she said, "but once you had been away a while I was constantly watching the TV news and more and more I realized just how terrible it was over there. I knew that something was going to happen to you, but I didn't know what. It was all the waiting I couldn't take. Now it's hard to stop worrying, even though I know you're safe."

"I know, it bothers me, too, especially after hearing about Doc Toner. It never seems to go away." We looked into each other's eyes, saying nothing yet each knowing what the other was thinking.

"Come on, Cheryl, let's get happy. We're together and that's all I care about now. Even if we never see each other again, at least I got my wish to see you once more. Sounds a little corny but it's the truth."

"It's not corny. That's what I love about you. Your ability to tell me just how you feel. I was worried that you might lose that tenderness."

The hospital's PA system interrupted. "Now hear this. Now hear this. Visiting hours are now over. Will all visitors please leave the hospital."

"Gosh, it seems like you just got here and now you're leaving. Drive slowly. The roads get awfully slippery this time of year. . . . I'm glad you told me you were going out."

"Good-bye, and thanks for understanding." She put her coat on, kissed me, and left.

Afterward, I tried to analyze my emotions.

I felt bad about her going out, not because I thought she'd fall for someone else but because I wanted so much to be with her. I was jealous that someone else would make her happy, and that someone else would have her attention for the whole evening. Of course, she'd kiss him at midnight. That thought probably hurt most. Someone else would be there to start her New Year.

I looked out the window and saw the steam bellowing out of the chimney of one of the buildings near the hospital. The wind was shifting the snow drifts, swirling the flakes against the windows. I remembered playing in the snow as a child, diving into the drifts.

Now I lay wondering if I'd ever have that joy again—to frolic like a child. The corpsman came by with the night meds. I fell asleep looking out the window.

\*     \*     \*

When I woke the following morning, I saw Sanford sleeping on his bed with his uniform still on.

Ron wasn't the poster picture of a marine. He was tall and lanky, almost skinny. (Everyone on the ward was thin; months in the jungle, with long brutal patrols, hot humid weather, bad water, a limited diet, malaria, dysentery, and massive wounds, had shriveled our bodies.)

Ron was nineteen years old. He had long, dark, wavy hair on top of his head, but Marine Corps white sidewalls on the sides and back. His light-olive complexion and dark eyes gave him the appearance of a Latin. He had the devil's smile and an easy manner. I'd heard that Ron was a real prankster, and I shouldn't be fooled by his quiet manner.

It wasn't until after breakfast that Ron woke up.

"Hi, Ron . . . what are you doing back so early? I thought that the passes lasted until tomorrow."

"Yeah, they do. I just figured that I'd have as much fun laying here as laying at home."

"Come on, tonight's New Year's Eve. Didn't you have a date with your girl for tonight?"

"I thought so, but she got an engagement ring at Christmas from some other dude and she took it. Man, I thought that everything was all right. Hell, she didn't even tell me that she was seeing someone else. She called me up at home to tell me, 'Welcome back, I'm getting married, and good-bye'!"

I saw the hurt in his eyes. But what could I say to cheer him up? How do you make someone happy who loses his girl and his foot at the same time? Ron said nothing for the rest of the day. He just lay silent and stared at the ceiling searching for an answer. He found none.

It was after lights-out that evening before either of us said a word. I'd pulled the TV over between his rack and mine and I watched an old movie, waiting for midnight to come.

"Say, Rick, do you ever feel like going back to the bush if you get better?"

"Yeah, once in a while. Why do you ask?"

"It's just that as bad as it was, it was simple and easy to understand. You stay alive or you die. Back here there's no reason for things to happen—there's no control over your life. I guess I've just been gone too long and I'm feeling sorry for myself."

I tried to change the subject. "Ron, do you think the doc's

going to save your foot? Or is it too messed up?"

"Hell, I don't really know. I'm just guessing that's what he'll do."

"How did you get hit, anyway?"

"I was just ditty-bopping across this rice paddy when some irate farmer opened up on me with an AK-47. I zigged when I should have zagged. Ruined my whole day, too."

"Damn, you're lucky. That was probably a sniper, and they usually don't miss."

"Yeah, he was probably all smoked up and thought I was a revenuer. What about you, Rick?"

"No big deal. I was teaching this new guy to walk point 'cause I was going on R and R. He tripped a booby trap and an ambush. I caught the booby trap—he caught his lunch."

"You always hurt the one you love," Ron said.

"Yeah, Ron, you're right. Start no shit and you get no shit."

"Look at this, only half a minute to New Year's. My girl's with her fiancé tonight. She'll be planting a nice big kiss on his lips just about now."

"Yeah, Ron. Someone's with my lady now, too." The television showed a big room full of people all going nuts and kissing each other. Ron reached across the space between the racks, and I reached back to shake hands. "Happy New Year, Rick."

"Happy New Year, Ron. Do you want this TV on anymore?"

"No, turn it off." Ron pulled the sheets up and turned on his side. I rang my call button for the corpsman. He just stood up at the desk in the nurses' station.

"Yeah, what do you want, Eilert?" he yelled.

"Pain shot."

The holidays were over. Now the business of getting better was here.

# 9

THE NEW MAN for rack one was wheeled in. He was hooked up to a machine that made a hell of a lot of racket. He was a small guy, really skinny, with bandages all over his body. Ron and I looked at each other, then back at the living dead man.

"Rick, I'm glad he's next to you. He's going to expire and they won't find out until he starts to stink."

"Thanks, Ron. You're a swell guy."

I turned to the new guy to introduce myself, remembering the doctor's request to watch out for him. I said hi several times, but either because the guy was so messed up or because the machine was so loud, there was no reply. "Hey, Ron, what kind of machine is that? It looks like he's in a spaceship."

"They call it an ingress-egress machine. It sucks the infestation out through one tube then pumps good stuff in through another tube. It grosses me out to watch that garbage going through those tubes."

"How can anything gross you out after you twist your foot every which way and let it flap in the breeze?"

"That's different. That's entertainment, not anything like this machine. Look who's gross—if my legs looked like yours I'd cut them off, then call my tailor."

Throughout the day the patients came back from home leave. Some of them looked good, as if the visit had really perked them up. Some came in with black eyes, cut lips, and scraped knuckles from fighting. Others came back looking really terrible. Dennis was one of those. The ambulance drivers pulled him back to his rack with his parents walking behind him. Once he was in his rack the duty nurse went back to get his vitals, taking one of the corpsmen with her. "Dennis, did you change your dressing like you were supposed to?"

He shook his head no, then his father answered.

"That's too much pain for him to go through. Why should he have to go through that every day, let alone three times a day?"

The nurse was furious. "He was put in your care with the understanding that you'd see to his health. That infection can spread very quickly. You may have set him back weeks in his healing. Corpsman, go get that dressing cart and change this wound. Now!" she snapped. Dennis had that old look of terror in his eyes. To go that many days without a dressing change meant that the gauze could be stuck to the inside of the wound, and when they pulled it out he was going to be in sheer agony. Dennis's parents were in a huff. But this wasn't civilian hospital care, and Dennis knew he was back in a world of shit. Still his father kept on the nurse's back.

"There's no reason that my son should have to be tortured like this."

"Sir, I'm logging this on his chart and I'll make sure the doctor sees what kind of care your son gets at home. This is the last time he gets out of this ward until those wounds are closed completely."

The corpsman brought the cart up and began to strip Dennis's clothes off and then his bandages. The nurse turned to the father and asked him to leave. He did. We spent the next forty-five minutes listening to Dennis scream.

"Man, what a cracker ass," Ron said. "I'd rather listen to this damn machine than listen to him moaning all day and night."

Smitty came in walking faster than ever. He was drunk as a skunk and wearing jeans with the top of his uniform. I tried to flag him down.

"Smitty, have a good time?" Smitty only smiled and staggered to his rack and passed out. Ron and I laughed.

By evening the entire ward had returned. I had to get used to the noise all over again. The TVs, the radios, the machine next to my rack, and all the laughing and yelling were deafening. It wasn't until after night meds that I was able to get to sleep. It had been a wild day, and I was beat.

*　　*　　*

The following days were very uneventful. Ron was quiet, brooding about his girl. The new patient was quiet, still not saying anything. Now that the holidays were over I didn't get many calls. I'd had only one phone call from Cheryl since her date on New Year's Eve. For everyone on the ward, after being home with family and girls, coming back to the ward was a real letdown.

However, since I'd moved to rack two, I was in another world. I was meeting all the new people and learning about their wounds and how they got them. It was actually becoming interesting, an easy way to make friends. Across the aisle and to the left was Martin. He had been shot in the femur and his balls had swollen up to the size of cantaloupe. Directly across from me was Sergeant Miller. The whole top of his hand had been blown off, much like Ron's foot, with almost all the bones gone from wrist to fingers. To my right was Sergeant Rey. He'd been shot in the femur and hip. Like Martin he had swollen nuts and needed a catheter every night. It would send chills up my spine to watch them shove that tube up his dick in the evening.

One day, after Ron had performed his magic with his toes, bending them back ninety degrees so they touched his ankle, they wheeled Winston to another rack and brought a new man into rack one, next to me. His face, arms, and legs were completely bound, like a mummy, and there were huge burned areas on the flesh that were not covered with bandages. Ron, not one to hide his feelings, yelled over to me, "Hey, Rick, you think you're fucked up—look at this guy." I knew that the new guy heard that because he turned his head toward Ron's voice. Once he was secure in his rack, I yelled over.

"Hi. My name is Rick Eilert, or Rick, whatever."

No response. The new guy kind of huffed and turned his head away.

Ron made another wisecrack. "Friendly son of a bitch, isn't he?" I motioned to him to be quiet. I felt that anyone who looked that screwed up had to feel sorry for himself and angry at the world.

After a few minutes Miss Noland came by.

"Rick, this is Al Jones." She waited only a moment to make sure the guy was awake, then continued, "Would you show him the clockwork for eating his meals, and if he gets any mail, read it for him?"

"Yes, ma'am, I'll be glad to." Still no response from my new bunkmate. The nurse began to explain Al's wounds so I understood why he needed help.

"Al's been blinded from his injury and is unable to do things for himself." Before she could continue Al jumped square in her shit.

"I'm not blind, you bitch," he yelled. "And I don't need anyone's help."

Sergeant Rey interrupted. "At ease, marine. You don't talk to her like that or I'll come over there and break your face."

Nothing more was said. Everyone settled back into his own thoughts.

The following morning Doc Bone came for rounds and started with Al. This was the interesting thing about new faces, watching the first dressing change and seeing the wounds and how well the patient was able to cope with the pain. The doctor began with the bandages on the head. With each layer of gauze removed, more and more burned flesh was seen. Finally, it got down to just the bandages over his eyes, nose, and lips. Part of his left ear was gone as were parts of his upper and lower lips. The damage was awful. Al was able to keep himself from screaming, but at one point he lit into the doctor.

"Ouch! You son of a bitch, stop that. You're hurting my eyes."

The doctor didn't take anything from anyone. He slammed back, "You keep your mouth shut. There are a lot of people on this ward that are worse off than you. Just take it easy and let's get you fixed up."

In reality Al was the worst off of anyone on the ward. But the doctor had to make him feel that there were other people in the same boat as he was, so he wouldn't feel alone in his misery.

Once the bandages were all off his face, what we saw was horrible. Most of his nose was gone. He had no eyelids at all, and just a shriveled-up eye in one socket and a dark void in the other. In addition his whole face was badly burned. Everyone on the ward was straining his neck to see the damage. And everyone felt badly. It's easy to hide lost limbs and body scars, but hiding a cruelly disfigured face is another matter.

The doctor removed the bandages from the rest of the body. Both his arms and legs were badly burned; his left elbow and kneecap were gone. His legs weren't broken, but large chunks of flesh were torn away. The doctor ordered his wounds to be tripped and changed three times daily, and the wounds covered with a gauze like that on my stomach. It had something like Vaseline on it. Blass made his notations, then they turned to me.

"Well, Rick, how are we doing today?" Doc Bone asked.

"Fine, sir, but what do I do about this gauze on my belly?"

"Take it off at your own speed, but the sooner the better." He pulled away the bandages. I took a deep breath and squeezed the bed frame. The doctor noticed a small area just below the kneecap that was oozing pus. He pulled a mini–surgical kit from the dressing cart following him, and instructed the nurse to get a shot of morphine. He pulled a scalpel out and began to probe the area with its edge. After the nurse returned with the injection, the doctor waited five minutes and then began to carve away at the infected area, removing the infected flesh and leaving a pool of blood in the hole he had created.

I didn't really get the numbing effect of the medication until after the doctor had finished carving. The pain was horrendous.

"There we are, all done. Take it easy now." I was perspiring and tears were flowing down my face. I lay back and tried to catch my breath as the doctor moved on to Ron's rack. I didn't have any desire to watch the doctor working on Sanford. I just closed my eyes and listened to the symphony of pain as the doctor moved from rack to rack. When he reached Dennis's rack he really got upset. Everyone who had been home over the holidays had probably missed a few dressing changes; the doctor had figured that would happen. But Dennis just flat out hadn't let his parents care for the wound as he had promised the doctor he would.

"Dennis, you crybaby. I trusted you to follow my instructions for your own good, and what do I get for that trust?"

"But Doc, it hurts real bad," he replied.

"That's a horseshit excuse, isn't it, Dennis?" The doctor then began to pull the packing out in big chunks.

"Look at this, that hip looks like it did three weeks ago. You're a damn fool." He turned to Blass, telling him to continue as before with Dennis's dressings.

It was three days before Al began to open up to anyone, but finally he started talking.

"Say, Rick, want to see a picture of my girl?" He fumbled through his wallet. "I was just with her three weeks ago in Hawaii on R and R. I gave her an engagement ring there. I would have left the Nam next month if I hadn't been wounded. Then we were going to get married when I got home. Gosh, I love her." He was able to pick out a laminated photo of the two of them. Al had his head turned sideways to me, as if he had trouble hearing.

"Man, Al, she's a knockout. I mean a real pretty girl, and what a body. You're really lucky." Standing next to her in the picture was Al. He really was a good-looking guy. Big and muscular, dark hair, almost like a Rock Hudson. *What a difference from how he looks now,* I thought. *What will his girl do when she sees him so screwed up? No way will she saddle herself with him like this.* "Al, is this you next to your girl?"

"Yeah. Isn't she out of sight, man? What a woman." Then he thought a moment. "Rick, you know as well as I do that there is no way she's going to stay with me. I'm blind and crippled. It would be nice if she did, but hell, she's so young and pretty. She's got the rest of her life to go yet. I know what has to be done. I know what's right.

"She's not the type of girl that would dump me. When I phoned her from Scott she said that she'd stand by me through thick and thin. But I'm nothing more than a burden from here on out. Just think of it. We go to the beach together: she's really pretty and all the guys are checking her out. She sees how nice they look and thinks of how easy it could be to love someone that's not all scarred and blinded."

"Maybe she loves you more than you know, maybe it doesn't matter to her what you look like."

"Yeah, Rick, I guess you're right."

"Say, Al, how did you get so messed up?"

"I was carrying a box of ammo when a mortar went off in front of me—the box exploded and the flash burned me." Al's head dropped to his chest. His body tightened and he took a deep breath.

"I was knocked cold. They say a NVA soldier ran by me and put a burst in me. Two rounds bounced off my flak jacket, broke some ribs, and left a bad bruise but no real damage. The morning before this happened I had to go to the battalion CP and identify the body of a friend of mine. His face was blown

154

away and I remember thinking to myself how horrible a wound like that would be."

I had expected a short, reluctant answer. Now I was worried that Al would become too upset or resent my questions.

Al seemed happy to talk about his injury. "Doc says I'm blind but I know he's wrong. There are times when I can see light. I'll be OK. I've got to be."

I knew that Al's eyes were gone, that there weren't any eye-balls left at all. A moment before he said he knew he was blind. Now, what a contradiction. Al's recovery would be long and hard, and I felt ashamed and guilty. My wounds seemed so small and insignificant. What right did I have to complain? I should thank God for what I had left.

"Al, you are one lucky dude. That blast could have taken your head off."

Al cocked his head in my direction. "Lucky, you say? I wonder."

I felt like crawling into a hole. There was no further conversation.

When dinner came, Al was propped up in a sitting position. The tray was put on a table in front of him. I took my tray and positioned it in front of myself with the plates in exactly the same position as Al's. I then instructed Al on the position of his food as if the tray were a clock. Potatoes at twelve o'clock, vegetables at one and two, meat at six, bread at eight, and des-sert at ten. From now on, every meal would be served in this exact manner. Al picked up the procedure very quickly and with fantastic accuracy. He spilled his coffee twice, but only because of his shaky grip.

"Say, Rick, thanks. This is a lot easier than I expected. Do you think I can learn how to screw by the numbers?"

"Hell, yes. Ron learned. One, two, three, four, I'd rather do this than go to war." We laughed. "But Ron can't last beyond eight."

Ron threw a handful of potatoes at me, but I ducked and the spuds hit Al in the face and chest. Al got very excited. "Who the hell threw that? Ron, I know it was you, you fucking crip-ple." Al took a handful of corn and tossed it in Ron's direction but didn't even hit his rack. Instead he hit me, and I fired a plate of cherry cobbler into Al's chest and crotch.

A student corpsman finally broke up the melee but only after

Martin and Rey had joined in. Everyone was laughing hysterically. Ron got in the last word, though. "Al, you're going to make one hell of a blind date. Remind me never to go out to dinner with you."

Martin couldn't stop laughing. Sergeant Rey, who was normally very quiet, joined in the fun. "Sanford, you ought to be a diplomat. You're so subtle."

Al wasn't at all offended by Ron's taunts. "Sanford, I'll be more fun at dinner than you or Stumps will be at a sock hop."

Everyone joked around until the trays were picked up and the dressing cart was brought out. Then the feeling of doom and gloom gripped the ward. Crawford had the dressing changes.

Al's wounds covered so much of his body that at times even the sheets covering his body were painful. Crawford tore into Al's dressings unmercifully. I tried not to watch. I had to psyche myself up for the pain to come. Watching other people's dressing changes was like hearing fingernails scratching a blackboard.

Al lay flat against his mattress. He tightened his body up and held on to the bed frame with all his might. The extensive burns were moistened with Dakin's solution fresh from the refrigerator. The corpsman rubbed the burned, blistered area with a four-by-four-inch piece of gauze. After ten minutes of that Crawford went for the open wounds, tearing away the dried dressings, scrubbing the exposed flesh, and then repacking the holes with long lengths of gauze. Al's body often lifted off the mattress, with convulsive groans and occasional curses. But never would he cry out. When Crawford finished with him, Al collapsed, exhausted and soaking wet with perspiration.

Crawford ripped off his dirty gloves then moved to my rack. He was meticulous and methodically cruel. He held the old dressing tightly, and while he tore it out he watched my eyes. As soon as he saw my terror, he pulled and pushed even more.

There was so much skin loss and muscle damage that almost every inch of flesh on my lower legs lay open. One almond-shaped wound lay on my right shin, the nerves totally exposed. Even the cool fluids used to irrigate the wound sent me into uncontrollable spasms. Crawford's tweezers hit the nerves while he scraped the exposed shinbone. Perspiration rolled off my face, hands, and arms. My breath was gone and I groaned when I gasped for air. I didn't scream or sob, but tears just poured out nonetheless. Forty minutes later I lay like Al, exhausted and motionless.

Crawford moved to Ron and after fifteen minutes of digging, gouging, and scraping, he finished applying the last strip of gauze. Ron looked over at me. "Hey, Rick." He stopped to get his wind, then continued, "Did you ever think being wounded was like this?"

I shook my head. "I thought you just bit on a bullet or a stick while they pulled the bullet out, then you put a Band-Aid over the cut and went out to defeat the Hun. You know what else? It seems that no matter where somebody was wounded, even in the legs, they put their arm in a sling. I guess it helps your balance."

"Yeah, I know what you're saying. The scars are always about two inches long and very neat. Hell, I thought we got one of those with our enlistment papers. In every war movie I've ever seen, nobody ever has to take a shit. Those tough guys hold it for the entire war."

"Ron, do you think it's going to be like this forever? You know, dressing changes."

"God, I hope not. I never thought about it. I thought the holes would just close and that would be it. Oh, no, this pain has got to go away."

I lay back and stared at the ceiling. Finally I rang the call button. A student corpsman responded.

"Pain med, Doc, most Ricky-tick." *God,* I thought, *what's it going to be like when the pain medication stops coming?*

My parents arrived a short time later, but I was out cold from my shot, so they visited with Ron and Smitty. They let me sleep. I didn't wake until two the following morning, and then only to get another shot.

Meanwhile, Al's nights and days seemed as one. There was no way for him to distinguish time aside from meals, dressing changes, and the noise around him. His rest was tortured, especially when everyone else on the ward slept. There were times, he said, when he thought he'd lost his mind. He'd wake up not knowing if it was day or night. The ward would be silent and he couldn't figure out if everyone was asleep or everyone was staring at him.

Al really believed that he would see again. His naïve understanding of anatomy and body functions was not his alone.

Almost all of the horribly wounded and deformed patients believed that they would fully recover, at least in the early stages of their hospitalization. Al believed that his injuries would heal—like all the wounds portrayed on TV and in the movies. Admittedly it was unbelievable, but the wounded in the movies were never portrayed as crippled and maimed for life. They never even hinted at what being wounded really meant. I remembered a movie with Jack Webb and Marlon Brando that dealt with paraplegics. Their pain was mostly mental, since they were numb from the waist down. It seemed that everything like this I'd ever seen was a sham. The actors knew that their portrayals were just acting. Now all this pain and terror was real, and forever. Just think of it . . . *forever.*

I knew these thoughts were running through his mind because he said that his beautiful girl friend, Peggy, was coming to see him tomorrow. His parents were driving in from Michigan and Peg was coming with them. Just three weeks ago they'd been together in Hawaii. She'd called him her bronze god, he said. He'd laughed about this to himself at the time.

Al's senior year in high school had been a storybook tale. He was all-state in football, one of the best high school quarterbacks in Michigan. He was also a wrestling champion. Peggy was the homecoming queen, and they were voted the king and queen at the senior prom. Peggy waited for Al, just as she'd said she would. She spent her evenings at Al's home sharing letters with his folks and making cookies to send to him. No two people could have been more in love.

Al had found himself sobbing a few times, but he couldn't understand why no tears fell. He so wanted to feel Peggy in his arms. Everything would be all right when she was by his side.

When I woke from my night's sleep I really felt relaxed for the first time in months. I'd slept soundly without pain or dreams. I felt strong, so strong in fact that I sat up in bed and let my right leg drop over the side of my rack. The pain hit with unbelievable ferocity. I passed out cold. Fortunately I didn't fall out of bed, because I was in traction.

Breakfast was over and the corpsmen and nurses had gathered at the foot of Al's rack to start rounds with Doc Bone. Chief saw me collapse. He lunged over, grabbed my leg, and gently raised the long leg case, resting it on the bed. There wasn't any damage, but Chief was stunned. He stood next to my rack until I came to.

"Rick, you all right? I thought you'd fall out of bed."

I winced. "Oh, I'm just great. Man, I never had pain like that before. What happened?"

"You've been flat on your back for six weeks. You just sat up too fast. That's what knocked you out."

I was amazed how weak I was. All my life I'd been strong. I ran everywhere: to the store, to school, to friends' houses, and just for fun. The Marine Corps had firmed up my muscles and wind even more. I was accustomed to long, difficult patrols. Now, six weeks after my injury, I couldn't even sit up. I was filled with rage and frustration. I was helpless. That frightened me.

Doc Bone was finishing up on Al's examination, and I braced myself as the entourage moved to my rack.

"Good morning, Rick. Enjoy your walk?" he chuckled.

"Oh, yes, sir. Remind me to wear my track shoes."

"You best take your time. It might well be another month before you can start getting out of bed. It's going to be hard learning to walk all over again, a lot harder than you think," the doctor told me, while he pulled the dressings away from my wounds.

"Will I ever be able to run again?"

"The peroneal nerve in your left leg is gone. Your leg will be paralyzed for the rest of your life. You'll have to wear a short leg brace. The muscle and nerve damage to your left thigh and right lower leg will hamper your ability to walk as well. You'll probably need crutches to get around on."

I felt a sick, empty sensation in my stomach. "My God . . ." I paused as tears welled up in my eyes and my mouth went dry. "I never thought I was hurt that bad. Won't I ever be able to get around without crutches?" There was a sense of urgency and my question was more like a plea.

"Maybe, but the pain will be terrible at first and later on you'll probably feel uncomfortable." Doc Bone always hated to relay such grim news, but he never underestimated our spirit and courage. In civilian practice such news might devastate a patient. But here, time and again he'd watched badly wounded men accept their disabilities as a challenge. Despite the agony, most exceeded normal recovery expectations.

My dressings had now been pulled away. I spoke very little while his examination was in process. I just put my death grip on the bed frame and endured another morning's torture. I thought about the moment I'd been wounded repeatedly, going over all the what ifs and maybes. It helped mask my pain.

The doctor moved on to Ron, then quickly through the rest of the ward. In his wake lay the exhausted bodies of his patients. It was then I decided I'd never go home to my family and friends until I could stand on my own. I didn't want anyone to see me struggling to learn to walk. I was embarrassed to think I was a cripple.

I rang and got another pain shot and fell asleep until noon chow. After lunch the dressing cart returned and once again I felt sick with fear. By the time Al's, my, and Ron's dressings had been changed, visiting hours started.

Ron was lying on his right side facing me and the nurses' station. Suddenly he reached across the aisle and grabbed my arm. "Look . . . over by the front desk," he whispered.

I turned my head. There stood a man and a woman in their late forties, and a gorgeous blonde. I recognized the girl as Al's fiancée.

Al was lying very still, as if asleep. I decided not to wake him. I'd leave that to his girl and his parents.

The nurse at the desk pointed and they turned around, slowly walking to the foot of Al's rack. All three stood there silently for four or five minutes, each with a tortured expression.

His girl spotted a printed card at the foot of his bed. It contained the patient's name, rank, and diagnosis. Apparently they didn't know he was blind until that moment. His girl and mother began to weep uncontrollably. They had to leave the ward. His father dropped his head and ran his fingers through his graying hair. He maneuvered around to Al's bedside and gently laid his hands on his son's arm.

"Is that you, Chief? I just had my dressing changed," Al snapped excitedly. There was a prolonged silent pause. Al was frightened now. "Who's there?"

"It's me, son," he said quietly.

"Dad . . . my God. Dad, is it really you?" Al's voice was trembling.

"Sure it's me, Al. How are you doing?" I could see that his father wished that he hadn't asked such a stupid question. It was obvious. His boy was blinded and mangled. "I've brought Mom and Peggy with me. They're both worried sick about you."

Peg and his mom returned. I watched the young girl's face. There was terrible hurt in her eyes, and an overwhelming look of disgust. She hadn't expected this at all. It was just a little over three weeks since she had been with him on R and R. He had changed so much.

Al sat up, and with his head cocked to one side, he scanned the area with his ears. "Peggy . . . oh, Peg. It hurts so bad," his voice cracked.

She moved to his side and gently kissed his cheek. Al's teeth were exposed where portions of his lips were torn away.

I thought she would vomit.

His mother moved in next to Peg. "Al . . . is it very terrible? Are you suffering much?" She was clenching her husband's hand.

"Ah, Mom, I'll be just fine. I can see some light already. I'm sure it won't be too long before I'm up and around." Al's words were confident but his voice wasn't all that reassuring.

His father read the diagnosis at the foot of his rack. It clearly stated, "Blind." "Did the doctor feel your recovery would be complete?"

"Oh, yeah, Dad. Sure."

Peggy touched Al's hand. His flesh was blistered and cracked almost everyplace on his upper body. She was clearly worried that he would hurt if she touched him. "Did the doctor say how long you would be hospitalized?" Her voice trembled. She tried to pick just the right words. "Do you think we can still hold to our October wedding plans? Your mother is helping me sew my wedding dress. It's really pretty."

"I bet you look terrific in it. Hell, you look great in anything. I've missed you so much. I didn't think it was possible but I love you more each day. Heck, it's another nine months away. I'm sure I'll be recovered by then." Al was losing himself in the make-believe that used to be his certain future. Deep down he knew that Peggy would suffer every day they spent together, but she was all he had, and to lose her would destroy him.

"Al, I've made your favorite chocolate chip cookies and baked a cake. I'll put the bag on your table here." His mother crumpled the bag and put it on the table firmly so that Al could hear.

It wasn't necessary. Suddenly Al knew this would be the way of things the rest of his life. Everyone thinks people who can't see are feebleminded as well.

Meanwhile, I received a phone call and was happy to have something to do besides watching Al and his family.

Peggy and Al's parents stayed for another hour exchanging small talk. After his parents said good-bye he had about five minutes with Peggy alone. Al tried to say all the clever, intimate words he was always able to come up with when he talked to Ron and me, but it was hopeless. Peggy sat holding his hand and staring at his scarred and bandaged face. She was grossed out. But I could see that she felt guilty. She really did love him. She'd thought nothing would ever change how she felt, but now she didn't have the same urge to love him. How could she?

Al grabbed for her hand firmly, and with a cracking in his voice he begged her to return. "Peg, when will you be back?"

"I'm driving home with your folks now. They said we'd be back in two weeks. Your father is taking a vacation day to drive down. I'll write often. I love you, Al. I'm so glad you came home." She leaned over and kissed his forehead. "Good-bye."

"Bye, Peg. I love you. Please write as soon as you get home."

Shortly after she left Al summoned Ron and me. Ron rolled out of his rack and into his wheelchair. I lay on my right side, propping my head on my hand. Ron rolled his chair between our racks so that the three of us were in a close huddle.

"Ain't she something?" Al asked proudly.

"That she is. What a body, and that face," Ron drawled tauntingly.

"She's all you said she was. She's one of those few ladies that are prettier than their picture. What eyes," I mumbled as I lit a cigarette.

"Eyes? Are you crazy? What a set," Ron laughed.

Al sat up. "At ease, you animals, at ease." Al paused, then almost timidly he turned toward me. "No way can she wait. Have you ever loved someone so much that you wanted never to see them again?"

Ron and I looked at each other. Ron shrugged his shoulders. Al wasn't as blind as we'd thought. I answered, "She's a wonderful girl, Al. I got a feeling she's the kind that would wait."

Al nodded. "I know Peg would marry me. She would stay with me forever, but man, that ain't right. She deserves so much more. At the very least a man to protect her and share life with her. Can you see her pushing me around in a wheel-chair, guiding me through stores and parties, even in bed. God, I don't know that I could handle anything like that if she were in my place."

Ron tried to reassure him. "It could work out. If you both really feel so strongly about each other."

Al was annoyed that Ron hadn't grasped his line of thinking. "Are you serious?"

"No, Polish."

"Look. All that Peggy and I had was based on a fairy tale. I've changed a lot in the last year, and now with this mess it almost seems impossible."

Ron became very apologetic. "I'm sorry, Al. Look . . . I thought I had the same type of girl when I was away. I loved her like I never thought I could love anyone or anything. I really can't figure it. I've learned to be cool—you know, take it as it comes. I've lost friends, but once they got blown away I could drag their bodies through the mud. When I went home over Christmas she laid her fiancé on me. God, that hurt. I didn't think I could be hurt anymore but she put me in a humm. I look at Peggy and I can see how lucky you are. I guess I'm jealous."

I was surprised by Ron's long oratory. I'd never heard him say so much before. Besides, Ron seemed so calm. Now that every-one else was in the open I thought it was time to say how I felt.

"Ron's right, I guess. Cheryl, my girl, was the only thing I thought of. She was all that touched me. Doesn't it seem strange that you can live with guys day and night, share every intimate thought you ever had, and they get turned into a pile of garbage and it's just over. Since I've been home there seems to be something between us. Something else is gone and I can't put my finger on it. It scares me that I'm losing her. She's all I have. But I know I've changed. She's still there, though. That counts for something."

Al signaled Ron to light him a cigarette. "Thanks. Man, you two are something else. Advisers for the lovelorn. I'm sorry that your girl dumped you, Ron. I didn't realize someone else had what I have, or felt what I feel. Rick, you sound like our situations are the same. Do you want your girl saddled with a gimp? Don't you think she'd hate you for making her a cripple, too? Hell, we're all mistakes of fate, aren't we?"

Ron laughed. "That ain't no shit. My captain was mad as hell when I got shot. He kept saying he just had to teach another dumb snuffy how to use the radio."

"You know what I mean," Al continued. "It's like, what right do you have to be alive? Being a little wounded is great, but get all blown to shit and you're an eyesore, a pain in the ass to look at. In all the other wars we'd have died, but the helicopter and modern medicine did us a favor and spared us."

"I've felt like that, especially lately. If someone tells me how lucky I am to be alive once more I'll go bozo." My voice shook as if I wanted to scream.

Al was really moved to talk. "Yeah, ain't we lucky?" he scoffed. "I've got to make Peggy leave me. It's only right. I'm not going to drag her down with me."

"Oh, hell . . . the dressing cart, and Crawford's got the duty." I threw myself back on my mattress.

The following morning I was wakened early for blood tests and the series of three shots everyone received before going to the OR. One of the injections was Valium and it knocked me out. I opened my eyes only once, just outside the operating room when the anesthesiologist put the IV in my arm, and I woke back in my rack on the ward. I opened my eyes slowly and the first thing I looked for was the traction bars on the left side of the rack. They were all gone.

The room seemed so open, so much bigger. I felt free, as if before I had been in bondage. I shook my left leg from side to side ever so lightly. It hurt like hell, but it was the first time I'd been able to move it in ten weeks.

"Looks good, Rick. Does it hurt much?" Ron smiled.

Al sat up and turned his head to the right. "Rick, are you back? How are you doing? Can you move?"

I smiled. "Yeah, you guys. I'm fine."

I received a round of applause from those near my rack. I clasped my hands together and raised them above my head, shaking them from side to side. I felt so free, so unrestricted.

After dressing changes were done and the corpsman gone, a nurse walked up to my bed carrying several injections and a plierslike instrument.

The nurse was a buxom beauty, Miss Altman. "Hello, Mr. Eilert. Remember me?"

I smiled. "Yes, ma'am, I sure do. Is all that for me?"

"No, no way. Just a few things. First try to roll up on your right side."

I did as instructed. My legs lay flat but I twisted at the hip. She got behind me and pulled my pajama bottoms down. "I'm going to take these wire stitches out."

I was embarrassed having the pretty nurse inspecting my ass. Ron was just behind the nurse, laughing hysterically. "Look, everyone, a new face on the ward." Even Miss Altman chuckled.

It hurt as she pulled the wire away. All these weeks of having it in had driven the wire deeper. She was gentle and very patient. Soon it was done.

"OK, one more thing, stay put. I've got a shot for you." She drove the needle into my buttock. "This is a Keflin shot, a real high-powered antibiotic. It may hurt. The liquid is thick like syrup."

My eyes teared up, it hurt so bad. I pulled the pillow over my face, trying not to scream.

The nurse knew how painful the shot was and said nothing. She pulled up my pajama bottoms and rolled me over on my back, the pillow still pulled tight over my face.

Ron laughed until the nurse turned to him. "OK, Ron, pull 'em down. Got one for you, too."

Ron's laugh cut short as he rolled over on his side. Just like me he pulled the pillow over his face as the thick serum filled his butt. The nurse picked up the rest of the shots and continued on to the rest of the men needing injections.

Ron and I pulled the pillows away from our faces at the same time. We looked at each other with terror and tears in our eyes.

"God, what was that?" Ron sighed.

"There has to be some mistake. Man, feel the bump where she gave you the shot. Feels like a golf ball. Hell, it hasn't even thinned out yet."

Ron turned over and looked for the nurse. She was at Dennis's rack.

"Hey, Miss Altman. How often do we get this shot?"

She looked at the cards the injections are ordered on. "Three times a day," she shouted.

"Damn." I sighed.

"Three dressing changes and three Keflin shots a day. Man, that's cold. I mean c-o-l-d, cold," Ron muttered.

I flagged down the nurse as she walked past my bed. "Miss Altman, I need my pain medication."

She went to the nurses' station and quickly returned with a little red and gray pill.

"What's this?"

"That's your pain medication. Darvon."

"No, ma'am. I get Demerol, a shot."

"Not anymore. The doctor took you off narcotics. The Darvon will help some."

I was scared to death. I thought of myself after one of Crawford's dressing changes, with my body full of pain. "But it really hurts."

"I bet it does, Rick. You've been on those pain shots for ten weeks. You'll get addicted to them, and that's all you need on top of all your other troubles." She handed the capsule to me and watched me swallow it with a cup of water. Then she left.

Ron leaned over. "It's rough at first. Those shots really take the edge off, but she's right. That Demerol is nasty stuff."

I knew that Ron was right, but the shots helped me sleep and forget. How was I going to forget now?

The next ten days were quiet on the ward. I got my ration of visitors and moments with Cheryl, but I could feel her slipping away from me. It hurt, but there wasn't a damn thing I could do.

Al and Ron each went to the OR. For several days they were doped up, so conversation was nil.

Al received three letters from his Peggy, but he tore them up. Then, a week after his operation, his parents showed up.

"Al, it's Mom," she said, kissing his cheek. "We brought Peggy to see you, son."

His father signaled for her to join them.

I watched her carefully. She was all that Al said—very pretty. But she seemed so young.

I could see her eyes searching Al's bandaged face. She was frightened. She still loved him, but couldn't stand the sight of him. The group exchanged small talk for nearly a half hour. Al asked his parents to give Peggy and him some time alone. They agreed and went into the hallway.

Al reached out with his right hand and Peggy took it in hers. She spoke clearly but tears rolled down her face. I looked at Al's face. His lip was quivering.

"Hawaii was great, wasn't it, Peg?"

"It was wonderful, Al. I never wanted to leave. I wanted us to stay there forever. . . ." She paused. "Al, it's just not fair. We had so much. How could this all be? I keep thinking it's a bad dream and I'll wake up and it'll disappear."

"I know, Peg. I always knew this would happen. Then after I saw you in Hawaii I thought I could never be hurt. I felt as if nothing could kill me. Now, look. How are your folks?"

"Oh, they're OK. They send their love. They hope you'll be home soon. You know, all that stuff." Her voice sounded strange.

Al picked it up immediately. "They know I'm blind and they want you to forget about me?"

"No, that's not true. My parents aren't like that. They've always liked you and cared about you. They let me come to Hawaii, didn't they?"

Al knew it was now or never. "Peggy, I've got something to say to you. Just bear with me. I've thought a lot about us since we met on R and R. The Nam has changed me. It's changed me a lot. The more I think about us getting married the more I think you and me aren't good for each other. It's best if we break the engagement now."

Peggy's tears grew bigger and dropped on the bed sheets. "Al, that's not true. Please don't say that."

Al was dying inside. He had never dreamed he'd say all this, but he continued. "There's no way of knowing how long I'll be in the hospital. I'm doing fine but it'll be some time before I see again, and maybe even longer before I can walk again."

She had a good idea of what was going on. Over and over she insisted that she had no intention of leaving him. "Please, Al, stop saying that. You know I'll never leave you . . . not ever. None of this matters as long as we're together, honest." But he kept right on.

"Peggy, I just don't love you the way I should. I can't trust you to be faithful to me as long as I'm up here. You used to screw around with every guy in town before I started taking you out."

"That's a lie, Al. I never screwed around before or after I met you. Please, don't do this." She was sobbing now, and almost incoherent.

"Just shut up and get out of my sight . . . you bitch!" Al yelled.

She ran crying from the ward and within a few seconds his parents returned. His father was red-faced with anger.

"What did you say to that girl? What's wrong with you—don't you have a lick of compassion? Have you any idea what she's been through? She would wait for you forever, you know that?"

"Look, Dad, I don't want her to wait. I don't love her and I want to be left alone!" Al screamed.

His father stood silent then picked up his and his wife's coats. "If that's the way you want it, you mindless bastard, then that's the way it's going to be."

Al's parents took him at his word. They stormed out. And they never came back.

I had a lump in my throat after Al's parents left. I knew, as did everyone around Al, what he had just done. We knew how hard it was for him. I wondered if I could have done that to Cheryl.

The only thing Al had to hold on to in the whole world was Peggy's love. He knew damn well he could never find a woman like her again. It was doubtful that Al would ever meet anyone ever again unless she was blind, too. He was so messed up, who'd even look at him? The ward was quiet as Al lay still for a long time.

Ron got into his wheelchair and rolled to the foot of Al's rack.

"Al, don't worry. Once she gets home and thinks about it maybe she'll decide she really does want you."

Al remained silent. If he'd had eyes he probably would have cried. With all he'd lost in the Nam, now it looked as if his heart had been torn out.

Everyone worried that Al would become bitter. Instead he began to pull pranks. He even had people laughing at him, which in his case was good. To be able to laugh at oneself makes hard times easier to take, something everyone on the ward had to find out sooner or later.

Ron took over the duty of helping Al eat by the clock. "OK, Al, mashed potatoes at ten o'clock, meat at one, vegetables at three, dessert at six, and bread at nine. Got that?"

While Al nodded Ron would rearrange everything so that when he reached for the bread he got a handful of mashed potatoes. Al would get so frustrated that he'd throw the potatoes while cussing and yelling at Ron. He'd even pull off his bandages to gross everyone out. Ron would taunt him back. One afternoon Ron said, "Hey, Al, long time no see." At first there was quiet, then everyone, including Al, laughed until he cried.

When people came onto the ward and they passed Al's rack, it was always "Long time no see, Al." It got to be that you could tell who his friends were by how much they joked around with him. Learning how to laugh at the wounds was as big part of healing as any. Al was an inspiration to many of the patients, because if he joked about his pain and disfigurement, how could they bitch about their wounds?

One morning after rounds a new nurse was touring the ward, talking with a few of the patients. Her name was Miss Scanlon. She was as simple as could be—at least that was the way she acted. Instead of starting with Al in rack one, she went over to the other side of the ward first. Ron and I had helped Al memorize the first page in a comic book. By the time she reached Al's rack he had the comic book in front of his face. Before she spoke to him she looked at the tail end of his rack, where a sign gave the patient's name and medical problem. It read, "Al Jones . . . multiple frag wounds . . . blind." She looked back at Al holding the comic book, pretending that he was reading. "Excuse me, Al . . . what are you doing?"

"Why, ma'am, I'm reading a comic book. Why?"

"Are you feeling all right, Jones?" She said straining her neck to see his face behind the pages. "Come on now, Jones, you're blind, and there's no way you can kid yourself that you can see."

"The hell I can't read." He lowered the comic book enough to show his face. Ron had taken all the bandages off, and when the nurse got a glimpse of that face she almost passed out. Then she rushed back to the nurses' station and brought back another nurse and a student corpsman. Unfortunately the other nurse with her was also new and hadn't met Al yet either. "Go on, Mr. Jones, tell me again what you're doing." Again Al pulled the book down low enough to expose his mangled face. Lips gone, nose and eyelids gone all or partially, one eye withered and the other gone, leaving a dark hole in his face. The student corpsman fainted, falling against Al's locker, then hit the floor with a thud. On his trip to the floor he knocked over a filled duck. It spilled out, splashing his face and hitting the nurses' shoes.

Chief was on duty that day and came to the aid of the student. But he didn't give the game away. He just smiled and held the other corpsman up while Al continued to toy with the nurse. "Here, ma'am, hold this." Al handed her the comic book. "I'm reading page twenty-three." He then rattled off the whole page word for word.

The two nurses just flipped. They exchanged stares, each hoping that the other had seen the same thing she saw. Miss Scanlon flagged down one of the doctors from another ward who was visiting one of the patients. He had no idea what the nurses were talking about. A blind boy reading a comic book? He sat down on the bed next to Al.

"What's going on here? The nurses tell me that you can read. We both know that's impossible, now don't we?"

"Sir, I can see just as well as you. See that tile in the ceiling, second from the right? There are," he counted, "twenty-nine holes in that tile"—the number I'd given him after counting them myself.

The doctor was as astonished as everyone else in the area. Then the doctor caught on to what was going on, shook his head, and walked away. The nurses followed him. Everyone broke up laughing. Miss Scanlon stuck her face back around the corner. Al was still lying there, counting. "Eleven, twelve, thirteen." There he was, no face, and he just kept on counting as he held his head looking up at the ceiling.

The patient on the other side of Ron had a colostomy bag attached to his side. He was laughing so hard that the bag fell off, bursting and throwing shit all over. Everyone broke up again.

That afternoon Ron and I had to go to surgery. The two of us were laid side by side in the corridor outside the operating room. The anesthesiologist came out to check on Ron. Ron began talking to him.

"Say, Doc, will I be able to play the piano after this operation?"

"Of course you will. The doctor is only operating on your foot."

Ron smiled. "That's good. I never could play it before."

The doctor left. He didn't even smile. When we were alone again, we continued to joke around. After a few minutes Ron fell asleep from the shots he'd received before going to the OR. As soon as I was convinced that he was really out, I reached over and pulled the sheet up over his head. He looked like any of the other corpses that were often lying in the corridor. When the corpsman came out to get Ron he saw only a corpse and me. Thinking that I was Sanford he wheeled me into the operating room. When Doc Bone walked in he recognized me, and rather than switching to Sanford, who wasn't to be found, he went on and performed surgery on me.

Meanwhile, Ron woke up soon after I was wheeled in. When he opened his eyes and saw the sheet over his face, he knew that there had been foul play. He decided to get even.

Ron moved his gurney back in the line and waited for me to be wheeled into recovery, then hopped in after me. He pulled the sheet over my face, pushed the gurney against the wall, and then hopped back to his place in line.

One of the corpsmen in recovery noticed the body and called the morgue to come and get it. So I woke up with the sheet over my head. I chuckled to myself, thinking that I was in recovery and Ron had been put beside me. I was thirsty as usual and pulled the sheet down to request a wet rag, only to find myself in a room in which nobody recovers. "Where the hell am I? . . . Get me out of here!"

There was a corpsman there, sitting at a desk writing. When he caught a glimpse of this body sitting up and yelling, he almost died.

"I said, get me out of here."

The corpsman was still shocked. "Whaaa . . . whaaa . . . whooo . . . *Oh, my God.* You aren't dead."

"No shit, Sherlock. Get me out of here." He rushed me back to recovery and went to the nurse to explain that this patient had just come back from the dead. She thought the guy had flipped. She sat him down and had him tell his story to her all over again. She went over and pulled my chart, then phoned the ward to come and get their Lazarus. She tried to pump some information out of me, but I wasn't talking. I was saving up for Ron.

Actually my left leg was really bothering me. The doctor had removed more shrapnel. Windows had been cut through the cast in a big area around the wounds. I asked the nurse for some pain medication, then went to sleep once the shot took effect.

When I returned to the ward, my reception was a little embarrassing. The patients were all applauding and laughing. Ron had relayed the tale and had also beaten me back up to the ward, even though he'd gone into the OR after me. Blind Al was holding his stomach laughing, and just the sight of him laughing got me laughing, too. Once I settled down I realized that it really was funny. But it had scared the hell out of me when I found myself surrounded by stiffs. "Ron, I'll get you. Someday I'll get even."

# 10

IT TOOK A week to learn how to live with two long leg casts. But the biggest moment was when Chief introduced me to a wheelchair.

He placed the chair next to my rack, picked me up, and sat me in it. I hadn't been up for three minutes when I blacked out. Chief picked me back up and laid me in bed. When I came to, Chief explained, "It's been so long since you've sat up like this that your body has to get its equilibrium back. For the rest of the day I want you to keep getting into the chair and sitting there for an hour or so until you get used to it." Chief picked me up again, sat me back in the chair, and left me there. Again I passed out. But I stayed in the chair. By the end of the day, I'd mastered getting out of my rack and into the contraption. The next day I passed out trays for the first time and lapped the ward a few times. It was a whole new life. I went to the other side of the ward thinking it would be different from my side, but it wasn't. Everything was the same, except the patients faced east where I faced west. But the ability to venture out of the ward by elevator was a gas. The different views of the outside world with its cars and houses were fantastic. Finally I felt that I was really getting better.

As the days passed, the nurses tried to wean me off the pain shots that I had been on so long. Like many others I was addicted, but not in the same sense as street addicts. My reason for taking the drugs was for a real physical problem, not to ease the pain of a mental problem. There were times, however, when I asked for pain med though I wasn't hurting physically, but mentally.

It wasn't easy. When I had real pain, the pills that I was given just couldn't compare to a shot to both ease the pain and make me relax. Sleeping was difficult. Especially now that I could dream. Slowly, slowly I did get off the shots, but it was a real bitch. Even though my wounds were healing, especially the smaller ones, the absence of pain medication made the thrice-daily dressing changes more difficult. It became necessary for me to put myself in a trancelike state. I'd concentrate on something or someone in the area, or I'd close my eyes and try to think the pain away. Neither method was all that good. But it beat the hell out of screaming.

Now that I'd joined the mobile population, I also had to compete in the ward wheelchair races. These races could be fun, but dangerous. If the chair was to flip or tip over, injuries could be aggravated. But it was an effective way to blow off steam. I had one of the old wooden wheelchairs. It was so big and bulky that once I got in front of anyone it was almost impossible to pass me. So I was able to win many of the races I entered. The winners of those races were pitted against the best from the other wards. Races were given names and the bigger ones were held once a month in order to always have champs on the wards. When someone got discharged, the races would have to be held again in order to determine a new champion. The Three East 100 and the Ward Three South Rally were two of the more prestigious. I wasn't good at races requiring speed, my chair being more for large pack races.

One day I went to the cast tex room to have a new cast put on my right leg. This leg was healing and the doctor wanted to see how well it was doing. Once the cast was off, I didn't have any real discomfort. The union of the bone fragments was doing nicely; maybe the leg would only have to be in a cast another six to eight weeks. A new cast was put on, and I got myself into my chair and went back onto the ward.

When I returned to my rack, I was greeted by several other patients, who told me that they'd entered me in a chicken race. I couldn't believe it.

"You mean to tell me that I'm going to collide with another gimp, for the humor of the ward? No chance. I just got this cast put on."

Ron smiled. "Listen, Rick, haven't I always been honest with you?"

I just smiled.

"Look, this guy on Three East challenged us, we've got to respond, and you're the only one who's got the heft with both those casts to be effective. Besides, that guy is a cracker ass and doesn't have any legs."

"That's great, Ron—you want me to demolish somebody with no legs. That's real nice."

Al was sitting on the side of his bed all excited. "Ah, come on, Rick. I can't wait to see that jerk smashed up." He chuckled.

"The guy's an Army dogface, a doggy," Ron said with a snicker.

I stopped my chair. "Bullshit, he is."

"Honest, he's a doggy." Everyone nodded his head.

"Really, Rick, he's Army all the way. Eleven Bravo, no less."

"All right, when's the race and how much you got bet on it?" I asked.

"The race goes off in fifteen minutes and we got a hundred fifty on the nose, even money. I took the liberty of betting twenty of yours," Ron said.

"For a hundred fifty dollars that guy isn't going to back down, you know. Somebody's going to get hurt." Ron put his hands on my shoulders. "Hey, Rick, not to worry. I've taken care of everything. Blind Al is the starter."

Al laughed, happy as a lark to be involved in something for a change. He could walk by now, kind of like Frankenstein, stiff-legged.

I was pushed out into the hall by Toby. The ward didn't want the champ to strain until the "go" was given. The race was to be held in the hallway next to the elevators, outside the ward, so that no nurses or doctors would see what was going on. The two combatants were to line up at opposite ends of the corridor. Then Blind Al, standing in the center, would drop a handkerchief and move to one of the walls, hugging it until the race was over. I took up my position and Blind Al was led to the center of the hallway. We waited for Three East's champ to arrive.

When my opponent wheeled up, my heart sank. The guy didn't have any legs, but he was as big as a house, and his wheelchair was all metal. I panicked.

"Ron, I thought you said this guy was a cracker ass. Hell, his legs might be gone but his damn torso is six feet high, and look at that damn tank he's driving. Where did they get that, out of war surplus?" I looked down at my long leg casts sticking straight out at my opponent. They now looked like Popsicle sticks instead of ramrods. The two chairs and their seconds were brought to the center by Blind Al, who explained the rules. We'd charge at each other and the first to turn away from the impact would lose the money. The "go" signal would be when Al dropped the rag. I smiled at my adversary, but got only a growl in return. The guy had a five o'clock shadow at one o'clock.

The two chairs were put into position and the racers got ready. I wanted to pass out. Al dropped the handkerchief and we were off. But Al couldn't find the wall. He kept walking in circles, yelling, "I'm lost . . . I'm lost." Meanwhile, the two of us were steaming right for him.

"Don't hit me. . . . Please don't hit me," Al yelled.

I started to laugh. Before the two chairs collided, with Al in the middle, we both turned at the last second to miss hitting him. I went into an elevator door. The new cast was still soft and offered no resistance to the impact. My right leg bent up at a forty-five-degree angle, breaking it right where it was healing from the original break. I passed out from the pain.

Meanwhile the monster from Three East turned in the opposite direction, crashed through the men's room door, and hit the corner of the toilet bowl, sliding down the chair with one stump in the bowl and the other dangling over the side, and smashing his face against the pipe on the back of the toilet. He was bleeding all over.

The patients from both wards grabbed their champions and tried to sneak them back into their home wards without anyone seeing them. The Three East people got one of their corpsmen to stitch up their man. Three South had more trouble. My leg was broken again so they pulled me, still passed out, into the solarium, and using ducks they beat the cast back down until it looked straight. With the help of a little water they smoothed the plaster out. When I woke I was in terrible pain. Now I was on Darvon only and that was hardly enough to ease the hurt. Word was sent out for everyone to ask for their pain meds, hide them under their tongues, then give them to me. That way they were able to keep me doped up for three days, until the pain eased.

After I recovered from the aborted chicken race, when dinner time came I gingerly slid out of my rack and into my wheelchair to pass out trays. I was handed one with double orders of everything on it for a new guy on the ward. His rack was on the far southeast corner, and I sped off with both legs sticking straight out, weaving in and out of the other wheelchairs waiting to take trays.

As I rounded the corner of the last rack to my right, I lost control of the wheelchair. I couldn't stop.

The new man's eyes got bigger and bigger as he watched me plow into the foot of his rack. Food was scattered everywhere and a handful of mashed potatoes, piping hot, landed in my crotch. I frantically cleaned it away, then looked the unhappy patient straight in the eyes. "Sorry about that," I mumbled.

"You son of a bitch," came the reply.

I knew how he felt. This was to be his first stateside meal in over a year. He was probably starving after the long trip from Da Nang. I thought he would start crying.

He searched the floor. The little tasty morsels were everywhere. He looked back at me. "You duffus."

My face turned red as everyone applauded. "Hey look, I'm sorry. I'll get you another tray." I returned to my rack and fetched my own tray. I wasn't hungry anyway. My legs were throbbing terribly. "Here you are. Bon appétit."

"Thanks a lot," came the reply.

I sat there and watched the man stuff his face as if someone would take the food away. I tried to make amends. "Hello,

there. I'm Rick Eilert. Everyone calls me Rick."

The man waited to swallow his food before speaking. "I can see where you make a lot of friends. What was your MOS? Truck driver?" He didn't wait for a reply. "My name is Markley. Steve Markley of the Kansas Markleys."

Steve was a good six foot two, with dark hair, longer than regulation. His right arm was in a cast from his hand up to and including his shoulders and torso. The cast had a post from his waist to his elbow, holding his arm up at a ninety-degree angle from his side.

"You say you're from Kansas? Does that mean you're a cowboy type? Bet they call you Slim." I smiled.

"Yeah, you're right. They might as well call me Slim," Steve snapped. He finished eating, then started to question me. "Rick, is it?"

I nodded.

"Where is your rack at?"

"Rack two. Up where you come into the ward."

"Are you next to that blind kid? He seems a little strange."

"Yeah. I'm right next to him. We call him Blind Al or Long-time-no-see Al. He'll answer to either."

"Man, that's crass, calling him names."

"'Crass'! What the hell is 'crass'? Are you a college type?" Steve laughed. "Yeah. I'm a college type except I was asked to leave. The only finals I took were in pantie raids and Mazola rolls."

I laughed. "I got cut out of college, too. Isn't that cast a little uncomfortable at night? It sure looks odd."

"What do you think! I sure as hell can't pick my nose with that hand," he replied as he worked at the scraps of food on his plate.

"How did you get hit?"

Steve paused a moment before he spoke. It was as if he hadn't thought about it since he was shot. "I was with Delta CAPs. We'd just caught one of our Popular Forces stuffing sand in the chamber of our sixty. After we beat the camel piss out of him we went to the position and started to field-strip the weapon. It was dark as hell. I was talking to a buddy of mine. All of a sudden there was a burst of small-arms fire. Next thing I knew I was on my back. I felt like I was hit with a baseball bat. The bullet picked me up and slammed me down. It blew out the ball and socket and the scapula when it exited. Man,

Charlie ruined that night. Now there's a whole shit pot full of bone fragments and gunk that's got to come out. On top of that it's infected."

I winced as I listened to Steve's story. "Man, you're lucky. That's one of those John Wayne wounds where you bite on a stick while a pretty nurse pulls the bullet out, then you wrap your arm in a bandana and go on to win the war. I thought shoulder wounds came with your enlistment papers," I laughed.

"Yeah, Rick, you're right. Just like in the movies. What price glory now, Captain Flag, or something like that. I hope I'm out of here in a few weeks."

I laughed heartily. "A few weeks? More like three months. You've got to go through Doc Bone's customizing shop first."

Steve looked surprised. "Come on now. Three months? I've got a bad case of getting shot, not VD."

"What can I say?"

"I've heard people talking about Doc Bone. Who's he?" Steve seemed worried now.

"He's numero uno, el jefe, the honcho. Doc Magic Fingers. You've lucked out—he's the best doctor around. The peoples' choice. He'll tell it like it is."

Steve seemed relieved to hear all this. "Good, outstanding. I tell you, Rick, everything is happening so fast. Five days ago I was part of an ambush and ran a six-kilometer patrol. Four days ago I killed an old man I discovered had booby-trapped a path frequented by my squad. Just four days ago I was wounded. God, another two inches to the left and that bullet would have hit me right in the throat. It wasn't until I arrived here that I really started to feel pain."

I saw tears welling up in Steve's eyes as he tried to find a comfortable position to lie in. He asked a passing corpsman for something to ease the pain and was quickly obliged. Cox walked in back of Markley and pulled his pajama bottoms down until he found a suitable target.

"Woowee, that burns."

Cox laughed as he wiped the buttock with a cotton ball. "There you go, Steve . . . enjoy."

"Thanks, Doc. I'll always think of you kindly."

Ron was dangling his legs over the side of his rack when I returned. "Rick, where were you before? You had a phone call and we couldn't find you."

"I was with Chief, over by the new guy's rack."

"What new guy? The one with the airplane cast?" Ron asked.

"Yeah, that's him. His name is Steve Markley. He was with Delta CAPs."

Ron swallowed a deep gasp of air. "Man, that's the shits. Those people in CAPs are nothing but human sacrifices. . . . They run three-man patrols and they have only about ten marines and some PFs. Steve looks like Al, you know, from that photo of him and Peggy."

I would alternately nod and shake my head while listening to Ron. "Yeah, I know. I noticed the resemblance when I was over at Steve's rack. You know, we had people actually volunteering for CAP units. Big units run into big shit. But little units get wiped out. Anyway, he's from Kansas. I guess he's one of those cowboy types with horseshit on their boots. Ron, did you get your pay record yet?"

"No, how about you?"

"Hell, I was in the Nam five months and never got paid. Now I'm back in the world two months and still no pay. I'm going to owe my soul to the company store if I don't get some dinero soon."

"No pay yet. Man, bend over some more. Uncle Sam wants to shove that shaft."

Just as Ron finished the sentence I got a visitor. I was looking at Ron so I didn't see the man coming.

"Hey, Rick . . . how are you doing?"

I rolled over and saw Scott, a friend of mine from college.

"Scott! Man, it's great to see you. How did you know I was here?"

"The grapevine. I saw Ed on campus a few weeks ago. He found out from Tuna, who talked with your folks. Damn, you look like hell. What have you got, terminal clap?"

"Yeah, you're right. The Black Syph. God, you look great. I'm glad you came up, but isn't this a school night?"

Scott smiled at me, pausing for a moment, then the tone of his voice went from joyous to depressed. "Yeah, it's a school night all right, but I've joined the marines."

I was startled. "Oh, no, Scott. Oh, my God. Man, what for? You've always had good grades."

"It has nothing to do with that. It's just that college seems like a waste. There's nothing but partying all the time, and studying seems useless. Besides, you and Larry enlisted. Why shouldn't I?"

"I'll tell you why. You're going to end up dead. If you're lucky, I mean real lucky, you'll only lose an arm or leg. Look at me. Does it look like I'm making an impact on the world? Look at my old roommate. He got shot up and now he's minus one leg and one nut. Don't do this, man."

"It's too late. I've already signed up. I've got to find out what Vietnam is all about. If it's really honorable, then I want to be a part of something. I've always wondered whether or not I would be a coward."

"You don't have to join the Crotch to find that out. Besides, what's a coward? Everyone reacts to danger differently. But everyone's scared. If you can't get out of it, then choose an occupation other than a ground pounder. Believe me, being in combat infantry is not like in the movies. If you're hell-bent on dying, then at least die clean and well stuffed with hot chow." I paused. "Man, Scott, you're a very special friend to me. I don't want you to get hurt."

"Thanks, Rick. I appreciate your concern, but it's just something I've got to do. Say, did you hear about Jack?"

I shook my head no.

"He took off for Canada. What do you think of that? . . . And he was once my friend."

"Listen, Jack may have more balls than someone who goes to combat. You people back here know more about the war than we do. We're too close to the problem. When you stand toe to toe with a man trying to kill you it's hard to see what's in back of him, and he's not about to discuss issues. The enemy is there to kill you, and you him. It's so simple it's insane."

"Damn, Rick, I didn't think you would take sides with hippies and draft dodgers." Scott was visibly angry. His voice trembled with frustration.

"Look, Scott. I'm not taking sides. I'm just saying that I was there and I don't know why. All I lost were my legs and my friends. After a while that's what I was fighting for, not my country. We've had some protesters come up here and taunt us, saying we deserve to be mangled like we are. They call us baby killers and the like. That hurts, but they aren't the worst. During visiting hours we get church and local groups, Red Cross volunteers, school groups, and veterans' groups. The ones that seem the worst as far as harassment are some duffers from the big war, World War II. We've been told stuff like we don't know what real war is like. Vietnam wasn't tough, they say, and in the big one they were in for four years. Hell, they make it sound like they fought twenty-four hours a day every day for four years. Shit, they would take an island or a hill, then set up defensive perimeters or go back to the rear. Can you imagine being in constant nonstop combat for four years? There would be no survivors."

Scott couldn't believe what he heard. "Come on, that sounds ridiculous. Who would say that kind of crap?"

Ron was listening to the conversation and had to join in. "Hi, Scott. I'm Ron. Nice to meet you." Ron kept talking. "I had one of those people tell me that the wounds were much worse in the big one. Can you believe it? A thirty caliber made a different hole in Germany than in Vietnam? As far as wounds go Vietnam is a breeding ground for multiple wounds. Hell, probably none of us up here would have lived if the helicopter wasn't in use."

Then Al chimed in. "Can you imagine joining his vets' group so we could listen to forty more like him?"

Scott stared at Al. He was so busy talking with me that he hadn't noticed Al. Now he was sickened by Al's terribly scarred and deformed face. He excused himself and went out into the hallway for some fresh air. On the way out he passed a college sorority coming in carrying goodies and cards.

By the time Scott returned, the girls had split up and each was visiting a different patient, either to play cards or just to talk. Scott was astonished that none of the girls had become nauseated.

"I'm sorry, Rick. This room is so stuffy and it stinks so bad. I just felt sick. How are you doing? What do the doctors say about your legs?"

"Things could be better. They're still not certain they can save my left leg and the bone marrow in my right leg is badly infected. They say I may never walk again, and if I do it will be with the aid of a brace and crutches. I can't pull my toes up on the left foot. I can push down, but the peroneal nerve was destroyed. No more sports, no more running. My sister's getting married this summer. I've decided I'm not going unless I can walk into that church on my own two legs without any crutches."

"Rick, that's impossible. If the nerve's gone, what can you do?"

"I can try. I don't have any choice."

Scott handed me a large coffee can wrapped in tissue. "Here, Rick, this will get you going. It's my Great Scott's Health Food . . . nuts and raisins. It's great stuff. It'll build you into a giant."

"Thanks a lot, and thanks for coming up here. It was great seeing you."

"I've got to get going now. My plane leaves for San Diego tomorrow morning. Take care, Rick, and keep on fighting."

I gave Scott a salty little salute. "See you around. Take care of yourself and don't mess with those DIs. They'll tear you a new asshole."

Scott left. I was upset by his news. It was so easy to accept my own mortality but to watch a close friend go off to war was too depressing. I felt so helpless and I wanted to protect everyone I loved from being hurt. When I'd enlisted I was worried that the war would be over before I got into it. Once in combat I wanted to be anyplace else, spreading manure if necessary, so long as I got out of danger. Now I prayed the madness would end before I lost another friend.

"Good friend of yours?" Ron asked as he rolled over on his side.

"Yeah, a real good friend. Maybe it'll be over before he gets out of ITR."

"Fat chance. Tet's going full bore, and good marines are dropping like flies. No, he'll catch his lunch, too. Hey, want to be cheered up some?"

"Sure, Ron, anything."

"I got a wedding invitation from my girl. She and Jody are taking the plunge this summer. Ain't that the shits? I hate her for what she did, but I still love her. Man, my insides are all in knots. I keep wishing my wound wasn't so bad—then I could go back to the Nam. Ain't that stupid? I feel like I did something wrong."

"It's not so stupid. I feel the same way. Especially now. Maybe if I was with Scott he might come home alive. Besides, I can feel my life with Cheryl slipping away. Sometimes when I talk to her I feel like I'm eighty years old and she's ten."

Al cut in. "Hey, I hear you. Maybe we ought to go out and hustle some seventy-year-old babe, someone long on wrinkles and short on demands."

I looked around the ward. We were all so young, naïve even. Our adolescence had been formed in the jungles and highlands of Vietnam. Many of these young men had never made love or even been away from home until they entered the service.

Seven months earlier Cheryl and I had been inseparable—madly, passionately, innocently in love. It was that very special feeling that only your first love has. Neither of us had ever been rejected before, never heartbroken, never touched by any tragedy.

Our love was truth, the kind of honesty that only exists with first love.

Now when I looked in her eyes I still saw innocence mixed with some confusion. My eyes were dead, the eyes one only sees in war. Some call it the thousand-yard stare. I'd seen so much terror and horror that when I looked into Cheryl's eyes I felt ashamed. I wanted so much to just hold her and forget all I'd been through.

Age isn't a measure of years. Age is a by-product of experience.

Dr. Boone was a wonder to watch. He was moving around Al's rack like a dancer, and he was quick to sight malunions of bone fragments, the reappearance of infection, or skin grafts that were breaking down. He was satisfied with Al's progress and was almost ready to send him up to Five for plastic surgery.

"How are you feeling, Al? Still got that pain in your head?" he asked.

"Doing fine, sir. The pain is still pretty bad but I'll live. Sir, when are they going to operate on my eyes? I swear I can see light at times." Al was serious. Once again he'd convinced himself that his vision could return.

"Come on now, Al. We've had this conversation over and over. There is nothing that can be done, not a thing. You'll have a tough road ahead but you can make it. Just be patient."

"No, Doc, I know I can see. Please, at least try to operate . . . please," Al begged.

Doc Bone grabbed his arm with both hands. I watched the doctor's eyes while he thought about what to say. He'd performed hundreds of operations, but I thought he would cry, the emotion on his face was so very apparent.

"Al . . . listen, son. You've gone through a lot and you've lost a lot. For me to tell you that everything will be fine would be a lie. In combat you accepted the loss of friends and the fear of what was to come. There's nothing different about this situation. Nothing will change. Your eyesight is gone. You just have to rearrange your life some, but you have to start now." Doc Bone exhaled a sigh.

Al shook his head, then paused. "Yes, sir. You're the doctor. I understand all that, but you see, I've lost my girl. She was everything to me, I mean everything. I never ever considered a life without her, and now I have to. Do you understand? I can never see her again. That's why I have a hard time with this. What am I going to do?"

"You're going to get by. You're going to make do."

"Yes, sir. Thank you," Al said quietly.

The doctor moved to my rack. "Good morning, Rick. How's it going? Have you been using your wheelchair?"

"Yes, sir. They got me on the tray taxi service. Are you going to send me home today?"

"Yeah, sure. Let's see what we've got here."

He began tearing away the bandages and long strips of packing. I gripped my bed frame tightly and perspired profusely. Just about the time I thought I'd scream the doctor would rip another piece away, and I'd gasp for air. My screams were silent, but screams nevertheless. Once the gauze was out, the doctor took a long Q-Tip and probed the interior of the wounds and rubbed their raw walls until they bled.

"Oh, yes, it looks pretty good. OK, we'll go into the OR tomorrow and try and skin graft that area. How does that sound?"

I must have looked a little apprehensive. "Fine, sir. Where will you take the skin from?"

"The donor site will be your right thigh or, if need be, your belly. Keep it up—you're coming along fine. It looks like you'll keep your legs."

I was in real agony but the news was fantastic. "Good God, Doc, that's great. . . . I mean, thank you. Say, listen, if you ever need some of my skin you can take it off my ass. Hot damn, Doc, you're a prince!"

Everyone around my rack laughed and applauded. The doctor flashed them a wide toothy smile, delivered a snappy thumbs-up, then moved on to Ron.

I was so elated that I paid no attention to the rest of the doctor's round. After he left the ward, a corpsman went from patient to patient informing us of an inspection.

"Inspection, my ass. Who ordered that?" Ron yelled.

Miss Noland came up from Ron's blind spot. "The captain ordered it. Now square away your area and clean up those night stands," she barked.

There were curses. Radios and record players were turned on almost full blast as the men hung from their beds or reached from wheelchairs to straighten out the area.

Ron pulled his Bronze Star from his table drawer and tossed it in the garbage can. I saw this and told Ron to retrieve it.

"Look, Rick, they gave me that thing for carrying my buddy out of an ambush, but he was dead. So what was it all for? Besides, the way officers have been writing each other up for medals I'd rather let them have it. You know, up around Dong Ha we had this FO, a boot lieutenant, get a Silver Star for calling in a fire mission. That son of a bitch was five hundred meters behind my squad, behind a big old rock. He wasn't anywhere near the enemy but he got the medal. I had this Tex-Mex with me that charged one of their gun emplacements and clean it out just before he got killed. His reward was a Purple Heart." Ron pounded his table in frustration.

"Yeah, Ron, I read you. Almost everyone I know saw the same type of thing. . . . Say, what's all the crap about an inspection? These people up here have a hard enough time brushing their teeth. Now some gung-ho ass-wipe wants to see spit and polish."

"You guessed it. Captain Grant is a strange bird anyway. He's forever pulling this stuff. At one time he wanted all the patients not in traction to change their own rack. We had this guy, Billingham—he had no arms. What was he supposed to do, use his feet? From what I hear, Grant hasn't got many friends. He stands about five foot five and just loves to boss around big, tall, hard-looking marines." Ron laughed.

"What's he going to do, cut my hair and send me back to Vietnam?" I joked.

"If he could he would."

The remainder of the morning was spent cleaning up the ward. The lunch cart was just an interruption. Immediately after chow the cleaning continued. Then came the afternoon dressing changes.

The corpsman had just finished with Ron when Steve came walking up to my rack. He moved slowly and without any rushed motion, careful not to hurt himself. He saw Al sitting

up in bed with all the bandages off his head and eyes. I saw
Steve looking at Al as he walked over to my rack.

"Steve, I want you to meet the ward lookout, Al Jones."

Steve burst out laughing. Here was this blind-as-a-bat, no-
eyes marine supposedly looking out for something. Al smiled,
or what he considered a smile. Nothing on his face moved except the right-hand corner of his mouth, which wrinkled up
some.

"Al, nice to meet you. I'm Steve Markley, the new guy on
the block."

"Yeah, Steve, glad to meet you. I've already heard all about
you. Didn't you paint a fresco on the wall yesterday when they
gave you an enema?"

Steve chuckled, somewhat embarrassed. "Yeah, I'm an im-
pressionist, don't you know. My best work is done in snow. . . .
Rick, I'm supposed to get some blood test. Where do I go for
that?"

"Straight down the hall to your left. You mean they're making you walk for those duffus things? Man, next thing they'll
have you pass out trays and juice."

"I know. They already informed me of my obligatory duties,
starting with juice tonight during visiting hours. Aren't I
lucky?" he drawled.

"Steve, this is Ron Sanford, a victim of Jody's smooth talk."

Steve nodded hello, then out of the corner of his eye he spotted Martin. Martin saw him at about the same instant.

"Markley, you cripple, you. The last time I saw you was in
Japan. How are you feeling?" Martin asked excitedly as he lit
up a cigarette.

"I'm doing OK. How are your nuts? Still swelled up real
big?" he laughed.

"Yeah, now they call me Buffalo Balls. Ain't that rich? Say,
that Dr. Boone is one hell of a guy, ain't he? Man, I'd cut off my
left nut for him. He'd have made some fine marine officer."

A nurse came to my rack carrying some small pieces of paper
and a robe. "Here, Rick, take these chits to the specimen lab
and get the tests done. Then go up to Four for a chest X ray."

"But I've never been off the ward. What if I pass out, or fall,
or get raped? There are some kind of sex-starved Waves out
there."

The nurse nodded. "Sure, Rick, don't you wish. Try to catch

up with Steve Markley. He has to get the same tests. Maybe he can wheel you. Besides, then he'll have something to hold on to."

I wheeled myself into the lab. Steve stood leaning against the check-in desk.

"Hey, Kansas. Reserve me a seat."

Steve looked around. I'd wheeled up under his airplane cast. He reached down and took my chits and handed them to the corpsman. Steve's blood was drawn while he stood up. They drew mine where I sat.

"You two animals go back to your ward and use a duck to get urine samples. I'm surprised they let you into society. Normally they have us visit the farm for samples."

Steve and I looked at each other, then back at the corpsman. Steve put his good hand on the corpsman's shoulder.

"Listen, squid. Keep talking like that and you'll be drawing blood out of your pecker. Do you read me?"

The youthful corpsman stepped back two paces. "Hey, come on now. I was just kidding. Man, you've been in the jungle too long."

I turned my chair around and Steve stepped behind it, pushing me through the halls and the elevator to the fourth floor and X Ray. At any other hospital it might have looked odd, but here the hallways were filled with the maimed and battered bodies of young boys wandering in every direction with every type of injury.

Arriving in the X-Ray Department we entered a huge waiting room. The walls were lined with patients lying on gurneys, then rows of wheelchairs, and benches of ambulatory patients. Steve handed in the ward chits. Then we waited patiently for almost forty-five minutes. When it became obvious this could take all day, I conjured up a scheme to speed things along.

"Steve, don't ask any questions. Just keep your good hand on the back of my chair and look straight ahead like you're blind, for Christ's sake don't say anything, and kind of let your tongue hang out of your mouth."

I wheeled the chair through the mass of wounded men to the X-Ray check-in window and summoned the clerk on duty.

"Corpsman, listen. I'm Eilert from Three South. I came up here with this fine young marine to get X rays for tomorrow's surgery."

The corpsman gave Steve a quick glance, then leaned back

and folded his arms. "So what. Everybody here is getting X rays. Wait your turn."

I persisted. I leaned forward and gave the corpsman a very sincere stare. "Listen. We have to be back down on the ward by fourteen hundred. The general is coming up here today to award Steve here the Medal of Honor."

Steve had to bite his tongue to keep from laughing.

The corpsman looked up at Markley and cocked a smile out of the corner of his mouth. "Bullshit. Him? For what?"

I continued with so much sincerity my eyes started to water. "Steve here . . ." I stopped to wipe my eyes. "Steve here saved two wounded corpsmen. He carried them both back at the same time. As soon as he dropped them off, a rocket exploded in back of him. It tore open his shoulder and side and the concussion blinded him. Now at times when he's been standing too long he starts to choke on his tongue."

The corpsman leaned forward and looked up at Steve. He noticed his tongue hanging out. The smile disappeared and an expression of deep concern came over his face. I knew I'd hooked a big one, so I kept pouring it on.

"Steve didn't stop there. Although he was blind and severely wounded he administered first aid to the wounded corpsmen and phoned in for a med-i-vac chopper."

By now everyone around Steve and I was listening and they began to demand Steve be taken. The corpsman jumped up, came out from behind the desk, and put his arms around Steve.

"Sweet Jesus. What guts. Follow me." He put his arms around Steve's waist and led him personally to an open room.

I followed behind, choking with laughter. Steve turned his head and gave me a wink.

After the X rays were taken we waited in the hallway next to the developing room. Almost all the naval personnel on the floor stopped by to shake Steve's hand. A tall, buxom nurse turned the corner and stood in front of Steve. She guided him into a chair, then put her arms around his head and pulled his face into her breast. "You poor, wonderful, brave boy," she whispered to him.

I almost had a stroke watching Steve wallowing in her chest. When she tried to push him back to look at him, she had to peel his head away as if he'd become glued to her. She planted a kiss on his forehead and walked away.

"Rick, I can't stand up. I have a hard-on," he mumbled.

"You son of a bitch, I'm the one who made up the story, and all I get to hold is the X rays."

When we got back on the ward, Steve kept mumbling, "It was all real. . . . It was all her." By the time he told everyone the story of what we'd done, the whole ward was cheering.

Corpsman Blake walked up behind Markley. "You best get to your rack. You and Eilert got dressing changes due you, and we mustn't miss our dressing changes." Blake saw the depression fall across our faces. "Hey, look at it this way. You two missed the inspection."

Steve was awakened at a little past seven that evening by Miss Scallion, a new nurse on the ward. She was very short and petite. Her hands were almost childlike. She reminded him of an old high school girl friend. At first he couldn't take his eyes off of her and it made her very uncomfortable.

"Something bothering you?" she asked curtly.

Steve was embarrassed that he'd been caught staring and fumbled for the right words to say. "No . . . uh . . . no, ma'am. You just reminded me of someone."

"You're ambulatory, aren't you?"

"Yes, ma'am. I can get around."

"Good. We need someone to pass out juice tonight for visitors. So get your tail up to the nurses' station and get the cart."

"Yes, ma'am." As quickly as possible, Steve moved through the crowd of wheelchair patients, traction bars hanging over the end of the racks, and visitors. As usual, during visiting hours, the place was bedlam.

Next to the nurses' station was a large shopping-cart-type rig. On the top shelf, waist high, were several cans of assorted juices and stacks of paper cups. Miss Scallion pointed Steve back toward the ward. "Go get 'em. Don't forget to offer the visitors something, too."

Steve slowly walked out to the first rack, Al's. "Hey, Al, want some nectar of the gods?"

"Who's that?"

"Steve Markley. Prince of the universe."

"Steve, oh, yeah. What do you got?"

"We got juice. Navy juice . . . red, orange, purple, and yellow in color. It's got saltpeter in it."

Al laughed as he listened to Steve rattle on. "Purple sounds good."

I watched Steve work. It wasn't easy for him. His right arm was raised in the cast up away from his body, and the cast was superheavy and uncomfortable. Part of it was wrapped around his waist. Only his left hand was free. He'd set a cup on the cart top, then pour, then deliver the beverage.

My parents were visiting, so when Steve came both of them ordered a drink. "Steve, this is my mom and dad. This is Steve Markley. He lives on the other side of the ward." Steve nodded.

"Hello, Steve. Are you from Chicago?" my mom asked.

"No, ma'am, Kansas. Like Dorothy in *The Wizard of Oz*. Nice to meet you, but I've got to get going and pass out this juice before I expire." Steve crossed the aisle to Martin, whose girl was visiting.

"Hi, Steve. This is my girl, Julie. She's staying down here for a few days."

"Hello, Julie. Nice to meet you. Greg talked about you for twenty-four straight hours while we were together in Japan. Would either of you like some juice?"

"Yeah. Two orange. Straight up," Martin laughed.

Steve went to the cart parked at the foot of Martin's rack. He set the two cups side by side, then filled them. He pinched the two cups together around the lips in his left hand, and slowly, so as not to spill anything, he walked toward Martin. "Ohhhh . . . aaahhh . . . help me, help me! My pants!" Steve screamed.

I sat up as everyone turned to look. His pajama bottoms had fallen down, leaving him completely exposed. He wore no underwear.

Martin's girl gasped, but everyone else laughed hysterically. Steve was so flustered he couldn't move. He looked like a bird just about to land, with his right arm propped up from his side by his cast and his left arm up at a ninety-degree angle holding the cups. Mercifully, Miss Scallion rushed to his rescue, but even she laughed as she pulled up his pajamas.

Martin, whose testicles were badly swollen, was laughing so hard his balls hurt and he began to cry. His girl, Julie, passed out, hitting her head hard on the floor. Two new corpsmen rushed to her aid, while Steve still stood there holding the cups. He placed the juice on Martin's tray and, red-faced, stalked back to his rack. Ron was in convulsions, as were my parents.

"Come on back, Steve. We weren't laughing at your privates,

just the size. What have you been doing, breeding on an ant farm?" Ron yelled.

The nurse followed Steve to his rack and assigned the juice duty to one of the corpsmen. It took half an hour for the ward to get back to normal.

"Come on, Markley. Be a sport. You have to admit it was funny." Miss Scallion smiled.

"Ge . . . ge . . . get me my pain med, please," Steve replied.

The nurse nodded. She wasn't certain which pain of Steve's was intolerable, the physical or mental.

# 11

THREE WEEKS PASSED. It was February and the Tet offensive raged. Casualties mounted daily. The news was always bad. My unit was under siege at Khe Sanh.

My right leg was still badly infected. I was scheduled for another surgery, my seventh this time. They needed to remove some dead bone fragments near the anklebone. I'd become used to the procedure—the shots, the pre-op shaving of the area to be cut, and the thorough explanation of the surgery.

That morning at six I was wheeled down to surgery and my gurney was placed just outside an operating room. Steve Markley was on a gurney next to me. We smiled and gave each other a thumbs-up signal.

Suddenly a doctor burst out of the operating room, cursing as he stormed down the corridor. Moments later a gurney emerged from the same room and was placed against the wall. A lifeless body covered by a sheet, with a name tag on its toe, lay in front of me.

Steve and I looked at each other, shaking our heads.

"Imagine, this guy lives through a med-i-vac, field hospitals, the long flight back here, and then he dies. I wonder how old he was, who he was," I slurred.

Steve shook his head slowly. "He's d-e-a-d. That's as old as anybody gets . . . and his mom and dad are eating breakfast now, reading their papers, thinking their boy's safe. Here we are, you, me, and him. I'm glad I didn't get to know him." Steve turned his head away toward the wall.

A corpsman came out of the OR and pushed me inside. I

remember seeing the first name on the dead man's chart as I passed his body. It read, "David."

I was put on the operating table and strapped in place. I felt the cold sodium pentothal. I said good-bye to David.

When I awoke in the recovery room I had a nurse on my right taking my blood pressure and Steve on my left sucking on a wet washcloth. I saw the nurse give Steve a pain shot and he quickly fell sound asleep.

I passed out and woke up again on the ward. I'd been given a new rack assignment, number thirty-three, on the other side of the partition. I rolled to my right slightly. There lay Steve, my new neighbor. He'd been moved too.

"There goes the neighborhood," Steve snapped.

"What the hell are you talking about? Property values go up when I move in. I attract a special class of people."

"Sure, Eilert . . . lepers."

"Markley, when are you going to learn how to talk? Listen to yourself. Who can understand that foreign tongue?"

"Look who's talking. A gimp who can't even carry a small tray twenty feet. They took foreign bodies out of my shoulder. Now they put one next to me."

Steve shook his head and continued. "Man, are you ever lucky you live so close to the hospital. I've been away from home for eleven months. Now I got however long it takes to get well before I can go back. I've got to get home, too. I've lost my girl and I've got to get her back. I know that's impossible, but that's all I have to go home for. I even re-upped before I got hit. And now that I'm home, I haven't heard from her. How about you—you got a girl?"

"Yeah. I do and I don't. She's going through that 'I don't know what I want' thing. I think that means she does know what she wants, and it's not me. I think Jody's been busy since I went away."

"I know what you mean. There wasn't one man in my CAP unit that had his girl when he got home, if he got home."

We were so awake that sleep was going to be hard to come by, without a pain shot or a sleeping pill. I decided to hold on a while longer until it really started to hurt. The corpsman came around with my Keflin shot.

"Do you want your sleeper and pain med now?"

"No, later. I want to try falling asleep on my own." The corpsman shrugged his shoulders and moved along.

"Unique idea, Eilert, falling asleep under your own power.

Think I'll try it myself one of these days. You know, it really doesn't matter what they give me—I still have trouble falling asleep." I nodded. "It makes for long nights, some of the longest I've ever known. I doubt that half the people on the ward get more than three hours' sleep at night. They all seem to grab an hour here and there, a full night's sleep only when they're doped to the gills."

When the lights finally went out, Steve looked down the row of racks. "Rick, look at that." He motioned down the row to the end of the ward. "You think these guys are sleeping safe and warm in these racks, or are they still in the bush?" I checked each of the racks and nobody made a sound. They were all perfectly still. When someone occasionally lit up a cigarette, he cupped his hands so as not to let the light be seen by anyone. This was repeated each time he inhaled until the butt was out. And if someone did fall asleep, the man next to him would stay awake as if he were on watch.

These were all unconscious actions. When asked why they weren't sleeping, the patients normally would say that they just couldn't sleep, or they'd had a nightmare. Yet every night the same ritual was played out. There was always an occasional giggle or cuss, and if there were conversations they always were in a whisper.

"Hey, Steve, what are you going to do once you get out of the corps?"

Steve shook his head slowly. "Hell if I know. That's why I re-upped. I never thought it would end this way. Now I don't know what to do. Maybe I'll go back to school. I wish I knew what's going to happen to me. My girl . . . the girl I used to have, her name was Anne. Man, I was in love with her. We went together all through my last year and a half of high school. I keep thinking I'll get her back, but I won't."

"Yeah. Everyone is having trouble deciding what to do. Why couldn't everything have stayed the way it was? The whole time I was gone, I'd dream for hours about parties, my girl, my friends, and my family. Now, it seems, the way I dreamed it would be like is gone. Yeah, Steve, everyone up here is a real mental case . . . except me."

Steve laughed quietly. I was right, though. It would be a long time before we could sleep the night away.

I rang for the night corpsman. My leg was throbbing. When the corpsman came both of us ordered shots.

"There's hope in dope." Steve grinned.

After breakfast the next morning, the ward went quiet as the corpsmen picked up the trays and turned off the television. Rounds were starting. Nobody spoke. I started to check out my new neighbors after the doctor had finished with me.

I was surprised to suddenly find that a man had been next to me, on the other side from Steve, night and morning. I hadn't seen him. The doctor pulled the patient's sheets back to his knees. Steve motioned to Miss Noland to come over. She moved away from the doctor's side and stood between Markley's rack and mine.

"Who's that? We've been here a day and never noticed he was there," Steve said as he craned his neck to see the patient's face.

Miss Noland smiled. "Oh, that's Craig. He doesn't say anything to anyone. He fell under a tank. His chest cavity and pelvis were crushed. I can't understand how he lived, but he's been on the ward almost seven months. He hasn't said a word to anyone all this time."

I shook my head. "Good God. Could you imagine laying under a tank track? With that sheet pulled up to his chin the only way I could tell someone was there was when he breathed—then the sheet moved slightly. That's one flat dude."

Steve smiled. "Let's call him Slim. You don't get any thinner than him."

Miss Noland put her index finger over Steve's lips and smiled. "Be quiet now. That's terrible."

I watched the doctor pulling Craig's dressings off his hip. The young marine didn't even moan or blink. Craig's face was boyish and his brown eyes looked as if they would burst into tears at any moment. His body was emaciated—red, black, and blue tank-track marks covered his chest, and holes showed where broken bones had broken through the flesh.

"Your holes are closing up real good. Give 'em hell, Craig," the doctor chuckled as he patted Craig's shoulder and moved on to the next patient.

I'd noticed this man before. His right leg was in a long leg cast up to his crotch, and the cast was spray-painted different colors. More than once I'd heard Doc Bone and the rest of the staff yell at his foolishness. If the spray paint got into the wound he could lose his leg.

"Well, Ryker, what have you painted on your cast today?"

"Got a nice red paint yesterday, sir. I'm going to stencil a picture of a bulldog on the kneecap."

The doctor was furious. He worked his butt off trying to save lives and limbs. A fool like Ryker thought he was being cool by flirting with disaster.

"Ryker, you are a dumb son of a bitch. Look at all this pus." Doc Bone yanked a length of packing out of Ryker's shin. It was literally dripping with pus. "Your wounds weren't serious when you came here. I could have put you back on your feet easily, but your dumb-ass artwork might have cost you your leg."

Ryker looked surprised. He'd been warned of such a possibility, but he never took anyone seriously. "You're not taking my leg," he snapped. "Nobody is going to take my leg."

"Fine, but if this doesn't clear up soon you'll lose it below the knee. If you keep screwing around, you'll lose it above the knee, then up to your crotch. If you let it go after that you'll be cold meat. It's your choice. I'm not beating my head against a wall. I order you to not paint on a cast again. You're going into cast tex and getting a clean cast. Do you read me?"

Ryker was speechless. Nobody had ever seen the doctor that upset. Ryker nodded. "Yes, sir, I read you loud and clear."

The doctor and his mob moved on to the next rack, too far away for me to see or hear.

I turned to Steve. "Nice neighborhood. That Ryker looks like one of the Jets in *West Side Story*."

"Yeah, he's a real sweetheart."

The entourage moved along fairly quickly, until they stood at the rack across the ward from Craig. I couldn't figure out what was wrong with this man. I heard two corpsmen talking while the doctor examined him.

His name was Johnson. He was very tall, at least six foot four, and thin. He was tar-black and always laughing about something. He was Army and had been stationed in Germany when he got his hand caught in a drill press. He lost the middle and index fingers on his left hand and got a few knuckles crushed. I didn't hear what the conversation was but everyone was laughing.

Directly across from me was Bridger, a black hillbilly. He'd gotten his right kneecap blown off and a severe belly wound. He let out a few loud moans when the doctor checked his dressings, but said nothing.

Across from Steve was a real hard-looking marine. His face was always dark from his beard, no matter how much he shaved. Everyone called him Turk. His voice was deep and gravelly, his face scarred, his nose flat. He had a generous number of chipped teeth and an upper body covered with hair, like King Kong. He'd been shot in the left thigh three times but was recovering quietly. I was surprised to hear that he shared a common passion with Doc Bone, classical music. It really floored me, especially when I was told Turk played the piano. Turk's fingers were so huge that it was a wonder he could get his trigger finger in the housing. He had an earphone for his transistor radio and would listen to the gentle music while the doctor removed the long strips of packing from his leg. For bets Turk ate glass cups.

Diagonally across from Steve's rack was Daniels. He'd caught a burst across his chest and was hit in both shoulders. He was just nineteen, of medium height and build, with black hair. He was in constant pain and rarely spoke to Turk. He had no visitors or family, just like Craig. In all the time he spent on the ward, his only visitors were the Donut Dollies.

As soon as rounds were finished Miss Scallion came to fetch Steve for the cast tex room. Two corpsmen accompanied her. Steve and his bed were wheeled away. I knew something was up. Steve was ambulatory, so why take him into cast tex on his bed?

Once he was inside the room Doc Bone, Miss Scallion, Crawford, and Quinn entered and closed the door. As Steve told it later, Crawford brought out a stainless steel cart with two bottles in brackets on the side. There was an instrument panel with several gauges. Two drains in Steve's shoulder were attached to the lines on the machine. After some adjustments it was turned on. Immediately cold fluid was pumped into the raw, tattered shoulder cavity while the other line sucked that fluid back out. The pain was unbelievably hideous, a deep throbbing pain like ice water over an exposed nerve in a tooth. The sound of the machine pumping away only added to his torment. Everything was checked to see it was running smoothly and then Steve and his pounding gadget roared back out into the ward. By the time he returned to his position next to me, the dressing changes were nearly over.

I lay on my side and watched the light yellow fluid pumped in and the dirty reddish-yellow fluid come back out. Steve's face was like stone. His eyes open wide, he bit on his lower lip. He lay motionless as perspiration gathered on his face, neck, arms, and hands. His face was pasty white and an occasional tear would drop out of the corner of his eye. He couldn't speak because the pulsating machine kept him breathless, and besides, it was so loud he couldn't hear anything around him.

In response all the radios, televisions, and record players were turned up. The ward trembled with noise. The entire day was a blur of sound and cursing. By evening chow the commotion had caused short tempers. It was hard to think and impossible to rest.

I got a few phone calls but had to cut them short because I couldn't hear. Even the shots weren't enough to let me rest. Steve ordered his pain med, too, but it never seemed to help.

By ten-thirty that night, tempers were gone. None of the sleeping pills or shots helped anyone. Steve was worried that someone would cut his throat. People yelled to the corpsman to turn off the machine, but that was out of the question.

At midnight I called the night corpsman over. "Doc, you've got to turn that off. I'm beat, and I can't get a lick of sleep."

The corpsman smiled and shrugged his shoulders.

At one-thirty I took matters into my own hands. I reached into the aisle between Steve and me and tried to turn off the toggle switch on the instrument board. I had to hold on to the superstructure over my head, then lean way out into the aisle and reach with all my might until my finger caught the switch and the machine shut down.

Steve had long since passed out, so he made no effort to turn the machine back on. There was a small quiet round of applause, a "Praise the Lord," and a few obscene comments. Exhausted, I lay back on my pillow and shortly afterward fell sound asleep.

At about 0500 I woke up. Steve's rack was empty and the machine gone. I rang for the night corpsman. "Hey, Doc, where's Markley?"

"Somehow the machine got turned off during the night. He got really sick and passed out. They took him to Intensive Care," he whispered.

"Oh, shit, you got to be kidding me."

The corpsman returned to the nurses' station and worked on the patients' charts.

I sat up and lit a cigarette. *Damn, I almost killed him,* I said to myself. I'd had no idea how important the machine was.

Later that morning after rounds and dressing changes, Steve was brought back on the ward, along with his machine. Once back in place Steve looked over at me. "Man, what a night. I was out cold. When I woke up I had tubes all over me and down my throat. God, I feel terrible."

"What happened?" I asked, as if I didn't know.

"I guess I hit the off switch during the night. Man, my chest aches where they were massaging me. I know this machine is loud as hell, but do you think somebody might have turned it off?"

I shook my head vigorously. "Uh-uh. Steve, who would do such a terrible thing?" I waited for a bolt of lightning to strike me.

On the morning of the fourth day the pump was stopped. The expression on Steve's face was one of ecstasy. The entire ward applauded. After dressing changes were over everyone took naps. It was the first quiet sleep any of us had had. We woke up for noon chow then went back to sleep.

I woke just before visiting hours. I knew Cheryl was coming and I was filled with fear.

Before I left for Vietnam Cheryl was my reality. We knew each other so well that we could almost read each other's thoughts. We constantly reassured one another of our devotion. A simple caress would calm my fears.

Vietnam had taken that away from us. Reality was the jungle, and day-to-day survival. Cheryl was a dream, my fantasy. I remembered lying on the sweltering jungle floor, while leeches crept up my body, mosquitoes clouded the air, and my very soul cried for fear of dying. I would think of Cheryl. Her eyes, her touch, her calming voice gave me a reason to live through those horrible hours, days, and months. I convinced myself that she was all the goodness, understanding, and love in the world, and somewhere along the way I forgot she wasn't yet a woman, but still a young girl.

The war had matured me in many ways, but in love I was still an adolescent.

Love was innocence, truth, trust, gentleness, romance, music, humor . . . and it was always honest. We had a mutual passion for dancing, skiing, long walks, and just being together all day. We'd spend hours on the phone at night.

Her cycle of life was to work each day as a receptionist, then home for dinner and out with her girl friends. Weekends were parties and dancing and friends. Her life was a social schedule. A happening was who met whom, who broke up; new songs, new clothes.

My life in Nam was who died or lost an arm or leg; how much ammo or food, how many cigarettes I had. When I got to

Great Lakes Hospital my life cycle became dressing changes, operations, and pain. Cheryl's visits were my reward.

Cheryl's life changed little after I returned to the States, at least in my mind. I was jealous of everything and everyone Cheryl was a part of. I encouraged her to go out on dates. I knew what dancing and laughing and being with friends meant to her. It hurt me that I couldn't be the one to make her smile or hear her talk. I trusted her yet I felt cheated of all the little things we had enjoyed together.

But Cheryl was changing, too. She hated her job. She felt trapped. She'd always wanted to be a flight attendant, to meet interesting people, to go to exciting places and escape from her little-girl life. She was dedicated to me and constantly worried while I was in Vietnam and at Great Lakes Hospital. She loved me, but she was confused about Rick who was lying broken in bed. Her dreams were of a family, a beautiful home, travel, nice clothes, and happiness. Now our marriage was two or three years away.

The war had been real to her because I was part of it. But she hadn't understood why we were there. She'd always worried about my dying, but she'd never concerned herself about my being wounded. Being wounded is an enigma. In the movies it's a red bandanna, a little blood, and within moments our hero is back on his feet. To say one is wounded almost sounds harmless. You can wound someone's ego, wound his heart; it indicates he still lives and is therefore basically well.

Cheryl was shocked and sickened by the twisted and shattered bodies of the young men she saw in our ward. She was heartbroken to see me so helpless and smashed up. She loved me deeply, but now the ugliness of war was there for her to touch and it frightened her.

To her I had changed. I talked differently. I seemed callous. My sense of humor wasn't just dry—it was arid. I seemed distant, as if I wanted to be back in the Nam. I was crippled, and never again could I do some of the physical things that had brought us together.

Cheryl was just twenty and faced with the physical problems that a spouse might have at sixty-five. She wanted all that life offers young women. She loved me, but for the first time in her life she had to weigh that emotion against all she would be deprived of.

The clock hit seven and in walked Cheryl along with a girl

friend. She introduced her friend to Steve and moved next to my rack.

Ron Sanford saw Cheryl come in and yelled to her from the other side of the partition, "Cheryl, will you spend the night with me?"

"Sanford, you maniac, my girl is a saint. Besides, I've been saving myself for marriage," I yelled back.

Steve looked over Betsey's shoulder and rolled his eyes. "You're saving what, your primitive mating skills?" he drawled, then looked back into Betsey's eyes.

Betsey had gone to school with Cheryl and now they worked together. She had huge blue eyes, light brown hair, a beautiful body, and strict morals. Great girl to look at and talk to, especially if one was bed bound and shot to shit. Steve used his silver-throated Kansas thrush routine on her, and she loved it. Even Cheryl was amazed by Steve's smooth talk.

Steve continued to lay it on. "Betsey, you're really beautiful. I know that sounds corny, but I've been around so much ugliness for so long that, well, you're all a guy could ask for."

Martin's rack was just past Steve's, beyond the partition. He began pounding his mattress. "God, Markley, I love that kind of talk. Say you'll be mine."

Steve was red-faced when he realized the TVs and radios had been turned down and everyone was tuned in to him. "You people are all beasts. You lack romance and appreciation for nice things."

I was amused but I couldn't concentrate on anything but Cheryl. She leaned over and planted a long, passionate kiss on my lips. For a moment I thought she meant it.

We searched each other's faces for several minutes. We both had so much to say and ask, but wanted to use just the right words.

"Rick, I'm so confused. I love you . . . I really do, but I've just got to get away. I want to join the airlines. I want to be on my own. I want to grow up." She talked quickly, almost apologetically. It sounded rehearsed.

"Wait, slow down some. I understand all that. I joined the Marine Corps for some of those reasons. What happens to us? What about all we planned?" I pleaded. My heart was pounding and my mouth got dry.

"I don't mean right now, Rick. It's just something I have to do. I need time. I'm scared. Sometimes when I'm with you . . . well, you're different. You seem far away. When I come up here to see you I feel awful. Our life was so wonderful before you got hurt."

Cheryl put her hand over her mouth and tears began to flow down her cheeks. She put her head next to mine on the pillow and sobbed.

I felt terrible. I knew what emotional torture all this was, but I was helpless to do anything. I constantly assured her of my love, but she was torn by her emotions, not mine.

"We have to go now, Rick. My parents want the car back early on weekday nights. I'll be back in a few days. I love you, Rick." She gently kissed me.

I held her hand while she stepped away from my bed. Steve gave Betsey a tender kiss as well, and held her hand as if they'd been going together for years. The two of us watched the girls leave, following their rear ends, which were framed by the superstructures of the racks, until they were out of sight.

Steve raised his hand to the ceiling. "The gods are with me. I'm in love."

"Man, Markley, you're a convincing fellow. Hell, I almost wanted to go out with you." I smirked.

"Yeah, Steve, you never talked like that to me in Japan," Martin yelled.

Then Al screamed, "Shit, I could go queer for a guy like you." Everyone laughed.

"I ain't shitting you, Rick. Betsey is one hell of a lady. Isn't she dating anyone?"

"Nobody I know of. She acts different on dates. Cheryl and I doubled with her and a friend of mine, Fast Eddie. She was holding on to the doorknob all night. She just ain't into physical displays of affection."

"That don't matter to me. Those eyes of hers could make a dead man come. Besides, I can talk with her so easy. What a personality. What a mind."

Al yelled, "What an ass." Again everyone laughed.

Steve noticed I was down. His mood changed quickly. "I know what you're going through. My girl, Anne, was every part of my life. We had breakfast at her house every morning. We'd drive to school together, have classes together, and lunch, and study hall. We'd go to the library and check out the same books. Her father was a really successful businessman and he had the neatest study and library in the county. Anne and I would study at night by the fireplace and listen to classical music while we cuddled on the couch. She's all I've thought about for the last year. I had it once. Shouldn't I be able to have it again? I mean, I know what I want. Trouble is, Anne is married and it looks pretty grim." Steve winced in pain and gasped for air. "Oww," he moaned. There was a horrible pulsating spasm still present in his shoulder, and he couldn't shake it.

After the girls left, Steve and I watched television. When the sleeping pills were passed out, we saved them by hiding the tablets under our tongues until the corpsman left, then we put them in our bedside tables. After lights-out we took my portable phonograph and a few records, and rolled into the head.

This was the first time I had been near toilets in eight months. For the last ten weeks I'd used ducks and silver saddles, and I never knew sitting on a toilet seat would be such a treat.

Finished, I wheeled my chair up next to a long window looking west across the hospital parking lot. It was weeks since I'd seen the ground outside, and I envied the people walking around. They were free to go where they wanted and enjoy female companionship.

Steve walked over in back of my wheelchair and sat on the windowsill. "This is terrible. Look at those two cars under the streetlight."

I craned my neck and lifted myself up on the arms of the wheelchair. "Yeah, I see. Damn, what I'd give for binoculars. Look at the windows steaming up."

We watched silently for over half an hour. Then I put on a Peter, Paul, and Mary album and we sat back and listened, letting our minds wander.

Alerted by the squeaking of wheels, Steve turned to the doorway. There was Ron Sanford in a wheelchair, pushed by Blind Al hobbling with the use of a cane.

"Got room for two more?" Ron asked as he led Al in. "Al had to see what was going on back here."

Ron moved into one of the toilet stalls and sat on the throne. "Man, this is heaven," he joked.

Al found himself a stall as well, and slowly, with the aid of his cane, found the toilet and sat down. "Damn, it's dark in here," he chuckled.

Then Smitty strolled in. "Hey, Smitty, welcome aboard. What's the matter, can't sleep?" I snorted.

"I was thinking shit and look what I find," Smitty replied as he took up position in one of the other stalls.

Steve turned to me with a big grin. "Now, Rick, what were we talking about before we were interrupted? Oh, yeah, Blind Al's sister. Eilert, what you said about his sister isn't true. She isn't as pretty as Al."

"Markley, you're going to get me knifed in my sleep," I chuckled.

Al stood up and walked toward the sound of my voice.

"Take it easy, Al. I said no such thing. She doesn't look like you at all except in the eyes." Everyone laughed.

Al took a wild punch at me but missed and hit the urinal.

"Next time we have a race that you start, duffus, find the goddamn wall," I laughed.

"I would have found the wall if someone hadn't moved it. Hey, I heard that the guy driving the other chair got all his front teeth knocked out on the top of his mouth, from hitting the pipe."

"Quiet, people, I came in here to listen to some music." I started the records and it mattered not what they sang or even the beat. It was doubtful that anybody listened to the words. Each went off into his own little world.

By the time that the first side of the first album was finished there were three more chairs in the head. It reminded me of the Nam, where everyone would gather around the radio bunker when they tuned in to armed forces radio.

Steve listened intently to the music. He sat on the windowsill, his back to the wall and one leg drawn up to his chest, with his chin resting on the knee. He stared blankly out of the window.

"*Oh, my God.* Rick, you got any binoculars?"

"No way." I rolled my chair over toward the window.

"Somebody's down there trying hard as hell to make a baby."

"Stop it, Steve. Don't toy with me." I tried to pull myself up to the sill to get a peek.

"Smitty, you got some extra eyes. Go get 'em. We got some of that dirty, filthy sex they've told us about. Hurry." Smitty was the wrong one to send; Fast was not his middle name. The deed had been done and the car was gone by the time Smitty got the binoculars up to his eyes. "Damn you, Markley, there never was a car down there, was there? You son of a bitch, was there?" I nodded there was.

"Honest, Smitty, a blue Buick Skylark. Hey, they're bound to be back again. From now on when we come in here just bring the eyes along."

Everyone returned to his rack, and word spread fast about the happy couple frolicking below. Although we all talked about sex, we'd forgotten that it was still done. We decided to meet in the head regularly at night.

Steve couldn't relax to save his life; between going to surgery in the morning and watching the parking lot he was all keyed up.

"Know what, Rick? I'm hornier than a ten-dicked billy goat. I swear I'd screw a snake if somebody held its head."

"Go to sleep. You're an animal. You belong on Five North with all the rest of them crazies."

"Who can sleep around here? I'm getting my pain shot. That should help." Steve rang the call button and the night corpsman responded quickly.

"Yeah, what do ya need?" he asked with a thick Boston accent.

"My good man, we'd like two shots of Demerol straight up. Now get on with you quickly," Steve demanded.

The corpsman shook his head and went to fetch the night nurse to open the medicine cabinet.

"Markley, what do you think this is, a restaurant? Say, why don't you take my sleeper? The pain shot should do the trick for me." I reached into my drawer and pulled out the red sleeping pill and handed it to Steve.

"Thanks, Rick. Tonight two sleepers are in order. You cut me a huss tonight, I'll catch you later."

Steve swallowed the tablets and washed them down with a cup of water. Shortly after that the corpsman returned with our pain meds. Steve squirmed and tossed for over a half hour before the pills and shot took effect. He was exhausted from the days on the machine and he was tortured nightly by dreams of Anne and the Nam.

I held off falling asleep until I saw Steve pass out. Only then did I relax.

The following day's dressing changes and all went well. There was a new man brought in who was raising a lot of hell but that wasn't unusual for new patients.

After dinner Steve and I wrote letters, read, and watched TV until after lights-out. Then we made our trek to the head.

We had our fill of nostalgia early and returned to our racks. We both tried getting to sleep but couldn't. We each lay silent for almost an hour thinking the other was asleep . . . but neither of us was. Rest was always welcome but sleep was a rare commodity. The ward was silent except for some whispers and an occasional groan.

"Do you think we'll ever be able to sleep through an entire night?" I whispered to Steve.

"Hell, I don't know. The way it is now, I can't put together two hours of peaceful sleep. At first I thought my problems were because of the constant throbbing in my shoulder. But every time I drop off to sleep I wake up sweating like a pig, with my heart beating so fast I worry that it'll burst."

"Me, too. It seems that I'm always running a patrol, usually at point. I'm always waiting for that explosion or gunfire that comes out of nowhere. It hardly ever bothered me once it got down to the shooting. It was the waiting that screwed me." I rolled to my right side on the edge of my rack and continued the whispered conversation. "I remember when I got in my first fire fight. When the first shot was fired I dropped to the ground. Before I got down to my knees I noticed everyone else was already on their bellies firing their weapons. It seemed impossible that anyone could react that fast."

"Really. Can you imagine how tight everyone is . . . so on edge that a twig snapping or cans rattling compel people to hit the dirt and start digging. Man, we must really be screwed up. I can see myself out on a date when a car backfires or a loud noise surprises me. I'll fall to the ground and my date will be embarrassed and leave me."

The two of us talked until almost two in the morning. By then we were talked out, but deep down we were still in the bush. For the next hour we lay silent, staring out into the darkness of the ward.

A little after three there was a terrible crash. It sounded like a rocket exploding. Everyone heard the noise, then someone yelled, "Incoming!" and almost every mother's son leaped or fell out of his rack to the tiled floor. I passed out almost immediately after hitting the floor. I got a cut over my left eye and both casts were cracked.

Steve landed on his right side, collapsing the bar that held his arm up and cracking the cast around his chest and elbow. He was choked with pain so severe that he bit through his lower lip. As he lay on the floor he looked under the long line of racks. There were broken bodies everywhere, including those hanging from the beds by the traction bars stuck through their limbs. The bodies squirmed and groaned aloud.

Steve saw me lying motionless with a small pool of blood next to my head. At first he thought I was dead. He crawled to my side just as I awoke.

Terror filled my eyes. My body was consumed with pain. My legs were on fire.

O'Hara was the night corpsman. When he heard the thuds of bodies hitting the floor, he leaped over the nurses' desk with flashlight in hand and raced into the ward. He couldn't believe his eyes. Almost every bed was empty and the horrible screams that echoed through the ward frightened him.

The night nurse was Miss Altman, who was working on Three East at the time. She heard the commotion all the way in the other wing of the hospital. As soon as she arrived on the ward she saw the extent of the damage and immediately called the doctors on night duty.

Patients' bones had been rebroken, wounds reopened, and an unbelievable number of cuts and scrapes caused. Several delicate surgeries performed weeks and months earlier were ruined. Emergency surgeries had to be performed and vast numbers of pain shots given. It was chaos.

I was lifted gently into my rack and then transferred to a gurney for surgery. Bone fragments had popped out of my knee and through the skin.

Once everyone had been picked up and put back into his rack a team of nurses, corpsmen, and doctors went from rack to rack checking each patient.

Steve's shoulder was split open and he, too, was sent to emergency surgery. I returned to the ward at 0730. There was Steve back on the machine. Chief was on duty and he helped me off the gurney and back into my bed. Mercifully, Steve had passed out. Chief made certain I was comfortable as he tucked me in with a warm blanket.

"Some new guy threw his silver saddle on the deck last night and that's what started this whole thing," Chief groaned.

"Is that son of a bitch still on the ward?" I inquired.

"No, they carted him off to Five South. They were afraid that someone would kill him if he stayed any longer."

"Believe me, Chief, nobody has to worry. He's a dead man. It don't matter where they hide him. Nobody's going to forget what he did."

The following morning the people at my end of the ward turned on the news for more information on the siege at Khe

Sanh and the battle for Hue. Jackson recognized one of the men we saw lying wounded on a tank. Three days later he was on Three South. Watching the news was like home movies to the men on the ward. We represented almost every unit that the Marine Corps had in the country.

It wasn't like a mother, father, sister, brother, or friend searching for a chance glimpse of someone in the service. When Three South watched the news every day we were all affected. If one of our units was involved, then in a matter of a few days another wounded man would come in.

All of us had grown so close to guys in our outfits that the personal involvement and constant worrying almost drove us mad. The doctors called it survivor's guilt. To us it was just more pain.

When Steve woke from his deep sleep I tried to cheer him up. That wasn't easy, especially with the tube stuck in his back.

"Hey, Steve. You alive?"

"Man, I must be—dead couldn't feel this bad. What the hell happened last night? I thought that they didn't rocket hospitals."

"That new guy got upset when nobody answered his call button and decided to leave Three South with his memory, so he tossed his silver saddle on the floor and yelled, 'Incoming!' They've been bringing guys back from emergency surgery all day."

"They best have the son of a bitch someplace safe. I could kill the fucker."

"Chief said they took him up to Five South. I think someone should send our greetings to the lad. Maybe cut off his nuts or a few fingers."

I watched a seventeen-year-old grunt hobble back to his rack.

"Man, what the hell did you want to go across the pond for?" I called out. "Didn't you have to get your parents' OK to get into a combat zone?"

The grunt didn't reply. Steve shook his head and started to laugh.

"Hell, we aren't any smarter than he is. It's a shame we had to get our smarts so late in life."

"Hey, tell me about it. I can't tell where smart starts and stupid ends. Were we ever young?"

"So they say. But it feels old, very old."

# 12

WE WANTED REVENGE and we were determined to get it. O'Hara had pulled the new man's chart when they transferred him to Five South, and found out that the stranger's name was William Osborne II. Osborne had some damage to the muscles in his legs as well as flash burns to his eyes. He wasn't blinded but he wore bandages around his head covering his eyes. It seemed Osborne was a pain in the ass everywhere he went. None of his wounds were permanent, yet he complained and screamed worse than any of the other patients. Osborne had spent all but one week of his tour in Vietnam. He'd worked in supply, a normally safe place, but a rocket sent him home early.

The gimps surrounded my rack and talked about their holes and how they'd been wounded, about R&R, women, and what they were going to do once they got out of the Green Machine. Then talk started about how to give Osborne a good-bye gift to equal his to us. At first killing him seemed very popular, any way from cutting off his privates to shoving him out a window.

Peterson suggested that we save the ward shit from the silver saddles that day then put it all in a shoe box. The ambulatory patients could sneak up to Five at night and shove it all in his face. We all agreed that should be the plan, but Steve thought not. "What happens if you do pull it off? Osborne is going to scream his fool head off. If you do this in the middle of the night, you're going to get forty swinging dicks from Five hitting the deck. No, this has to be an assassination of sorts in daylight. We got to get him off the ward, say to go to X Ray. Then, like a pie in the face, leave him stranded in his wheelchair."

"Good idea, and the only corpsman to plan the snatch is O'Hara," I suggested. "Now, whoever gets Osborne off the ward will have to be a patient that nobody on Five knows. It can't be a corpsman because the nurses on Five would remember who it was that took Osborne away. O'Hara can get us a chit for X Ray, then take him over by the patients'-elevator door. Then, when the deed has been done, everyone hops into the elevator, comes down to Three, and gets back in their racks."

"Sounds good, Rick. The world is safe as long as you never have any authority."

"Thanks a lot, Steve," I laughed.

The assassination was set for the following morning, when the fewest people would be in the halls and no civilians would have to watch Osborne being attacked. O'Hara got the X-Ray chit and had someone he knew who worked over at mainside make the snatch. Johnson, Sanford, and Toby waited outside the elevator and Peterson was the wheelman holding the elevator door for the escape.

It all went off without a hitch. As soon as Osborne was brought to the waiting elevator and the coast was clear, the demons attacked. Nobody said anything so Osborne couldn't recognize any voices. Toby ripped off the bandages on Osborne's face, then Johnson and Sanford let him have the shoe box pie. His chair was pushed against a wall and the getaway was clean. When the commando team returned to the ward they were greeted like heroes, and then they returned to their racks. The nurses and corpsman had to get everyone to quiet down, but they had no idea what was going on.

Before Peterson got back to his rack, Steve stopped him for a situation report.

"Everything went off great. He started to scream, but he got a mouth full of yesterday's prune juice. It was beautiful."

"Well, all right!" Steve yelled.

Later on that day it was all over the hospital that the asshole who'd done a number on Three South had been dealt with. All the ward elders felt that the punishment was just, but that it should have been more severe. The nurses and corpsmen knew why it had happened and which ward had done the big nasty, but they couldn't prove who was involved.

The following morning Steve was returned to the ward minus his machine. He was happy as a lark and so was everyone else. Later that day mail call delivered a letter to Steve from his mother. She was coming to see her son. It was the first time since he'd been wounded that he was able to think of something besides his wounds, Anne, or the Nam.

"Hey, Rick, my mom's coming to see me. Ain't that great?" he roared with delight. Then his face went emotionless, almost frightened. "Rick, what will I say to her?"

"Hell, Steve, don't ask me. I was scared to death about seeing my parents."

Steve nodded. "I just don't want to be different to her. I know everyone changes some, but I want to be her little boy same as before. I mean, I don't want to be treated like a gimp or a sick person or an old man."

"I'd treat you as being kind of strange because you are, but you're still going to be her little Stevie. I'm sure of it."

We both knew we'd changed a lot and our lives would never be the same. I thought about the first visit I'd had with my family. I loved them all so much and missed them so terribly that I thought my heart would explode. If Steve was half as close to his family, his first visit with his mother would allay all his fears. All that he worried about would pass and all the happiness would prevail.

"Does the letter say when she's coming?"

Steve skimmed over the pages until he found a date. "Febru-

ary twenty-fourth. Ain't that great? I can't wait. What's the date today?"

"Listen to the cowboy poet." I smiled.

Steve asked everyone who passed his rack, "What's the date today?"

After a few shrugs and blank stares a nurse replied, "Today's the twenty-fourth."

Steve's mouth dropped open and his face turned pale. "Good God. That's today. Damn, that's too early. I wanted to be in good shape when she got here. Hell, I'm all gimped up. I've got to clean myself up. Innkeeper, my chariot," he yelled.

A passing student corpsman helped get his shaving and washing gear together. Steve had been off the machine a very short while since Osborne's blitz and he felt awfully weak. The corpsman placed Steve in my wheelchair and helped him into the head. Steve shaved, sponge-bathed, and washed his hair. The corpsman helped him on with a clean pair of pajamas.

The cleanup at least made Steve feel human, and the anticipation of his reunion numbed his pain. He returned to his rack to psyche himself up for the possibility that he would gross out his mother.

After lunch, his afternoon dressing change didn't even bother him. He lay in a trance.

My dressing change was far more eventful. My fall out of bed had rebroken the fibula in my right leg and the break was exposed by an open wound. It seemed that whenever gauze was thrust into the wound the fibers would snag on the bone. Each time this happened the corpsman had to probe with a tweezers to free the gauze. In addition, a wound on the inside left calf had torn open. It was as raw as when I first was hit. Shortly after the dressing change I received my thrice-daily ration of Keflin, and as always the whole procedure left me exhausted.

Steve lay quietly with his head cocked to his right, watching

for his mother. As soon as the clock struck 1400 hours and visiting hours commenced, she appeared rounding the corner. His aunt Helen was at her side.

Steve froze. His heart pounded frantically and the palms of his hands got moist. At first he thought he might cry. His lips quivered as he called to her. "Mom . . . Mom, over here."

She'd been looking at all the racks and you could see her heart sinking as she thought about her Steve being so horribly wounded. When she heard his call and saw him sitting up on the side of his bed she broke down crying, as did his aunt. She ran up to him and gently, yet warmly, embraced her son.

"Oh, Steve . . . my boy. I've missed you and worried so much about you. Are you OK? Does it hurt terribly? Are you eating well? You look so thin." She rattled on, not listening for a reply. She had all the questions but now the answers weren't important.

Steve wrapped his good arm around her neck and pulled her tear-filled face against his. For a moment he looked as if he were six or seven years old, safe and protected in her embrace.

"Mom, God how I've missed you. I'm just fine, just a little flesh wound," he assured her.

I heard that remark and rolled my eyes. *Just a flesh wound*, I thought. *Who's he trying to kid?*

"Aunt Helen, thanks for coming with Mom. It's good to see you. Did you bring me some of your chocolate cake? Say you did."

"Here you are, German chocolate, just the way you like it, moist and covered with heavy frosting."

Steve was in seventh heaven. His face beamed with delight. He wanted to keep hugging both of them; at the same time he wanted to just listen to their voices.

"How's Dad and the kids?"

His mother held his hand and kissed it. "Your father's fine and misses you very much. So do your sisters. Lord, Steve, you look so good. The telegram we received painted a gloomier picture. The first word was that you were in serious condition."

"Ah, Mom, you know how exaggerated those things are. Say, I'd like you to meet Rick Eilert. He's my guardian angel."

Steve's mother stood between Steve's and my racks. She just had to turn around to see me.

"Hello, Rick. Nice to meet you." She smiled.

I nodded my head to her and Steve's aunt. "Nice to meet you.

Steve talked about you and home often. Did you know Steve's on a strict diet? He's not to eat any sweets. Maybe you should just leave the cake box over here so as not to tempt him in his weakened condition."

Steve let out a huge groan. "Ooohhhhh, you son of a . . . gun," he caught himself. "Don't listen to him, Mom. He's got a head wound. He got hit in the ass."

Steve's mother laughed, as did Aunt Helen. Mrs. Markley looked at my legs buried in two long casts, and at my heavily scarred hands, arms, and face. She knew the anguish she'd felt when her son was wounded and I could sense her imagining the pain I must have endured and grieving for my parents and everyone's.

Steve's enthusiasm prevailed, but often during the visit his mother and aunt were almost overcome by the heat, stuffiness, and horrible odor that filled the ward.

Mrs. Markley talked a good fifteen minutes straight, asking questions about Steve's friends in the CAP unit and about Australia, but he just listened to her voice and seemed to dream of home, of when he was a kid . . . two years ago.

It was an emotional visit and all of the patients shifted their attention from the TVs and radios to Steve and his mother. Steve felt that he'd start crying, and had to cough to get the lump out of his throat. His mother couldn't ask enough questions of her boy, and Steve was filled with the same curiosity about home and friends, and especially his girl.

After they had visited a reasonable length of time, the rest of the patients came hobbling up to introduce themselves. I had the impression that Steve was so excited that he'd forgotten where he was and that everyone around him was sharing in the reunion. As the wheelchairs started to pull up Steve introduced each of the guys. He even forgot some of their names and that embarrassed him no end.

The patients were so happy to meet the parents of all the other guys. After sharing so many days and nights of talking about home and family, each of us felt part of every other man's family. In addition, the other guy's mother or father was the next best thing to having our own around. This was a time in all our lives when family was still a big part of each of us.

She stayed in town for two more days, coming day and night to see Steve. The last evening that she came up, she brought a pizza. After she laid it on the table next to Steve's rack, he yelled, "Pizza, anyone?" Within three minutes it was gone. She and Aunt Helen just laughed. Their good-bye was a tearful one, but it was certain that she felt a whole lot better after seeing that he was being well treated and cared for.

After lights-out, Steve and I stayed up talking about home. We talked for several hours, then fell asleep. We were content that we'd survived and come home. All our other fears would have to be handled when we got out of the service.

When we woke up the following morning we continued our conversation, this time going back to our childhood, then coming forward to our high school years. All the parties, girls, drinking, and pranks. The wonderful carefree days, when the biggest decision was where to go on a date, or what party to go to first.

As the day worked its way into night we still talked. And when the lights went out Steve and I and some others went into the head to listen to the record player and shoot the shit some more. Within a half hour the place was packed, the ambulatory patients sitting on the toilets. The wheelchair patients jammed their chairs in tight against each other to get close to the phonograph. For some reason, during the day we all stayed close to our racks, but once the lights went out we all came together. It was nice, too. There was always someone to talk to about all our problems. We didn't solve too many, but we at least got them off our minds.

Many times it was because of visiting hours that people got depressed. The long months of healing, the constant dressing changes, the Dear John letters all left everyone down at one time or another. It wasn't getting better that was always on our mind, either. Often it was the going home that seemed so hard. Living like a human being again was even harder to think of. In the Nam life was very simple—you fought like an animal to stay alive, and if you didn't, you died. Life at home was far more complicated.

I had the phonograph propped up on the windowsill overlooking the parking lot. Steve was seated sideways behind the phonograph, leaning against the window itself. He perused the parking lot below with my binoculars.

"Man, there are a hell of a lot of cars down there tonight. Most every window is fogged up, too. *Hot damn*, Eilert, passion—real get-down, dirty, filthy sex. See that white Mustang just below in the first slot?"

Everyone rushed to the window, crawling all over one another to see the show. Even I lunged forward, propping myself up on my forearms.

"No shit, Steve, give me those looking glasses," I pleaded as I craned my neck.

Steve refused to surrender the binoculars.

I continued to plead. "Come on, Markley. Help the handicapped. What's going on?"

"That pervert is the physical therapist up on Nine. Those squids have it made. *Woowee* . . . look at that turkey's moves . . . a right to her blouse, a left to her thigh, a right to the blouse again. That deviate is using his head for leverage. . . . Man, that Wave is blocking every shot in his arsenal. She should be a goalie."

We all fought for position, trying desperately to see below. Ron crawled up on the sink and looked out over Steve's head. I continued to grab for the glasses.

"Let me see. . . . This ain't fair. . . . My God, it looks like he's taking her clothes off." Steve got up on his knees. "He is. . . . Holy cow. He's got her coat off now. Oh, look at this—just like a sailor. He's stroking her hair and face. Lower . . . much lower, you fool."

I finally got hold of the binoculars. "Ooohhh, you're right. Oh, yes, lower . . . much lower. That's better."

Two more wheelchair patients entered the head and jammed their chairs up against the others in front. The newcomers raised themselves up on the wooden arms of their chairs. Ryker even stood up on his chair and peered down over everyone's head, only to see the car's roof. "What's going on? I can't see a damn thing," he grumbled. I could hear him grinding his teeth.

"Some squid investigating a Wave's blouse."

Ron pounded on the wall next to Steve's head. "Man, that ain't fair. It's been sixteen months since I've even touched a woman. Give me the binoculars."

I refused, and pressed the glasses even tighter into my eye sockets.

Martin, who was way back in the mob, yelled forward. "You asshole . . . if you won't let me see, then give us a blow by blow—no pun intended."

I decided to oblige them. "Her eager lips bid him to come closer. Her heart pounding, she surrenders to his will and unbuttons her blouse. Her hot lover fumbles all over himself as he consumes her quivering lips."

"Damn you, Eilert. You don't have to be so graphic. I'm starting to sweat," Martin mumbled.

Ryker, who still couldn't see, asked me to continue. "Don't listen to Martin. Keep going." The others agreed, so I continued. "She pulls him down on top of her trembling body, digging her fingernails deep into his back. Now she plunges her fingers through his hair." Groans and moans were coming up from several people. Ron slipped and fell into the sink basin with a terrible crash. I continued, "He's got up. . . . *Oooh*, he's taking off his pants. Oh, *no* . . . oh, *please, no!*"

"What's the matter?" Hans yelled. "Don't stop!"

I put my forehead down on the windowsill. "It's a *damn blizzard*. They were just about to do the *big nasty* and now I can't even see the parking lot."

Steve had his face pressed against the window. He turned around and lit up a cigarette. "This is outstanding. What a day. First Doc Bone reams out my shoulder with a foot-long Q-Tip. Then they get my dinner tray mixed up so I get an all-liquid diet. Eilert lets me sleep through a visit by the Miss Wisconsin contestants, and now just before I have an orgasm . . . it snows. Rick, turn on the record player."

"OK, zouns? What will it be? Peter, Paul, and Mary, the Beatles, or Bob Dylan?"

"Peter, Paul, and Mary," Hans demanded. "But we best keep it down. I saw the night nurse on the ward just before I came in here."

We formed a semicircle around the record player. Steve took out a pack of cigarettes and passed them out. Ron struck a match, lighting his, then offering the same match to Markley, then me. I blew it out.

"I know this sounds stupid, but I was third on a match before I got hit." I lit my own.

"No shit, so was I," Ron laughed.

Hans chimed in, "Me, too, but I don't really believe that superstition stuff."

I put on the record, turning the sound up just enough to be heard.

Steve said dejectedly, "I believe in all that. What I can't believe in is being here. I'll be twenty-one in two months and I feel like I'm eighty. I started out with this romantic notion of God and country. I wanted to go to the Nam, win a chestful of medals, be a hero, and come home to my faithful sweetheart."

"Too bad it just weren't so. I know what you mean, kind of like Lawrence of Arabia, Beau Geste, Dr. Zhivago, Prince Valiant," I offered.

"Gunga Din," said Ron.

"George Gobel," laughed Martin.

"You gimps are really sick. Can't you ever be serious?" Steve snapped.

I defended the mob. "Hell, Steve, all of us felt like that at one time or another. I'm not sure of the author—anyway, he said, 'Men march off to war because the women are watching.' I felt gung ho all through my first fire fight, until I saw my first dead marine. All of a sudden I realized that it wasn't a game. Everything I did mattered. Every step, every decision. Now it seems I'm the other guy—everything always happens to me. I was the oldest guy in my platoon at nineteen years, eleven months. My platoon commander was twenty-three and the platoon sergeant twenty-one, but I was older than everyone else. Hell, they called me Gramps. There were times I felt so old I thought I was getting senile. Now I sit here wearing powder-blue Navy pajamas and forty pounds of plaster. I've been on this planet twenty years and I know where I've been, but I haven't the foggiest idea where I'm going." I sat back somewhat winded. I hadn't put that many words together in a long time.

Ron sat in the sink basin shaking his head. "No screaming eagle feathers. Every day I was in that lousy, stinking jungle all I ever thought about was coming home . . . and all the time I figured I wasn't coming home alive. Now I'm here, and I'm scared to death to go home. Home was the one constant thing in my life. I guess I'm afraid it might have changed as much as I did."

Martin slammed his fist down on his long leg cast and clenched his teeth. "Why don't people understand us? What did we do that our fathers' fathers didn't do? I've heard people call us baby killers and warmongers. I never shot no kid and I never knew anyone who did. How can any intelligent creature think *grunts* like war? Hell, every waking minute is spent waiting for that bullet that will kill you or maim you for life." His expression changed to sorrow. "I wanted to come home so bad I felt like crying. Now that I'm back home I feel like I should go back in the Nam with my friends. You know, in the bush I felt like I made a difference, that I was needed. I trusted my friends with my life and they trusted me. Do you understand that? . . . with my *life*, not my money or my girl, but with my very being. Now nothing I can say or do here means diddley shit!"

Steve looked very tired and emotionally exhausted. He handed Martin a cigarette and lit one for himself. "How is it we got out so cheap? I was up in Physical Therapy to see one of the doctors. I passed some poor snuffy on this tilt board—you know, one of those boards they lay you on and strap you down. Anyway, this guy was paralyzed from the neck down. I tried to talk with him but he had this huge scar on his neck and could only blink his eyes, which were filled with tears. What gives me the right to be here when my friends died? Hell, they all had something to live for, like wives and kids. One minute they were right next to me and the next minute their bodies were all torn and twisted, and I haven't got a scratch. I never wanted them to die. It scared the hell out of me, but I just as soon get hit as them. What right do I have to be with a woman or have fun, or a family? Or happiness? They lost their lives and it seems at the very least I should have to give up something for being alive."

I nodded to Steve's plea for understanding. I'd always had trouble saying exactly how I felt. "I wanted nothing more than to come home. I got to where I didn't care how many arms or legs I lost. I just wanted to get home alive. But, like you guys, I feel like I should be back with my unit. We had a lot of casualties up at Con Tien and our company was really low on people, especially experienced people. We started getting replacements just before I got hit, but they didn't know shit, and there wasn't enough time to get them squared away before another good marine got dinged."

"Steve, do you think you'll ever forget all this crap? I mean, will your mind and feelings ever be back home or will they always be back in the bush?"

"Ron, I couldn't get my head and ass wired together before. I doubt anything will change now. Every time I hear a loud noise I want to crawl under my rack and hide forever."

A song on the record player caught everyone's attention. Conversation stopped and we listened carefully to the words. The song was "Risin' of the Moon," sung by Peter, Paul, and

Mary. The men switched the words around to fit their situation and all chimed in quietly.

> *How well they fought for dear old America,*
> *and how bitter was their fate . . .*
> *oh, what glorious pride and sorrow*
> *filled the year of sixty-eight.*
> *Yet I thank God while hearts are beating;*
> *each man bears a burning wound . . .*
> *for the fight must be together*
> *at the risin' of the moon.*

A new man on the ward stood in the back of the head, not certain he was welcome. I spotted him and motioned for him to come over. The new man nodded and slowly walked toward our wheelchairs.

One of his arms was in a cast and the other in a sling. He wore no pajama top. He had a scar on his chest from his throat to his navel. A colostomy bag was strapped to his waist.

"Hi, I'm Bob Norton," he said quietly with a New York accent.

Steve laughed. He'd never been around any New Yorkers and his speech sounded strange. "Welcome aboard, Bob. I'm Steve. This turd is Rick Eilert or Captain Ugly. You'll meet everyone else later. Man, what hit you?"

Bob smiled. Until he reached Three South he'd considered himself really messed up, but everyone in the head looked as bad as him or worse.

"I was with One Nine up near Gio Linh. We were out on a platoon-size patrol when we got hit with rockets. Everyone made their bird. While I was running I fell in a man-trap and flipped over on my chest. Three stakes went through me. Man, I was lucky. One stake just missed my balls and ended up between my legs. Another missed my throat and clipped my ear." He winced. It hurt him to even talk about it.

"Yuk . . . that's the berries. I'd rather be shot or raped," Ron laughed.

"Must be like getting skewered on a stick. How did they get you off the stakes?" Steve got goose bumps at the thought.

"It wasn't easy. The corpsman and two others had to lower themselves in the pit without impaling themselves. They cut the stakes under me rather than trying to slip me off. They lifted me out, stakes and all. Man, the helicopter ride was a bitch. They couldn't lay me on my stomach or back because of the stakes sticking out of me. Luckily I passed out."

*What a lousy way to get wounded,* I thought. "How long have you been back in the world?"

Bob shook his head, lowering his eyes down to the floor. "Two days . . . long enough to get a Dear John. She said it was for my own benefit. She said she was confused and very lonely. How can she be lonely? She's been around family and friends for the last thirteen months. Her biggest fear was discovering a tear in her pantyhose or fighting the dreaded frizzy hair. I swear, she made it sound as if she's been a POW."

"I know what you mean. Let's face it, you've probably changed so much that it scares her. Remember, she's still a little girl and you've turned into an old man."

"Hell, I'm only nineteen. All I thought about the whole time I was gone was my girl. I loved her so much. All I wanted was to come home, marry her, buy a little house, raise a family, and be left alone."

I nodded. Bob had said it the way it was.

"That's the problem . . . that's all any of us wanted. My girl, Cheryl, just started dating and now I want her to start married life. I feel like you do, but I can see how smothered she must feel by our old-man attitudes. Cheryl and I had the tightest relationship going—I called her every night, even after I had just dropped her off. We saw each other every minute we could spend together. We even talked to each other about getting married and having kids. But since I've been home every time I see her it's like we're talking two different languages, like we're strangers. She sees me differently physically and mentally. I'm not the seventeen-year-old kid she fell in love with. Now she has to decide whether she wants to try to catch up to my level of maturity or grow with someone else. The decision isn't mine. I've nothing to say to her. I want her but does she want me?"

Hans, who had his chair stuffed into one of the stalls, started talking. "I'm the luckiest guy up here. My girl waited, and even though I'm busted up, I'm alive and all my organs function. I understand everything you guys are saying. It seems that most of my talks with Pat go over her head. I understand how she feels and she tries to understand me, but I know she never will."

"That's great. I'm happy for you," Steve said sincerely, "but since I lost my girl I realized it's best that I start a relationship with a lady that never knew me before the Nam—at least that way I won't have to explain how much I've changed. I met a really terrific girl in Australia. Man, I know I could fall for her, but just ain't no way I'd ever get back to down under."

I did nothing but think of my relationship with Cheryl. I was sitting in the head because of my thoughts of her, and the Nam. I decided to try to change the subject. "Do you people believe in God? . . . I guess that sounds stupid, but when I left for Vietnam I felt like a religious fanatic at times. I thought if I believed as hard as possible that God existed then I wouldn't worry about dying. The only trouble was . . . I was always scared."

"I believed there was a God at first," Ron said angrily, "but after watching my two best friends die for no damn good reason, I lost that trust. How could any God let innocent people die such hideous deaths? Hell, my only sin in life, before going in the corps, was being an eighteen-year-old virgin . . . for that transgression I got my damn foot blown off. Good thing I didn't play with myself."

Hans got so worked up he started to tremble. When he started to speak he stammered. "Ro-Ro-Ron is right. Our sin was being poorer or dumber than other kids our age. For that I got mutilated for life. My friends and peers carry nothing through life but the amusing memories of protest marches in the streets and parks, and a smug notion that they sacrificed some energy condemning what I was forced into doing. If you didn't have money for college, you got drafted. If you couldn't pull grades you got tossed out of school on your ear and got drafted. So the choice boiled down to enlisting in the branch of the service with the neatest uniforms or moving to Canada. That left all those arrogant bastards the privilege of passing judgment on me. They never sacrificed a thing. They don't have to carry pain day after day forever. They skate through life. God lets it happen. God made me this way. American justice and God's mercy. Where would I be without their help?"

Norton shuffled in close. He was caught up in the bull session and looked relieved to finally say how he felt. "When I'm lying in a rice paddy up to my armpits in mud and leeches, and I'm tired and scared, lonely and being eaten alive by mosquitoes, who has the right to say I'm a murderer, a baby killer, or anything? Charlie might have an opinion worth hearing . . .

but the guy who went to Canada? Some rich kid who's living off of Daddy for everything including his pizza and car? Some ass-wipe that hides in college or trade school, then comes out on Saturday to call every poor kid a stupid shit for being drafted? Those are the people that belong up here. God has his eyes closed. All that crap about a rich guy on a camel passing through the eye of a needle. Hell, you ain't going to see a poor kid on a penny passing through that needle to heaven either. I really wish I knew what was going through God's mind."

Steve was really upset. "Didn't you all pray to God to get you out alive? Didn't you all beg him to get you back home? I bet you prayed like hell that you not end up a vegetable for the rest of your lives. We all just got done saying how cheap we got off. It could well be all this has a purpose. Did you ever consider that maybe God wanted us to never let anyone forget what horror war is? It could be that our wounds add more credence to what we have to say. We have to persuade everyone to never let this happen again. I've thought about all this a lot. If I do anything, I'm going to make sure my kids never have to go through this."

I started laughing quietly at first, then hysterically. I could see Steve and some of the others were getting mad. I held up my hand and waved it around. "I'm sorry, Steve. I wasn't laughing at you. I was just thinking about some of the prayers I made . . . I remember up at Khe Sanh, when we were getting mortared really bad. I prayed to God as hard as I could, 'If you get me out of this alive, I'll become a priest.'" Everyone started to laugh. "Another time I said, 'God, I'll never screw again, not *ever again*. God, I'll be a monk.'" The laughter increased. "Then there was 'God, take my first male child,' and I can't remember how many other mindless promises I made. I think the Lord took payment this way." I stopped laughing and got very tense. "What if this is just a down payment?" Laughter erupted again. "Enough of this serious stuff. Ron, what happened to you in that race with Three East?"

Ron's face got rigid. He closed one eye and opened the other one wide. "What happened? They put that gimp out there with me that's got a colostomy bag taped to his side. When we hit that second curve by the service elevator, his bag dropped off and got caught under my wheel. When the bag broke I skidded off into that guy with one leg and no jaw from up on Six South."

"Next thing you're going to tell us is that it was a setup,"

Hans scoffed. "When Rick and that tank from Three East had that chicken race, and Blind Al drove Rick into the elevator door, Rick broke his leg and didn't make any excuses."

"So what?" Ron snapped. "Rick didn't hit a bag of shit."

Hans broke the laughter but kept his voice quiet. "I saw on the news that Three Twenty-six was getting their ass waxed up at Khe Sanh. That's your old unit, isn't it, Rick?"

I nodded. "Damn, Hans, I feel helpless."

Steve stared out the window into the mini-blizzard. "Last night they showed the area where my CAP unit used to be. It was just smoldering rubble. They didn't say what happened to the marines holding that position." Steve's voice cracked. "But nobody could have pulled through that. There were only eight guys out there. Kelly, Croft, Randy, and Jo-Jo held the southern edge of the perimeter, by the communication bunker. Morton, Nick, Ski, and Tobin had the north end and the PFs filled in the holes. Those guys were like brothers to me. Hell, we knew more about each other than a husband and wife. God, we were tight. I should have been there."

"What could you have done?" I pressed. "Instead of eight dead marines there would have been nine."

Ron broke in. "When is this feeling going to end? When I was there I wanted to be here. Now that I'm here I want to be there. Find any logic in that?" Ron cleared his throat. "Do you remember the first man you killed?"

"I'm not about to forget," Steve drawled. "It happened so fast. I didn't have time to think about it until it was over. He was on one side of a dike and I was on the other. We both stood up at the same time, about three feet from each other's barrel. We fired at the same time, but since he was so short, his weapon fired into the dike and I fired into his chest. What a surprised look he had on his face. I sat on the dike watching his body floating in the rice paddy. The water was red around his body, and the leeches were swimming from all directions to drink their fill. I didn't hate him. I didn't know him. I was scared of him, so I killed him. Man, what a lousy day. What about you, Ron?"

"It was a lot like your story. We walked into each other on a jungle path. I just saw him first. I felt wrong about pulling the trigger . . . you know, like I froze. He looked like he was seven feet tall. After I killed him I got real sick and puked all over his corpse. He was such a little fellow and so young. He carried a picture in his breast pocket of an old woman and a little boy. I remember thinking about what his mother was doing at just that instant.

"I felt sorry for her, even more than I felt badly about killing him. Doesn't that sound odd? It's not as if I had a choice, but I wonder—if he'd killed me, would he have cared at all?

"Dying didn't frighten me because of the pain. It bothered me that no one would know I was dead and my body would stay lost in the jungle."

Hans shook his head. "I wonder if that's the way we're supposed to feel. I wonder if killing people was easier in other wars, like World War II. There was an easy choice of good over evil. When they killed the enemy it meant he wouldn't live to invade the States and kill there."

"What the hell is going on in here?" The men looked around and there stood a very angry Miss Altman. "You heard me, what are you people doing in here? It's past two o'clock."

Steve shuffled up close to the tall, buxom nurse. He winced in pain, mostly for show. "Why, Miss Altman, we all had trouble sleeping and rather than bother everyone on the ward we came in here. We're sorry if we've been too loud."

She smiled. I could see that she wouldn't stay angry at us. She shagged us out of the head and back to our racks.

# 13

THREE NIGHTS LATER, after evening dressing changes, Cheryl returned with Betsey.

The sight of Cheryl walking toward me made all my pain disappear. I reached out my hand to her. She took it cooly, walked briskly to my bedside, gave me a short kiss and a lifeless hug. Her face was emotionless, her eyes were fixed—hard and determined.

I smiled, hoping she would do the same. "God, I'm glad you came tonight. I've really missed you."

She looked around the ward constantly when she spoke. "Oh, I didn't know we were coming until an hour ago. Betsey drove. How are you feeling? Do you think you'll come home for Easter?" Her voice was a monotone.

I took her hand and pulled her close. I was confused. "I'm getting better. Really, I'm feeling stronger every day. I haven't asked the doctor yet, but there's a real good chance I can come home at least for Easter weekend. Won't that be terrific? Just to be alone together sounds too good to be true."

"Oh, it'll be great. Even for a few days. Home cooking, and all your friends will be home from school."

"I'll be happy for all that. But most of all I just want to be with you."

Cheryl stepped back from my bed and lit a cigarette. "No, you don't understand, Rick. I'm going to Florida with my girl friends over Easter."

I was dumbfounded.

anned this a month ago. I had no idea you would be here by then. Please don't be angry."

"You mean you'd rather go to Florida than spend the time with me?"

"No, Rick. It's not like that. It's just that I made a deposit on the room and bought my ticket already. My friends planned on my sharing the expenses and all."

"Well, if that's all, I'll give you all the money you need to reimburse your friends. That way you won't lose any money and you won't short your friends."

"No, you just don't understand. I want to go. I've really been looking forward to it."

"I can't believe it. For the past eight months I've done nothing but think of you. You mean your friends are more important than me, don't you?"

"Rick, you just don't understand." Cheryl wheeled around and stormed off the ward. Betsey turned to me when she spotted Cheryl leaving. "What did you say to her? What's wrong with you? Don't you have any idea of what she's been through?" she said in a huff. Without another word she took off.

"Eilert, what's with you? I was mentally abusing Betsey's body when you ruined my perfectly good, almost sexual experience. Cheryl looked madder than hell."

"Steve, forget it. I'll never understand it. Betsey's got the brain of a pea. Imagine her saying I have no idea what Cheryl's been through. What does she call being blown to shit?"

"Come on, Rick. What's the matter? Don't tell me. . . . I thought you and Cheryl were going to be the exceptional couple. You know—staying together, forever in love, the girl that waited."

"She asked if I might come home for Easter. I told her I may be able to, at least for a few days. Then she said, 'Well, that's too bad. I'm going to Florida with my girl friends.'"

Steve smiled and shook his head. "Ain't that the shits? At least she told you she was finally able to make a choice. You or Jody . . . you lose."

"Steve, you're a comfort. You have a talent for turning the knife. Oh, God, when is this going to end? I know she's confused, but this is crazy."

That evening Steve left me alone. I lay there for hours trying to sort out all that had happened over the past year. Cheryl and I were so happy. Was it the grenade that had changed my life, or the war, or was all this destined to happen?

My sleeping pill was welcome that night. I wanted to forget. I was tired of losing people I loved. I was tired of all the pain. And I was helpless to change anything.

The following day Steve and I were up at the nurses' station. We heard some interesting information. The Navy was doing a study of the effects of combat and severe wounds on the mind. The doctors up on Five North were conducting interviews with patients from wards on Three, Four, and Five.

We on Three South were first to go, and we were reminded that "this is America . . . home." We were no longer at Con Tien, Khe Sanh, Hue, Dong Ha, or Da Nang. So they told us to watch our step and no funny business. I pitied the poor doctors that would have to see us.

We all felt uncomfortable about seeing any doctor besides Doc Bone. He always treated us fairly, and he was always honest with us. We'd have done anything for him. He was one hell of a man, besides being a great doctor. And nobody wanted to go to Five North. All the mental cases were there. Battle fatigue, they called it, but each of us had, at one time or another, suffered from shell shock.

Steve and I returned to our racks. Ron followed and sat between our beds. "Either of you been up to Five North?" Ron asked.

We shook our heads no as Ron continued. "I went up there once to see a friend of mine. He was sedated. But there were a few of them in the halls being escorted by a couple of huge corpsmen. One guy was stalking the bush. I mean that guy was in the jungle, only his body walked the floor. The other guy was carrying a dead body. That's what the corpsman told me later. This guy had both his arms out in front of his body and refused to put the corpse down. I came back to my rack that day and thought I was going to cry. It's one thing to be paralyzed but to forever be in one combat experience has got to be living hell. I thought fire fights that lasted two minutes were too long. I just can't fathom something like that."

Steve closed his eyes and shook his head. He laid his head in his hands.

"Man, what madness. I don't mean their insanity, I mean war and the military leaders that forget what effect combat has on the human body and mind," Steve said in a disgusted voice. Then he smiled. "Hey, you know what we ought to do?"

With my index fingers I formed a cross, as if to cast away vampires. "Away, you leper. Not another screwball idea."

Ron got excited, eager to do something to break the boredom of the uneventful days. "What you got on your mind?"

Steve flashed an ever widening smile. "Listen, now. When we go up to see the shrink, freak out on him. Start to twitch and bob up and down, then start to see things in his office that aren't there . . . you know, like cows and ducks. Let's see what happens, what he writes on his report. Maybe we'll get some strict bed rest, no serving juice or passing out trays. Hell, we're getting out of the corps anyway, so what's the harm?"

"Genius. What talent," Ron affirmed.

We disbanded for afternoon dressing changes and as usual they left us in exhausted heaps. Steve watched television and listened to music for the remainder of the day. Steve stayed awake until after midnight, saying nothing, just standing watch. He took his sleeper and shortly afterward fell asleep. When he awoke the following morning I was sitting up eagerly, eating my breakfast.

"Hey, Eilert. How's it going?"

"Fine, Steve. Are we still going bananas up on Five?"

"Sure. Proceed as planned. Let's just make sure we pass it around that other people should do the same thing. We don't want to be the only two from Three South to go bonzo."

Steve and I went into the head and cleaned up. Then we went to the nurses' station and got robes and chits to go up to Five North. Steve got behind my wheelchair and pushed me to the elevator and then into the waiting room to see the doctor.

While we were talking, Ron came rolling up in his wheelchair.

"Ron, what are you doing up here? They started on your side four hours ago."

"I was in yakking with Bone. They're going to cut my leg off below the knee. I guess they want to find out if that's going to fuck me up. You know, shell-shocked and limbless."

Steve went over the battle plan with Ron, who couldn't wait to get started.

Steve went in first. He was in the office for about twenty minutes when the door opened and he came sliding out like the hunchback of Notre Dame. He was twitching and rolling his eyes, with his tongue hanging out of the side of his mouth and drool dripping from his chin. Every other step he would whisper, "Incoming, incoming." The doctor led him to the door and called a corpsman to come up and fetch him.

As I entered the doctor's office, Ron started to go nuts. "Somebody get that cat. Please, get that cat before he eats my food." I went in and sat down. "Marine, do you know either of those patients?" the doctor asked.

"No, sir." I let my head swing from side to side, blinking constantly and flinching every once in a while. I couldn't believe that this guy was buying all this garbage, but he remained very serious. He asked questions and wrote frantically on a pad of paper in front of him, pausing to bite the eraser off his pencil.

"Do loud noises bother you? Like explosions." I almost choked. I'd been blown fifteen feet into the air, and this asshole asks if explosions bother me. I just nodded yes. When the interview was over, he called the ward and asked that a corpsman fetch another patient. Then he sent for the next man.

It was O'Hara who came to get me. He had a big grin on his face when he saw me sitting in my wheelchair outside the doctor's office.

"What the hell is going on? You're the third joker that I've had to come and get."

"Nothing going on, Doc. But that shrink is really weird. He should see a doctor. Man, he had three pencils chewed in places all the way down to the lead. And every pencil had the eraser bit off."

When I returned, Markley and Sanford were waiting. They'd told everyone on the ward about their act. When they spotted me they all broke up in hysterical laughter. One by one the rest of the men came down, escorted by a corpsman.

The following day the psychologist came down to the floor to talk to those patients who were unable to get out of their racks. Each one of those he interviewed knew the shit that the others had pulled and followed their lead. The doctor was pissed off, and made no bones about it. He went into Doc Bone's office yelling his fool head off about insubordination and other complaints. The ward was laughing hysterically. The shrink left in disgust, beating his hand against his clipboard.

The nurses looked baffled but Bone knew exactly what was happening. He stuck his head out of his office with a huge grin on his face.

Since the shrink thought we were all fruity we decided to prove it to Doc Bone. We decided to order fruit the following morning and save it for morning rounds. When the good doctor came on the ward for rounds he started with "Listen up, you animals. You shook the hell out of that poor doctor from Five North. I had to tell him that you were just pulling a prank on him, and that you're really all right."

We pulled the fruit from under the sheets and pillows and started throwing it at him. Everyone, even the doctor himself, started laughing.

"The only normal thing about you marines is that you're all nuts," he cried out. Then he came in and did the rounds, still cracking up every now and then. The usual sounds telegraphed his location—"Oooh . . . ahh . . . Chrrrist"—but after almost every groan was a laugh.

Steve and I often talked about the doctor with the others. The one thing we all believed was that he really hurt to see so many young men torn apart so horribly. He also knew that when we had thrown the fruit, it was to let off some steam after being imprisoned in plaster and traction for so long, and he would rather have us toss a bunch of fruit than take swings at each other. He never made anything of the incident, although most of the other doctors would have put us on report.

We were starving for new and interesting ways to amuse ourselves. One night, while shooting the bull in the head, Steve came up with the idea of going up to Maternity.

I couldn't figure out what the hell was on Steve's mind. "What do we want with a bunch of babies? Talk about dumb—that machine sucked your brains out."

Steve went on. "Well, according to Collins, every time he goes up there he gets to see those pretty young mothers breastfeeding their babies. Some of them are almost naked. When's the last time you saw bare tit?"

I shrugged my shoulders and the others shook their heads and rolled their eyes.

Steve sat smuggly on the toilet. "Yeah, I thought so. Now it sounds like a great idea. Should we give it a try?"

We saw no reason that such a fine idea shouldn't turn a profit. We thought a modest fee could be charged. Five dollars seemed decent. Two for Steve, two for me, and one buck for Collins to push our chairs up for a peek.

We coaxed Collins into joining forces. All he had to do was take people with him every time he went to Maternity and we'd pay him a buck. Considering how many times a week he had to go up there, we could all make a lot of extra money.

Steve and I took the first tour (any good tour guide tests the water before he sends people out). We checked off the ward and made our way up in the elevator. When we reached the nurses' station in Maternity we got more than just a few dirty looks. Markley and I were craning our necks trying to see a naked body running around, or even a few hungry kids. We couldn't see anything at all. The drapes were all pulled around the beds to allow the mothers privacy.

"Nothing. We came all this way for nothing. There go all those wonderful dollars."

"Easy, Rick. Why do we have to tell them that we saw nothing? Hell, they might be just as happy to see women, period." Steve and I returned to the ward and to the anxious faces on the floor. Peterson couldn't stay quiet. "Well, tell it like it is. Was it great?" I jumped in. "It was out-fucking-standing. They were having a circle-nurse. Ten beautiful mothers offering the nectar of life to those little brats. It was a regular skin show." Then it was Steve's turn. "That's right. Well worth the trip. Ticket sales are at rack thirty-three. The tour leaves three times a day from the patients' elevator number three. Five American dollars. Only one patient per tour."

There were bookings for the first week and a half within a half hour. When the patients did go, they very rarely, if ever, saw anything, but when they returned to the ward they made it sound as if it were the greatest thing since round doorknobs. They were embarrassed because all the other guys said they'd seen something and they didn't want to be outdone. Meanwhile, Steve and I were raking in twelve dollars a day.

Miss Altman started to get a little suspicious, so she called Markley and me into the doctor's office. We were afraid of what she might say, so we asked the ward to back us up. But only four chairs could get into the office and even then it was very tight.

"What the hell is going on with you people? I've gotten complaints from the nurses up on Maternity, no less," she said angrily.

"Well, ma'am, you see, we all have been getting kind of strange being up here so long without the benefit of female companionship. We just wanted to see the real thing, that's all." I mumbled with my head down.

She leaned back in her chair and started peeling an orange. "You marines are nuts, real fruitcakes." She tossed the peels into the crowd of us. "You're all animals." Then she started laughing. "It's true. You've been away too long, but going up to Maternity . . . come on, that's a little out of line. No more trips up there. Do you read me?"

We all agreed. It had been fun, but we were glad to be out of the business.

We got a new nurse on the ward, Miss Bixby. Her first major duty was to put a new long leg cast on me. At nursing skills she excelled. At common sense she was a zero. She wouldn't accept any advice from corpsmen or patients.

Late one night she was going through the ward checking on the patients, flashing a light in their faces. She made a big mistake. Standing right next to Brandy, she put the flashlight in his face. He awoke out of a sound sleep and in one fluid motion put his fist right in her face. She fell to the floor. It happened so fast that she couldn't even scream. When she pulled herself up off the floor her nose was streaming blood. She went back to the nurses' station until the bleeding stopped, then returned with a security guard and a corpsman. Brandy was very apologetic but to no avail. He'd just been transferred to the ward from Three East, and he wasn't well.

"I'm going to get you court-martialed for striking an officer. This is unforgivable!" she yelled, and tried to make all of the patients near Brandy's rack describe what had happened, even though they were asleep when it occurred.

Everyone on the ward felt badly that she'd been hurt. We understood that she had every reason to be upset. But she refused to listen to any explanation on Brandy's behalf.

"To tell me that he hit me out of reflex is so much bull. If he gets away with this, that would condone everyone who wants to get even with a nurse or corpsman, using the excuse that they were asleep when they did it."

Everyone agreed that what she described could happen in the future, but the fact was that this time it had been a reflex on Brandy's part. The doctor was asked by the men on the ward to try and make her understand what had occurred. He understood, but his hands were tied. She had made the charges. Only she could drop them. We decided that we would have to help her reconsider.

Blackmail was the only solution. We needed a photo of her in a compromising position with one of the patients. I was chosen. The plan called for me to strip naked and make an attempt to sit on the toilet. Then have the nurse come in and grab me. It mattered not how she grabbed me just as long as her arms were around me. I'd pretend that I was slipping off the toilet seat. Someone on the ward would have her come in and try to help me back up on the shitter. Someone else would hide in the adjacent stall and take a picture. Wheelchairs would block the entrance to the head, and once the picture was taken the camera would be passed back from man to man to O'Hara, who'd be waiting on the emergency staircase.

The day arrived. All was ready. Everyone took his place. Instead of my hanging half-on-half-off the pot, they laid me naked on the floor in the stall. Miss Bixby was summoned into the head, the wheelchairs following right behind her. There I lay, moaning and groaning on the floor—my two long leg casts up in the air, still on the wheelchair.

As soon as she saw me on the floor she sent for a corpsman to assist her. In the meantime, she knelt next to me, putting her hands up under my armpits to sit me upright. As she did the flash went off, and the camera was immediately given to the men blocking the door and passed on out to O'Hara. He then rushed down the stairs to the second floor, where a friend was waiting to develop the picture.

Miss Bixby was surprised by the flash. At first she hadn't any idea of what was happening. When it dawned on her, she let go of me. I fell back down, hitting my head on the base of the toilet bowl. She sprang to her feet and raced out after the camera.

When the picture was printed about an hour later, O'Hara put a nice five-by-seven in her purse when she was off the ward. The photo had turned out very well. My privates were exposed and it looked like she was hugging me.

Brandy set up a meeting in the solarium and Miss Bixby was sent for. He explained what they would do with the photo, and they sat her down and tried to reason with her. They no more wanted to embarrass her than they wanted Brandy court-martialed. It was as if a bolt of lightning had hit her—all of a sudden it was clear to her. The patients all knew that they really couldn't get away with their threat, and that nobody would really believe she was fooling around. But she dropped the charges. The subject was never brought up again, and she really started to let her hair down. Soon she became one of our biggest supporters, and often straightened out differences between the nurses and patients. She ran errands for us, cashed checks, phoned parents, and nearly always listened to our point of view before making a decision. She became one of the best nurses we ever had and we loved her like a sister.

Each month a new class of corpsmen would train on the ward prior to going overseas. To a marine, a corpsman is second only to his weapon in importance. The corpsman is the one who has to expose his ass to tend a wounded man. His speed in the field makes the difference—not only between life and death, but also in saving limbs. When the corpsmen worked on the wards their jobs were all the dirty ones, like cleaning ducks and silver saddles, and bathing the bedridden. Once those duties had been performed, they could assist in dressing changes and other patient care. They took a lot of ribbing from the patients, but they knew that it was all in fun, and they learned to laugh at themselves as well.

The nurses followed the same path in their training. Once they left the wards they were usually sent to the Nam. Most of them went to field hospitals, or to the regular hospitals either in-country or where the med-i-vac flights landed on their journey back to the States. Others went to the hospital ships in the Gulf of Tonkin.

Many nurses had received their training in civilian hospitals, and were not used to servicemen as patients. Before coming to our ward, they got some coaching in military courtesy. Nurses and officers were supposed to be different classes of creatures from enlisted men. But that didn't matter to the wounded, because they knew that they were getting out of the service, and whether they left as privates or as sergeants didn't mean diddley shit. Still, the patients treated the nurses with respect in most cases.

I couldn't sleep one night so I went to the head. Inside I found no one around the long line of sinks or shower stalls, but I heard plenty of gibberish. The door to the urinals was also closed, and with my long leg casts protruding out in front of my chair I nudged it open.

I found a party going on. Almost everyone was present. The room was filled with cigarette and cigar smoke. Two bottles of Scotch sat on the windowsill, one empty and the other well dented.

Ron sat glassy-eyed in a nearby sink. "Hey, Ricky-ticky, come on in and join the funeral."

"Thanks. Who are we burying tonight?"

Steve stood up and quickly staggered back to a nearby toilet seat. "We're burying *bad times*. Who was it who said, 'War is hell . . . but combat is a mother fucker'? Come on in, Rick. Have a drink," Steve pleaded.

Hans, who was wrecked, tossed the Scotch bottle across the room. From one end of the toilet stalls a voice sang out a little rhyme:

> *Here's to it. . . . Birds do it flying in the sky.*
> *Bees do it, stick to it, then die.*
> *So here's to it, let's do it,*
> *Baby, you and I.*

First a hand appeared from around the partition door, holding a pint of bourbon. Then O'Hara stuck his head out. "Hi, there, Eilert. Come join us. I've got my orders for the Nam, or so I'm told. They're going to ship out a bunch of us in the next forty-five days. Why take me? I'm a lover." Everyone laughed.

I opened the bottle and took a long swig. It took my breath away, burning all the way down into my stomach. "Woo, that's good. Man, that's the first drink I've had in months. Hey, isn't this bad for us? You know, taking medication and all."

O'Hara laughed as he offered Ron another drink. "Yeah, you can get real sick."

I looked at all the others getting plastered. "Oh, I just wondered. Can I have another?"

Steve, who had the bottle, now stood up briskly and handed me the shrinking volume of nectar.

Our conversation was totally different from the earlier ones. Blass came into the head for the first time at night. He was the only corpsman on the ward who had been in Vietnam. He was highly respected by patients and hospital staff alike.

"Blass," O'Hara slurred, "I got my orders for the Nam. Come on in and get sick with us."

Blass smiled. Normally he would have been outraged, but he understood the seriousness of the occasion. Corpsmen didn't last long in the Nam. Blass picked up the bottle and fired down several quick slugs. "Good luck, O'Hara. Listen to everything those jarheads tell you once you get in the bush." Blass shot down another swallow, then helped wheel the drunken patients back to their racks.

Later he took O'Hara out and they drank the night away.

We were all sorry to hear of O'Hara's misfortune. If he was

lucky, real lucky, he'd get his leg blown off or get wounded badly enough to end up at Great Lakes.

In the Nam we went through corpsmen very fast. Most of them were killed. We were treated daily by walking dead men. We knew it, Blass knew it, but fortunately the green man going to Vietnam didn't see it that way.

Doc Bone discovered that I had osteomyelitis in my legs, a disease of the bone marrow, and I had to go to the OR again. Ron and Duffy also were going to the OR, to have their legs cut off. Ron's right foot and Duffy's left. They were put in racks next to each other, so that they could compare their pain and stumps and share their feelings with each other. They could also share shoes, since their sizes were similar. Otherwise they both would have tossed out the other shoe.

All three of us were prepped, put NPO for surgery, and taken down to the operating room at the same time. We waited in line, one behind the other. The doctor came into the hall and went to Ron's and Duffy's gurneys.

"All right, you two, this won't be a long procedure at all, as I've already explained to you. We'll keep a pretty close eye on you today, so you might be in the recovery room longer than usual. Don't let the phantom pains fool you. Your feet can't hurt because they're gone."

"Yes sir, and thank you," Ron said, as Duffy just smiled and nodded.

Ron was the first to go in. They wheeled him out within a half hour. Then Duffy went in. I had a lot of respect for their courage. It's easy to talk about letting someone take your arm or leg, even your finger. To actually do it is another matter.

Duffy was pulled out and I took up my place on the operating table. The doctor, who had left to change into a clean smock, returned.

"How's it going today, Rick? Let's see, what are we going to cut off today?" He picked up a huge knife and let his hands start shaking. I knew that he was just goofing around, but still the idea that I could have been Ron or Duffy gave me cause to worry.

"Don't worry about those two. They're both in good shape. They'll be knocked out for a while. In fact, they'll probably wake up about the same time you do, so you'll see them in recovery."

The doctor signaled the anesthesiologist to start putting me under. I was told to start counting backward from one hundred. Instead I started at ninety. At first the anesthesiologist wasn't paying attention, but when I said, "Eighty-six," the room broke out in laughter.

The next thing I remembered was waking up in recovery. A woman was right next to me and Ron's and Duffy's gurneys boxed in her rack. As usual I was very thirsty and asked the nurse to bring me some water. She returned with a rag for me to suck on. When I looked around the room I saw Ron sucking on a rag, Duffy sucking on a rag, and everyone else sucking on rags.

When patients were coming out from under the anesthetic, we weren't held responsible for our actions. Anything we did or said was let slide, even grabbing a nurse. Ron took advantage of that. As soon as the nurse returned to Ron's side to get a blood pressure reading, he grabbed her breast. Then he pretended to pass out, and the nurse let it go. She walked away shaking her head. As soon as she had gone Ron opened his eyes and smiled, hoping that she would return, but she didn't.

Duffy started to mumble. At first he couldn't be understood, but his voice got clearer and clearer. "That sheet . . . that woman's sheet . . . it's going to fall."

I checked it out and sure enough, whoever it was that laid the sheet over her had done a lousy job and it was falling off. So everyone lay there watching, waiting. It had been a long time for all of us, so the idea of seeing a naked female body was really exciting. The woman was wearing a big green pizza hat, so it was hard to see her face and hair. For some reason she had a towel wrapped around her throat. All the patients just kept staring. I looked at Ron, and he was puffing away and so was Duffy. The closest anyone was to her gurney was four feet away, so blowing at the sheet wasn't going to make it fall. Even so, I decided that I would blow, too, and soon everyone in the recovery room was blowing. It got the nurse's attention but she had no idea what was going on. The sheet fell, there she was. A seventy-year-old woman, if she was a day. Suddenly we were all ashamed of ourselves.

The nurse saw what had happened and ran over to cover the old woman. Fortunately, she remained unconscious.

Both Ron and Duffy were very uncomfortable. Both complained of phantom pains. Ron kept telling the nurse that his toes hurt. I was almost embarrassed to ask for a pain shot but did so anyway. She brought pain shots for all three of us.

"This is better than an opium den," Duffy said. Meanwhile the nurse phoned the ward to send corpsmen for the three of us. Chief, Crawford, and Snyder came down and brought the musketeers back to the ward, where we were met with applause for Ron and Duffy. Everyone realized what they still had to go through and just wanted to let them know that they had support.

Ron hadn't received any word from home since he had been back at Christmas, when his girl dumped him. Duffy, too, was a long way from home, so visits from his family or friends were rare. The only people that cared at all were the men on the ward, and that helped them a lot.

The operations that they'd just gone through were serious, and the other patients worried about them. We took turns checking on them, and they were never left alone for long periods of time unless they were asleep. I felt good inside to see so many badly wounded men worrying about their friends first, just like in the Nam.

That evening my parents came up to visit. My mom brought sandwiches as usual. I'd told her in advance that Ron and Duffy were having amputations, so she purposely brought extra rations. She was very close to Ron, and on evenings when I was feeling poorly or was knocked out, she'd often visit with the other men on the ward. Ron wasn't much of a talker but my mom was an exception. He'd talk to her about anything and everything. She proved to be an adopted mother for many of the patients whose families were far away.

When she arrived on the ward that evening I was out cold. I'd had a pain shot just an hour before and would be out for a long time. Steve was eager for conversation and kept my father talking while my mom visited Ron.

When she walked around the partition to Ron's rack, she saw him and Duffy in their beds, side by side. Duffy was playing his guitar and both men were sitting up with their stumps crossed over their other legs, swinging rhythmically to the beat of the music. It really cracked her up.

She walked up next to Ron's bed and laid a kiss on his cheek. "How are you doing, Ron? Does it hurt very much?"

Ron looked at her with eyes big as saucers. "Oh, it's great, Mrs. Eilert. They got me so doped up I might just get the other one chopped off, too. Say, did you bring any of those great sandwiches with you?" he mumbled.

She winked and provided a brown bag filled with goodies.

"You know I did. How could I forget. Say, why don't you introduce me to your neighbor? I've seen him before but never met him."

She walked around Ron's bed until she stood between the two racks.

"Hey, Duffy. Meet Mrs. Eilert, Rick's mommy." Ron smiled groggily.

Duffy was dizzy with dope as he laid down his guitar and shook her hand. "Nice to meet you, ma'am. I've seen you up here a lot and I've shared your sandwiches with Rick. Thanks a lot, that's really nice of you."

"Were you a grunt, too, Duffy?" she asked quietly.

Ron laughed and answered before Duffy could. "Duffy a grunt? Please, Mrs. Eilert, don't give him more credit than he deserves. Duffy got gangrene in his leg. He fell down the steps of one of those houses my mama always told me to stay away from."

Duffy laughed. "I was a truck driver. We hit a land mine and it blew the truck and all of us to shit—I'm sorry, I mean heck."

My mother smiled as she patted Duffy's hand. She couldn't help but love every one of the guys on the ward. She sat there the rest of the evening exchanging jokes and listening to stories of home and girl friends.

Meanwhile my father kept vigil over me. He'd endured World War II so that his son would never have to be put through all the suffering such insanity produced. Yet there he was, next to his son's twisted, torn body. He had another son at home. He was still too young for the draft, but would he, too, have to be crippled or killed someday for some nebulous reason?

"Steve, did you know what you were doing in Vietnam?"

Steve hesitated. "Mr. Eilert, I can't rightly say. I went for all the right reasons, but it got down to keeping my people alive. You watch the news and count how many Vietnamese soldiers you see fighting. Most of the ones I saw were in the rear selling drugs, whores, American gear, and holding their good buddies' hands. I thought I knew, but I don't. I wish I was born a hundred years ago. Life may have been harder but it was a lot less complicated. It seemed people fought wars for reasons, something they believed in. If someone stole your horse or cow you hung the son of a bitch. Nowadays they let the bastards go because they can't spell, or a hundred and fifty years ago someone in their family was a slave. Hell, I don't understand it. Today I watched people on TV carrying a NVA flag and yelling about how the American imperialists should be killed. What would they have done in World War II if someone carried a Rising Sun or Nazi flag down Michigan Avenue?"

My father chuckled. He looked up at Steve. "They would have drawn and quartered the fool . . . if he was lucky."

"Then what happened? I must be crazy, because something ain't right." Steve dragged deeply on his cigarette. He looked over at me to make sure I was quiet and comfortable.

My father watched TV with Steve, exchanging stories and political ideas. Steve especially enjoyed these conversations with Dad, because of his knowledge of varied subjects and his commonsense approach to most problems. My father worked as a design engineer in the aerospace industry. He also worked with optics for scopes and high-altitude photography.

I woke shortly. Dad was talking with Steve about a news brief on Vietnam. "Two hundred seventy Americans were killed in Vietnam last week," the announcer had said.

"Shit, Dad. I hope none of my unit got it," I mumbled.

My father moved next to my rack and grabbed my hand. "I hope it's none of your buddies, either. I went through this often during World War II. You worry about your friends, neighbors, relatives, and it can drive you crazy. It gets worse. Wait till you have a son go to war. You worry about them every minute of every day. You're my son, not a marine or an adult. You're my child and it's hard to think of you any other way."

My father was visibly moved. So was I. When I was with him I felt like a youngster. I depended on his strength and his wisdom. I never really realized how much I loved him until that moment. I cried.

Visiting hours were over. Mom returned from Ron's bedside still laughing from the joking around. She laid a brown paper bag on my nightstand and kissed my forehead as she left. Steve shook my dad's hand and bade them good night. Everyone felt better from the visit.

Steve and Chief filled me in on my parents' visit. Chief especially liked my parents and was touched by my mother's visit with Ron and Duffy. Steve, too, was good about letting me know all I missed. It wasn't long before I zonked out again.

Steve woke me to eat my breakfast. "Hey, duffus, awake. The chef has been up all night watering those eggs."

I opened one eye and looked around my rack. I sat up and

looked at my plate of food and held up a short, skinny sausage link. "What the hell is this?" I asked with disgust as grease dripped from its tip.

"Why that, my boy, is a Frenchman's dick—Le Pepe, so to speak," Steve replied with a straight face.

"Imagine what it must look like soft," I laughed.

Suddenly from my left came laughter from Slim's rack. The sheet was pulled up just over his mouth, but I saw the covering popping up and down. His laughter came in squeaking and snorting yelps. Even his bed shook. It was the first sound he had made since he'd come on the ward.

Slim quieted down and made no further noise. "See, Eilert? See what you started? Don't ever touch a Frenchman there," Steve said. Slim started laughing again, and everyone joined him, glad to have him back in the world.

When the corpsman came for my tray he brought a surprise as well. "Damn, Sam Blass. Hey, Doc, where have you been? I haven't seen you in weeks, since O'Hara got news he was going to Nam," I said excitedly.

"Rick, you've improved since I last saw you. You got color in your face and you're a lot more alive," Sam replied. "I had some shrapnel come out of my arm. Doc Bone dug it out, but it wasn't infected so he put me on Five South for two weeks. And I had two weeks of casual duty in the barracks. Man, that sucks. It's good to be back at work. Doc Bone said I could start assisting him in the OR. Can you believe that? What other doctor would give me a break like that? He knows I want to go into medicine and I'll tell you, I want to be like him. Some guys' heroes are Mickey Mantle or Johnny Unitas. If I could be a doctor half as good as him, I'd give my left nut for it. Can you dig it? I'm going to be in the OR with him. Hell, I wouldn't care if I mopped floors in there. Damn, he's a man."

"You're not going to get any arguments from me. Hell, I don't mind going to the OR with him, and I'm under the knife."

"Sam, do you mean the doctor wants you to clean instruments and all that?" Steve asked.

"No, nothing like that. He said I can observe him. Holy shit, I'd re-up for this." Blass grinned. He picked up my tray and started to walk away, when Steve stopped him.

"Hey, Doc, want a good laugh?" Steve inquired with a devilish smile. Blass nodded his head vigorously. "Take this weenie and hold it over Slim's face."

Sam put down the tray and picked up the sausage link, holding it like a baby's bonus between thumb and forefinger. He stepped lively over to the flat man's rack and presented him with the ugly morsel. At first there was no response, but slowly Slim began to snicker. Each time he exhaled the sheet over his mouth would hop up and down in quick, small, jerking puffs, until he exploded into loud, hilarious laughter. Again those around him couldn't resist the unusual sound and joined in. At first Blass thought he was crazy, then he, too, was consumed by the hilarity and doubled up with stomach cramps and happy tears. He staggered his way back to the breakfast cart and didn't return until he'd composed himself.

Blass was a seasoned combat corpsman. He'd spent eight months in the field with grunts, and was highly decorated and wounded twice. Sam had been senior corpsman on the ward for more than a year and was respected by the nurses, other corpsmen, and especially Doc Bone. Blass had every natural talent needed by a doctor. He was intelligent, quick to learn, and blessed with perfect recall. It was Blass that Doc Bone relied on to ensure his instructions were carried out. Sam needed only to be told, "Change this dressing," and he knew exactly how to do it properly and relatively painlessly. We were thrilled to have him back.

Soon the sound of the doctor making rounds was heard. Grunts, groans, and occasional curses were audible up and down the other side of the ward. Once he got to our side of the ward, Steve and I braced ourselves for his greeting. When he reached Steve's side, the sounds of gauze being torn away hurt almost as much as the touch itself would have.

I tried to block out the noises but couldn't. When all the bandages and packing had been cleared away, the doctor inspected the wound closely, even shining a flashlight into the cavity.

"Looks good, Steve. The infection's clearing up and the tissue is growing back. Time for physical therapy . . . yes, PT, starting tomorrow. Blass, get him scheduled for twice a day!" Steve had come along far better than he expected and the bone grafts were successful. "Let's cut that cast off, too, and put his arm in a sling. How does that sound, son?" he asked Steve.

"Great, sir, just out . . . um, standing, sir," Steve replied enthusiastically. At last, signs of improvement. Now there would be a chance to see how much mobility he had.

I was next. I was holding tightly on to the bed frame, anticipating the pain to come. The doctor wasted no time and quickly stripped the gauze away. He looked over the packing and bandages for pus but none was found. Twice in one day. He was pleased.

"Blass, take Eilert into cast tex and put walkers on his casts. Rick, you're going to PT, starting tomorrow. It's time to get you back on your feet. OK with you?" he smiled.

"Best news I've had all day, sir. Thank you, sir," I beamed. The pain that rocked my body seemed to disappear momentarily. I was only out of the OR a little more than a day, but the news was overwhelming.

The entourage moved on to Slim's rack. "Good morning, Craig," the doctor said cheerfully as he removed the dressings. "Yeah, just as I thought, you're closing up real well. It's time for you to get out of this rack. You start physical therapy tomorrow just like your amigos. Corpsman, take this cast off and get him cleaned up. We'll start with the whirlpool treatments twice a day."

Once the doctor was out of earshot I gave out a quiet but audible yelp. "Sell my clothes—I'm going to heaven. PT, Steve, can you dig it? Physical therapy. Hell, we'll be out of here in a few weeks. I promised myself that I wouldn't get out of my wheelchair in front of my folks unless I could walk under my own steam. I'm not going to let anyone see me stumbling around on crutches. I've just got to learn to walk. My sister is getting married in June. I can't go to the wedding party like a cripple."

"Man, you're crazy. You'll be lucky to stand aloft with two crutches and a brace. Have you any idea what you're in for?"

"Come on, Steve, nothing is that bad."

As soon as the doctor's rounds were finished, Blass and a student corpsman took Steve into the cast tex room. Steve sat on an examining table while Blass moved around the huge case with the power saw. Plaster dust filled the room.

Blass cut the body cast in half first, then cut the cast from shoulder to wrist in two. He called in another student corpsman to assist. One corpsman grabbed the lower half of the arm cast, the other corpsman the upper section. Blass inserted the blade of the cast separator in the saw cuts and pried the cast apart. The pressure of the sections pushing away from each other caused Steve some unexpected pain. His arm had rested in the cast at a ninety-degree angle to his body for eight weeks. Now his arm still hung out away from his body.

The stench was nauseating. Blass hurried to open the window to let in fresh air. His plan worked, but the temperature outside was approximately twenty degrees. When the blast of cold air hit Steve's shoulder he almost passed out from the pain. Blass closed the window and sent a corpsman for a nurse and some room deodorizer. Meanwhile, he soaked the large section of cotton gauze stuck to the flesh with Dakin's solution. He let the solution soak through, then gently tore the gauze from the skin. Quickly he washed the area covered by the cast, then fitted Steve with a sling.

My turn came and the procedure was easy. Blass merely put rubber pads on the bottom of my casts and sent me on my way.

We had appointments at 0900 with the doctors in the PT Clinic.

Steve was first. The doctor had him sit on the examining table, where he measured the range of motion in his arm. The wrist would flex thirty degrees in all directions, the elbow twenty degrees, and the shoulder ten. The doctor charted all his measurements.

"Steve, I'm Dr. Graham. What we're going to do up here is have you exercise using weights, isometrics, and whirlpool. Whatever you do, don't be discouraged by little or no progress. This is rough, painful work. Don't try to liken this to work in a gym class. You're never going to experience this much prolonged agony and frustration again. Just don't give up. Take this chit down to room three. You'll report there twice a day, at oh nine hundred and thirteen hundred sharp. Don't miss an appointment. Excuses are like assholes—everybody's got one. Any questions?"

"Yes, sir. How long does this take? Will it all come back?" Steve asked, not really wanting to hear the answers.

The doctor gave Steve a tight grin. "This might not ever stop. We're just going to get you started. A lot of these exercises can and should be done a little every hour or two. You need to get flexibility back. If you skate between appointments, you'll only get stiff. It might be years before it really comes back. You've had a lot of damage, so don't expect much. I doubt you'll ever get your arm up over your head, and maybe not even away from your side. Raising and lowering it may be the best you can do. Now, let's get hot. Send in the next man."

"Yes, sir, and thanks." Steve felt like he was back in the military.

He found me sucking down on a cigarette in the waiting room. "Hey, Rick, doctor wants you."

"Steve, what's this guy like?"

Steve smiled and held up his hand like he was saluting Hitler. I crushed out my butt. "He says he's a doctor but he looks like he's twenty years old. He's got more pimples than I did at sixteen. He sounds like a coach at half time when you're losing by a hundred points. I've got to get going. See you out here after they're done with us."

I went in and got the same type of pep talk. "I'm Dr. Graham. You're here for one reason, to get up on your feet and to ambulate on crutches. That's a lot harder than it sounds, especially with two long leg casts. You're stiff-legged and carry forty pounds of plaster. How long have you been in these casts?" he asked very matter-of-factly.

"Four and a half months, sir."

"That's a long time to be off your feet. Don't be surprised if you pass out a few times.

"The first time you stand up, the blood will rush to your feet so they swell and turn purple. The toenails will cut into the skin and you'll bleed some. Then you'll pass out cold. Just make sure someone's around to catch you. Take this chit down to room five next to the parallel bars. Any questions?"

"No, sir, none yet. Thanks."

I wheeled out of the room and down the hall to the parallel bars. There was a tall, blond corpsman barking curses at a patient trying to get up a series of stairs with long leg casts and crutches. Once that was accomplished, he released him to return for the afternoon session.

I handed the corpsman my chit and waited for some instructions. "You're going to be trouble, Eilert, and I don't like trouble. That means I already don't like you. Move up to the end of the parallel bars," he ordered.

I placed myself at the end, in the middle of the bars. The chair's wheels were stopped by blocks set into the floor for just that purpose. The muscular corpsman walked to the other end of the bars and commanded me to stand up.

"You got to be shitting me. What am I, Lazarus, that you command me to rise? How can I stand? I can't bend my knees with these casts up to my crotch," I snapped angrily.

"I got another bad-ass marine. Listen, you chicken-shit mother fucker, get up on those walking casts. Use your arms."

I reached up to the bars. I released the leg braces on the wheelchair and my casts crashed to the floor. The vibration ran up my legs with unbelievable pain. When the pain subsided I opened my eyes. The corpsman was laughing his ass off. I grabbed my casts and positioned each leg in back of blocks on the floor so I wouldn't slide when I pulled myself up. Once my arms had been solid and strong. I could carry a thirty-pound mortar plate or forty pounds of ammo all day through the jungle. I could pump off a hundred push-ups and not be winded.

Now my arms felt like jelly. No matter how hard I pulled I just could not get myself up from the wheelchair. The Gestapo graduate came back around me and lifted me up under my armpits, until I stood erect on the parallel bars.

My first sensation was amazement. I felt ten feet high. The past four and a half months I'd been three and a half feet tall lying flat on my back. I didn't realize people's noses were closed on top, always seeing the two nostrils staring at me. Then, as if lead weights filled my casts, each leg grew increasingly heavy. Suddenly my legs swelled until I thought the casts would explode. I looked down at my feet. The toes were swelling to several times their normal size. They were almost black and blood dripped onto the floor where the toenails cut through. The pain of it all was dreadful, as I bore my full weight on each leg. My face felt as if pins and needles were pricking it and there was a world of spots. I fainted, falling stiff to the floor with no way to break my fall.

I landed on my right hand. The right side of my head slammed onto the floor. There was a pad, but because of the unusual way I fell I missed it and hit the tile. The goose-stepping corpsman made no attempt to break my fall and was the last to my side.

When I awoke I found myself on the floor. My legs throbbed and my head ached. There was a small puddle of blood next to my face. When I reached forward to push myself up I saw a clean, deep cut on my right hand just over the knuckle. Dr. Graham was kneeling next to me as two new corpsmen lifted me into my wheelchair.

"You're supposed to take it easy, Eilert. Wait until someone is next to you before you try something like that." Dr. Graham turned to the corpsman. "Shultz, what the hell is going on here?"

"You know these people, sir. They don't listen. They just complain."

Before the doctor could reply I was tearing at the parallel bars to get Shultz. "You lying cock sucker, you puke!" I yelled.

By now the hall was filled with other wounded men. Steve came to my side.

The doctor held his hand in front of my face. "Watch your mouth, marine. My people don't have to take that crap from you or anybody."

I found a new hate in my heart. More hate than I ever felt for the enemy. Crawford was a prince compared to either of these assholes, I thought. "He knew I was falling. He set me up, and didn't lift a finger to help me," I shouted.

Dr. Graham looked back to Shultz, who shook his head in disagreement. "Eilert, you do as you're told up here. Do you read me?" he said with a sneer.

"Yes, sir, loud and fucking clear," I snapped.

The doctor's eyes widened but he said nothing as he walked away. Steve stood near me as I was cleaned up and bandaged. "Rick, you all right?"

"Yeah, Steve, just peachy. This asshole gives puke a whole new dimension."

"Shut up, Eilert, and get back up on those bars. This time on your own, you crybaby," Shultz commanded.

Markley and I looked the tall corpsman in the eye. If looks could kill, our expressions would have melted steel.

"You, cripple with the bad wing. Get out of here," Shultz yelled to Steve.

No more words were necessary. Steve went back to his therapy room and I positioned myself for another shot at the parallel bars. When I looked down to the other end I saw Shultz standing there. I found new strength and pulled myself up on the bars.

The same sensations ran through me just as before, but this time the pain was worse. I felt nauseated and dizzy, but I pressed on. I put one hand in front of me, then one foot, then the other hand and the other foot. Each time I bore my full weight on each leg, cold chills shot up the bone and hot, burning pain through the muscles. My toes hurt so bad from the swelling that I almost passed out from the pain itself. My progress was slow and agonizing but I persisted, for each step I was closer to taking a punch at the therapist. Finally, as I neared the end, Shultz moved away and returned with my wheelchair.

He helped me into the chair and elevated my horribly swollen legs with the leg braces on the chair. I lay back exhausted, in agony and soaked with perspiration. Shultz said nothing more to me. Instead he left me alone and disappeared into the therapy room where Steve was.

Shortly thereafter another corpsman appeared next to my chair. "Hi, I'm Gordie. I'm going to be your regular aide, so from now on report here to me. Shultz give you a hard time?" he asked with a tone of concern.

"Man, that turkey is in the right line of work . . . now that concentration camps are all closed."

"Pay him no mind. I can't figure him out either, but Dr. Graham thinks his shit don't stink, so who's to say? Come on now, back up on your feet and let's try to cross again." Gordie helped me to stand, then got in front of me, between the parallel bars, guiding my every step and watching my face closely for signs that I would pass out. It was pure torture, but I felt much more secure and followed Gordie's instructions. Once we reached the other end, the wheelchair was placed so that I could slowly turn around and lower myself into it. Then my legs were elevated and I was able to rest.

"Say, Gordie, that's a strange accent. Where are you from?"

"Glasgow, Scotland. I came over here two years ago to join up so I could go to Vietnam. My accent isn't that thick, is it?" he asked with a wide grin.

"No, not much," I laughed.

Gordie was a stout man, not quite six feet tall but with wide shoulders and huge arms. He had bright red hair, green eyes, and a freckled complexion. The more I looked at him the more Scottish he looked. All he needed was a tweed suit and a collie running at his side.

After a brief rest, and once the swelling went down and the color returned to my toes, Gordie had me up for another trip. I felt no more enthusiastic about standing than the first time, but I followed his instructions.

Meanwhile, Steve was in a room that resembled a combination trainer's office and weight room. Bodies were everywhere, performing every conceivable form of exercise. Steve was seated on a training table, where he waited for someone to help him.

It was the tall, blond corpsman he'd seen in the hall near me. "You Markley?" the corpsman asked with some irritation.

"Yeah, Steve Markley."

"I'm Shultz. Are you going to be a wise ass, too?" he barked at Steve. Steve figured that this guy had been dealing with torn, broken bodies for so long that he imagined himself to be superior to everyone else because of his strength and size.

Shultz took Steve's sling off and grabbed his arm. First he had Steve demonstrate what he could do on his own. Dissatisfied, he took the arm and slowly, yet firmly, pushed it into positions he thought it should reach. Steve's eyes watered and he gasped for breath each time the arm was moved even slightly. The wrist and elbow hurt, but not as much as the shoulder. Shultz demonstrated his instructions rather than describe a point in detail. A few times Steve thought the shoulder would snap off at the socket, but Shultz managed to stop at just the right instant. The two men worked for over half an hour, then Steve was shuttled across the hall to the whirlpools. Here the corpsman sat up in a chair next to the whirlpool and had Steve lower his arm into the warm, swirling water up past the elbow, being careful not to get water in his wound. It was heaven. The water was so soothing and relaxing. Steve felt as if he would fall asleep. While he held his arm in the water he was told to flex his elbow and wrist, trying to work out the stiffness. Steve was amazed how good he felt after thirty minutes of that soaking. His sling was reattached and he was dismissed.

He waited in the hall for me. While he waited he inspected his arm. The water had washed away the weeks of blood, perspiration, and pus that had dripped down his cast. In addition there had been grime and scaly, flaky skin covering his arm. This, too, was gone.

I wheeled up to Steve and we went to the elevator immediately. "All I want to do is lay down. Man, am I beat," Steve sighed.

"Don't be ridiculous, Markley. By the time we get back downstairs it'll be time for lunch and afternoon dressing changes, then right back up here."

"Damn, what a day this is going to be. The doctor's rounds, dressing changes morning, noon, and night, and side trips to the tower for an hour's worth of torture. I'm going to be a wreck by the time I leave here," Steve replied with some agitation.

"Dressing changes, man, I'd forgotten how bad they were. That Shultz really knows how to get your attention. I wonder why nobody's killed that son of a bitch."

We were exhausted and back in our racks. Miss Altman arrived to get our thoughts about therapy. "Well, how did it go?" she asked.

"Oh, it was just delightful. Those physical therapists are real sweethearts. Especially that Shultz. There is a prince among men," Steve answered sarcastically.

Miss Altman smiled as she moved next to Steve to inspect his shoulder. "You sound like everyone else. Shultz is a real terror, but then he's not there to be liked. He's there to get you back on your feet. Did you ever consider that his attitude is for a purpose? He's trying to get you motivated to get back on your feet. Being nice doesn't always accomplish that."

I shrugged my shoulders. "Sure, I considered it, but I've had drill instructors get more out of me by treating me like a baby instead of scum. There is a fine line between cruelty and motivation. We can only do what we can to get back in shape."

"Yeah, Miss Altman, Rick's right. That jerk was moving my shoulder around like it was brand-new, and look at Rick's face and hand. He didn't get those cuts from constructive criticism. He was abused and taunted. Honest, Miss Altman, that Shultz is a dead man, and I'm not just blowing smoke up your skirt." When he realized what he had said he got flustered. "I'm sorry, ma'am. I just got carried away. I'd never blow smoke up your skirt . . . I mean, I'd love to . . . oh, hell, look what I've done," Steve said shyly.

Miss Altman laughed. We talked briefly until the lunch cart came. Then she took off to pass out trays.

It was now mid-March. All my wounds were nearly closed. The largest hole was only a quarter inch in diameter, located on my right calf. This hole ran almost all the way through the leg and had to be packed with gauze. The other wounds were closed or only open superficially. The scars were tender but dressing changes weren't quite so bad.

Every part of my legs was more sensitive. Steve had the same sensation. By the time we were done with dressing changes we were exhausted. And we had fifteen minutes to get back up to PT for an afternoon's entertainment.

I reported to Gordie at the parallel bars and Steve checked in with Shultz, who waited with a menacing smile.

"Well, lookie here, my tough-guy marine. Ready to pull your crybaby routine again, or do we get on with your therapy?"

"Yeah, you're right, Shultz. Let's just get it over with," Steve said as he sat on the examining table next to his tormentor.

Shultz stood next to Steve's right side so that his hip was just a few inches from Steve's right arm. "OK, tough guy, push against my side with your arm and hold it as long as you can."

Steve looked at Shultz and smiled. *Big deal*, Steve thought, until he tried. The task seemed easy. With his arm dangling, cocked at the elbow, Steve was to push out away from his side. He didn't raise it half an inch before the pain hit him. What made it worse was that he was hurting himself. It felt like something was tearing inside his shoulder.

The whole time Shultz stood there laughing. "Hell, you cracker ass, I'm not going to waste my time on you. Stand next to the wall and try the same thing there. When you get tired of raising your arm out away from your side, try lifting your hand up toward your chin. Here's a rubber ball. Carry it everywhere and squeeze it constantly. When you can get your arm three inches from your side and you can straighten out your arm some more, call me. I'll give you the next step." Shultz walked away in a huff, as if Steve had wasted his very valuable time. He went from table to table, checking the progress chart of each of the patients.

Steve went immediately to the wall and started a long, agonizing session of trying to move his arm in almost every direction. He had no idea it would be like this. All this pain to just nudge the arm. *I'll never do it*, he thought.

I was well through my second trip between the parallel bars when Shultz arrived. Perspiration poured off my forehead and soaked through my pajama top. Tears streaked my cheeks and little drops of blood dotted the floor from where the toenails pierced the flesh around my toes. My legs throbbed, as they swelled and pressed against the inside of the casts. My biceps burned from bearing so much weight on my arms. I'd just reached the end of the bars where my chair sat when Shultz stepped in and kicked the chair away.

"Come on, shit-for-brains, turn around and go back."

I wanted to cry. I hurt so bad. My frustration with Shultz made my head pound. I couldn't even curse him because I was so winded. I lay across one bar, putting all my weight on my belly, as I tried to gather strength and wind.

"Come on, Shultz. That's crazy," Gordie protested.

"Shut up, Scotty. You've got nothing to say about it. Now get his chair and take it back to the other end," Shultz shouted.

I looked up from where I lay bent across the bar. "Shultz, you bastard . . ." I put full weight back down on my legs, then reached around my back for the other bar. Once my hand held it tightly, I pressed up as hard as I could to face my body back down the parallel bars to my chair.

Gordie moved up in front of me to encourage my movement, but mostly to catch me. It was a wise decision. I hadn't gone two steps when my face paled and I fell forward like a falling tree, stiff. Gordie broke my fall and let me down gently to the floor pad beneath me.

Shultz went crazy. "What the hell did you do that for? He only did that because he knew you would catch him. As soon as he opens his eyes, make him start all over again." Shultz stormed off.

When I came to and saw the ceiling above me I immediately knew what had happened. Then I saw Gordie's smiling face and knew that everything was all right. "Thanks for catching me. Want to help me up?"

Gordie came from behind, pushing me up by my armpits. As soon as I was back on my feet the dull ache hit me. I felt nauseated, but I slowly dragged myself down the length of the bars. Gordie turned me around, insisting I continue.

When I made a slow about-face I saw Shultz standing at the other end, and just behind him Steve crossed the hall to the whirlpool room. I pressed on, ever so slowly. It was pure agony, every little step. It took over twenty minutes for me to make the fifteen-foot hump, but I did it. Shultz walked away while Gordie helped me back into my chair.

"Way to go, Eilert. That's the way. Boy, I love to see Shultz mad. He likes moaners so he can ride them. You did great. That's plenty for today. See you tomorrow morning at nine. Go back down to the ward and take it easy." He patted my sweat-soaked back and helped push me part of the way down the hall to wait for Steve.

We said nothing until we got back into our racks. "Say, Steve, how did it go today? Are you and Shultz getting to be good buddies? Maybe you should have a few nights alone with each other," I teased.

"Yeah, you're right, duffus. That's one cock sucker I could kill and be allowed right into heaven. That wouldn't even be murder. More like mercy killing."

"Hey, Steve, watch this." I wheeled my body around, letting my legs drop to the floor while I held on to the superstructure above my head.

Steve winced as he watched my toes turn beet-red, then blue, then almost black. He looked at my face and pleaded with me

254

to stop. "Come on, Rick. Don't overdo it. You're going to mess yourself up. Save it for PT," he said as he waited for me to faint.

"I got to get used to this. I've just got to walk again, even if I have to stand all day."

"OK, Rick, go ahead, but go at it slowly at first."

Finally the pain became so intense that I lay back and pulled my long casts back onto the bed. I lay motionless, holding my breath, trying not to scream. As soon as the pain subsided some, I relaxed.

It had been one difficult day. Unable to sleep we watched television until the dinner cart arrived. We hustled to pass out the trays and settle in for the night.

The evening dressing changes were almost the straw that broke the camel's back. Over the past ten hours we had endured three dressing changes and two PT sessions. Just as we began to get over the pain of one thing, another arose to cause more excruciating moments.

It was pure ecstasy after the last dressing had been applied and the last injection given. There would be ten or eleven hours of deliverance from all that suffering.

I looked forward to visiting hours. I hoped Cheryl would show. She didn't. Nobody came. But halfway through visiting hours, just after eight, there was a loud commotion from the other side of the ward. Yelling, cursing, and screaming in pain. Someone shouted, "You deserve all this, you murderers! They should have killed you—you're robots, mindless robots!" Then there were muffled voices and choking sounds.

Steve and I cleared out of our racks, as did everyone else. At the corner near Young's rack we were stopped by a logjam of wheelchairs and corpsmen. I craned my neck to see what was going on, but my view was blocked by too many heads. Steve could see, however, and people kept asking him what was happening. Before he could speak, a young bearded man was escorted from the ward with his head a mass of blood and a tattered NVA flag wrapped around his torso.

"Man, I don't know what's going on but I want a piece of the fucker with that flag," Steve yelled as he tried to press through the mass of people in front of him.

Several security people appeared, as well as duty nurses. Everyone was ordered back to bed, and reluctantly we went.

O'Hara came around with McCarthy. O'Hara stood at the

foot of Steve's rack and held his hand over his head until everyone shut up.

"Some new patient on the other side had two visitors of the flower children persuasion. They started taunting the rest of the patients around their buddy's rack, especially Duffy and Ron, telling them they deserved losing their legs, calling them baby killers. You know, all that good stuff. Brandy was in a wheelchair next to Duffy when one jerk pulled out this NVA flag, saying he hoped Uncle Ho wiped out every American in Vietnam.

"That's when the beds cleared and all the cripples attacked those two assholes. Brandy pulled Duffy's straight razor out of his shaving gear and cut into the turd with the flag. Toby started choking the other one. It was crazy. All those gimps dumping their wheelchairs and crawling on the floor to get that flag.

"The rest of the guys blocked the corpsmen so we couldn't break it up. By the time I got there, Brandy had scalped one mother and any number of people had punched, bit, scratched, or otherwise pounded on the two of them. Anyway, Security arrested them and they're out of here."

Everyone applauded and laughed, then got increasingly angry.

O'Hara held up his hands and called for quiet. "Look, I understand you might be disturbed, but your reaction was rather extreme punishment, wasn't it? I mean, you kind of confirmed what he said."

Steve got hot, almost uncontrollable. "Hey, that had nothing to do with the war being right or wrong. The last time I saw that flag it was flying over one of our Delta CAPs bunkers. They killed every kid in the compound and mutilated and burned the bodies so bad we couldn't identify them."

I cut in, my voice trembling with emotion. "I found one shoved down the throat of one of our corpsmen. Hell, that's when the North Vietnamese told the world they weren't even *in* South Vietnam, and all these stupid Americans believed that shit. Half the wounded up here are from Tet. Where the hell do they think we got wounded? Somebody blew the shit out of us, and they carried that damn flag."

A strange voice interrupted. It was Slim, the man who had been crushed by a tank. Everyone was silent. "Do you want to know what I owe a country that lets pukes like that carry the NVA flag?" Slim reached down and pulled out his penis. "I owe those American brothers Dick Shit. They owe me the fucking world."

# 14

I AWOKE THE following morning to the clang of a breakfast tray on my bedside table. I ached all over. My muscles were stiff and burning. It was the same sensation as the morning after a really tough football game.

Steve felt the same. Still, we had developed healthy appetites from all our physical labor, and we were surprised how much stronger just one day's therapy made us feel.

Soon, however, the corpsman gathered up the trays and turned the radios down, and the agony of morning rounds started.

Steve assumed the position the doctor always had him take for dressing changes. Doc Bone had done a super job of reconstruction on the shoulder joint and scapula. Steve's wound had shrunk considerably, so that the opening was just wide and long enough to thrust a Q-Tip in. The cavity on the inside was larger, and the wound had to be kept open to allow it to heal from the inside out.

Steve closed his eyes to the dull, pulsating ache caused when the packing was pulled out. He let out a frightening groan as he exhaled.

"Looking real good, Steve," the doctor affirmed, as he moved on to my rack.

"Good morning, Rick. How was PT yesterday? I heard you fell pretty hard."

"Yes, sir. PT is a bitch and I did keel over a few times, but what price progress?"

The doctor plunged his index finger into the wound and retrieved several feet of packing. I held tightly on to the bed frame and clenched my teeth. *What a lousy way to start the day,* I thought.

After Doc Bone finished looking at each of the wounds he asked, "What time is your morning PT session?"

"At nine, sir."

"OK, fine. Report to the Dental Clinic immediately afterward. You lost a lot of teeth on the left side from that explosion and there are still a lot of bone and metal fragments in your jaw, gums, and tongue. We've got to get a partial plate made. Then you can start eating on both sides of your mouth again, not just on the right side. Keep up the good work. It's worth it. But don't get your hopes up too high."

"Yes, sir. Thanks."

The doctor hadn't left the ward five minutes when the dressing changes commenced. Crawford had the duty, so the morning started off with disaster.

Crawford worked his magic effectively. When he was finished I pulled my pillow over my face and screamed into it. By the time I felt better, it was time for PT.

Steve walked behind my chair and pushed me through the

halls. When we got to PT, Steve reported to the weight room and found Shultz's smiling face waiting for him.

"Good morning, Markley. I've got a big day planned just for you. Have you been squeezing that ball like I told you?"

"Yes, I have. All day."

"All right, start with those isometrics I showed you yesterday, and I better not catch you faking it." Shultz gave Steve a menacing stare.

"Don't worry about me, Shultz. I wouldn't shit you—you're my favorite turd."

"Don't press your luck, ace. I'll eat you up." Shultz stormed out of the room and went down to the parallel bars.

I was already midway through the bars. Shultz walked up next to me and taunted me. When I made it to the end of the bars, Shultz had me turn around. I lay over one bar and twisted my body around to face the other direction, toward my chair and Gordie. It looked like a hundred yards away, but I slowly pushed myself down the length of the bars. Each step gave the word "torture" a new dimension.

I finally reached Gordie, and Shultz insisted that I turn around and take another trip, but Gordie talked him out of that. He helped me into the chair and elevated my swollen legs. After a five-minute breather I was up again. This time I concentrated on trying to walk again. I just had to solo if I ever hoped to win Cheryl back, and I pushed myself hard. When I reached the end, near Shultz, I automatically turned around and started back for Gordie. Once near my chair I turned again for a third trip. The pain was so terrible that I started to cry, but I pressed on. My legs were swelling terribly. So were my toes. Again the nails punctured the flesh. Halfway through the third run I began to feel faint and nauseated. My legs began to go numb, and I finished the last ten feet using arm strength alone.

Gordie grabbed me and lowered me into the wheelchair. I was unconscious and stayed out for more than four minutes. When I came to, Dr. Graham was leaning over me, holding my wrist to check my pulse.

"Eilert, we understand your desire to get back on your feet, but you don't have to kill yourself doing it. From now on, hold your sets down to two. We want to build up strength and stamina. Do you understand?"

"Yes, sir. I'll slow down. But I've got to walk on my own."

"I told you that it would be difficult just to get you up on crutches. So settle down," the doctor demanded. "You've got a chit for Dental, don't you?"

"Yes, sir. Right after PT." I continued trying to catch my breath.

"Then go right on up there. You've had enough here for to-day." The doctor grabbed a towel and wiped the perspiration off my face, arms, and hands.

I now wasn't strong enough to push the wheels of my chair, so Gordie took me to the elevator and put me on board. When the elevator stopped and the doors opened at Dental, I pushed the chair as hard as I could. My arms burned and tightened, but I rolled right off the elevator and through an open door straight into the clinic.

As I wheeled in, I passed patients with all sorts of horrible facial injuries. Jaws bent and broken. One man had no lower jaw, while others had open holes in the sides of their faces. Their wounds seemed far more horrendous than mine because they were visible.

I moved up to the reception desk and checked in. The Wave on duty had me wait in the corner of the room near two civilian women, probably wives of servicemen. They seemed sickened by the hideous wounds that surrounded them, and when they were called in to see the dentist they were obviously relieved.

A short, dark-haired corpsman came into the room and called my name. When he saw me in the chair, he came over and pushed me into the next room. There, next to the dentist's chair, was a table filled with instruments. I was lifted out of my chair and into the dentist's chair, where another corpsman prepared me for the examination.

"Hello, I'm Dr. Deeds. What hit you?" The voice came from behind the chair.

"A grenade and gunshot, sir," I answered, looking around the room for the source of the voice.

There, to my rear, stood a skinny little guy with cropped hair, a thin moustache, and tiny eyes. He read my chart through. Once seated he moved quickly, probing all over the inside of my mouth, carefully investigating the wound on my left jaw just below the lip.

"Man, that must have been one hell of an explosion, or you must have been very close to the blast," he observed.

"I was almost on top of the grenade, sir," I mumbled with his fist in my mouth.

Several X rays were taken and a tooth-by-tooth examination was made. As he probed the teeth he noted the tooth number and filling location. After checking one filling, he stopped and corrected himself. "It's a piece of shrapnel . . . hell, I thought you had some silver in that tooth," he laughed.

He gave me several shots to numb my mouth. Once the anesthetic took effect he began digging out bits of bone, shattered teeth, and shell fragments. One piece of my jawbone had been blasted back into my throat. It had to be cut out. A tooth fragment was cut out from the bottom of my tongue, and another pulled from the roof of my mouth. Several teeth on the left side had been blown clear off at the gum line. The root and remaining parts had to be extracted—eight extractions in all, not including the incisions made for fragments.

I left the office with my mouth packed with cotton balls and small pieces of gauze. My next appointment was in three days. I must have looked as if my mouth were filled with walnuts.

When I finally got back to the ward, it was time for lunch. I passed; obviously I had to be on liquids for a while.

I was totally miserable. Besides my mouth, my legs throbbed, my arms burned, and I felt sick. When I saw the dressing cart pull up, I went crazy. I couldn't speak but I mumbled loudly and tossed all over my bed. This was all I needed. *It just isn't fair*, I thought.

"This wounded crap ain't all it's cracked up to be," Steve quipped.

"Want an aspirin?" Turk asked with a muffled laugh.

I pressed my head deep in my pillow. Hearing the comments I searched the room for a gun or a bat to silence the group, but the more it hurt the more I felt like laughing or crying. So I laughed. By the time O'Hara finished my dressings I was giggling, with some difficulty, because of the gauze in my mouth. My eyes teared and the pain didn't stop. Miss Altman brought a Darvon, but it didn't help.

Then came the final blow, time for PT. Steve cracked a smile as he walked over to my rack and helped me into the chair.

When I wheeled up to the parallel bars, Gordie wasn't in the area. From behind came the unmistakable voice of my pal Shultz. "Get up on them damn bars," he snarled. I turned my head to flash a mouthful of blood-soaked cotton balls and gauze. I couldn't speak clearly but my eyes begged for leniency. Shultz laughed and picked me up under my arms and planted me on the bars.

I didn't think anyone could feel as bad as I did and still be alive. I could feel the blood rushing to my feet and the pain building. I tried to concentrate on moving down the bars, and fought my way along.

When I reached the end and turned back toward my chair, I began gasping for air. All the cotton in my mouth hampered my breathing. Shultz didn't care. He pressed me even harder to finish the exercise. I was near the breaking point, but not the quitting point. Shultz's smug expression made me more determined than ever to make it. I pulled and pumped my arms, dragging my heavy plastered legs, inch by agonizing inch, until I reached the chair.

Shultz said nothing, possibly because he was impressed. He slowly lowered me into the chair and adjusted the leg braces to elevate my throbbing pins.

By now blood was trickling out of the corners of my mouth. More blood ran from my toes as the toenails continued to dig into the swollen flesh. And I was gasping for air. Just as I started to panic, Gordie reached in and pulled the gauze out of my mouth. I could breathe, but my mouth hurt like hell. Gordie took me to Dr. Graham's office, where the doctor put in fresh packing and wrapped my toes.

"Haven't you got a lick of sense? I told you not to come back here today. If you don't feel any better tomorrow, stay in bed. Slow and easy is the way I want you to go. No more pushing yourself. What's in your head, a woman?"

I paused before I answered. I told myself that I just wanted to be like I was before. But deep down inside I knew I wanted to be the same because of Cheryl. "Yes, sir. I can't be a cripple. I don't feel like a cripple. I feel like me." I wanted understanding and reassurance.

"Get out of here, Eilert."

"Yes, sir."

I returned to the ward. As I passed the nurses' station I spotted Doc Bone and decided to beg for relief. I pulled up behind the doctor and tugged at his coat. "Excuth me thir. Can I get a thot for thith pain?"

I must have been a pathetic sight. I had fresh tear tracks on my cheeks, blood smeared around my front teeth, sweat-soaked pajamas, and bandaged toes.

"Had a hell of a day, Rick?" I nodded. "Just get back from PT? How did your dental appointment go?" The doctor asked with genuine concern.

"Aaaagh," I groaned.

The doctor smiled and peeled away the gauze strips around my toes. "Yeah, you've been to PT all right. Have you met Shultz?" I rolled my eyes to his question, again the doctor smiled. "Nurse, give me Eilert's chart."

The nurse went to the chart cart and pulled my file. He wrote some instructions. "Get Eilert a shot of Demerol. One hundred milligrams, IM." Then, looking at me, he said, "It's been one of those days when you don't know if you should shit or go blind. Get back to your rack and get some rest. I've ordered a shot for you now, tonight, and tomorrow after your one o'clock appointment at PT. I don't want you depending on these shots after PT, but considering your day at Dental, you rate some peace." He grabbed both of my shoulders and gave me a wide Texas smile.

I had tears running down my face. I hurt so bad, and I was so happy the doctor saw fit to help me. "Thank you, thir. Thank you."

Then the doctor saw my hands, blistered and torn from the parallel bars, and he wheeled me back to my rack and had the corpsman help me into bed. Without another word, he left for his appointment in the OR.

*What a wonderful man*, I thought. *That's why the patients love him so. It's not just his expertise as a surgeon, but his compassion. He didn't have to visit the ward. He didn't have to do all the extra things he did for us. But if it weren't for him, a lot of us wouldn't make it.*

The next three weeks were a monotonous schedule of dressing changes and physical therapy. The pain seemed never-ending, as we drove ourselves and each day brought some progress. Finally, I was weaned from the parallel bars to crutches.

They were a new terror. Teetering back and forth with little control of my balance was frightening. To come this far and rebreak a leg was too awful to contemplate.

Meanwhile, Steve went from the boring, painful isometric exercises to the use of weights and stretching exercises. He regained almost complete freedom at the elbow, but he couldn't lift his arm away from his side. His wound was healing slowly but nicely.

During those three weeks visitors were few. Cheryl and I talked on the phone frequently, but never about Florida.

She was confused and I understood she had to get away. That

she wanted to leave when I could possibly come home was difficult for me to handle, but I loved her and was in no position to make demands.

Steve's growing closeness to me made my visitors Steve's visitors. So he didn't feel excluded, except when Cheryl made visits alone.

With each visit to see me, my parents got to know more and more about Steve. They began to feel that he was like another son.

I had several dental appointments, none as bad as the first. Each visit to Dr. Deeds helped rebuild my mouth to its original form. A permanent partial plate was made for the upper left jaw and a removable partial plate for the bottom left.

But the big day came following one of the afternoon therapy sessions. Doc Bone summoned me into the cast tex room. I was afraid a new hole would be cut or some horrendous probing would be done. Instead, the doctor stood off to one side while Crawford removed the casts from both legs.

"What's the matter, Doc, do I need new casts?"

"No, not quite," the doctor responded.

Crawford had removed the top halves of both casts, leaving the cotton gauze wrapping the legs, and the plaster bottoms, still in place. Doc Bone took his scissors and cut through the gauze from crotch to toe. He peeled it back. It stuck from months of perspiration, blood, pus, and drying skin. It hurt but not with normal pain. The area was so sensitive after five months in the plaster, and the room was cold. The nerve endings previously exposed were now under thin layers of skin. Instead of a sharp, hot pain it was a dull ache, like an exposed nerve in a tooth, amplified by the size of the wounds.

Then the doctor grabbed my left leg under the knee and ankle, and held firmly while Crawford pulled the bottom of the cast away. The same procedure was performed on the right leg.

Both my legs were exposed on the examination table. The doctor grabbed each one and tested the union where each break had healed by trying to move the leg at that point. I groaned, but the unions held.

"OK. That's it, Rick. Now you get fitted for a drop foot-brace on the left foot."

"You mean the casts are off for good? Oh, my God. Oh, sweet Jesus. Honest, Doc?" My eyes filled with tears as the doctor nodded. My legs had been saved. The doctors in Nam had wanted to cut, but Doc Bone had saved my legs! I grabbed the man I owed so much to and gave him a huge bear hug. I was so excited I couldn't speak.

"It's been a lot of work, son, but you stuck it out. Don't quit now when we're so close to getting you up on crutches," the doctor said with a happy smile. He shook my hand vigorously and left for surgery.

Crawford worked quickly. Five months in a cast left an unmistakable odor. Even I got a little sick, but I helped Crawford as best I could. It took well over an hour just to get the crud off, and at least I was presentable to the ward population.

Just as Crawford was opening the door I looked down. I'd seen my legs when I was washing them, but now for the first time I noticed how skinny they were and was embarrassed. They were so skinny and formless . . . like two sticks with kneecaps. I felt naked and I pulled my pajama legs down to cover them, but my feet still showed.

"Oh, shit, Eilert—so they look terrible. I ain't staying in here. Now get out!" Crawford yelled as he flung the door open.

I wheeled quickly through the ward. As soon as I pulled myself into bed I threw the sheets over my legs. At first nobody realized the change. Steve sat up to do some isometric exercises. "Hey, Rick, what did Bone do?"

"Nothing, just looked at my legs."

Steve looked. At first it didn't register. Then it hit him. "He took off your casts. The doctor took them off. Far *East*. Hey, everybody, Eilert got his casts off!"

Several people gathered next to my rack to watch the unveiling.

"I'm not showing you deviates my legs. Why don't you all just go home?"

"Come on, Rick. We aren't going to laugh or nothing," Steve pleaded.

When it appeared that they weren't going to leave, I resigned myself to fate. "Oh, all right, but if one of you assholes laugh I'm going to stuff your mouths with two-day-old pus."

"Gross me out, Rick," Ryker cried.

I took a deep breath and slowly peeled back the sheet until it cleared my feet. I waited for a moment to make certain that no one was going to mock me. Then I pulled my pajama bottoms over my knees. Everyone's eyes widened. They'd known I was messed up but hadn't realized the extent of the damage. Both legs were covered with scars, skin grafts, holes where chunks of flesh were gone, and still-open wounds.

Steve held up his fingers to form a cross. "Man, those things look like tree stumps," he chuckled.

"Don't get near a pack of dogs, or they'll be lifting their legs all day," Ron laughed.

The comments and the laughter continued. "Woowee, they're ugly." "Give me some slack." "Man, you've been kissed."

I immediately pulled the sheet back over my legs. "See, I told you this would happen."

"Eilert, I'm going to buy you some Bermuda shorts," Steve laughed.

"Remind me to go to the beach with you. I'll yell, 'Shark attack!' and have the whole place to myself," Turk laughed, holding his belly.

"All right, go back to your holes, you animals . . . you trolls." I was angry, not at my friends but at myself. How could Cheryl or any other woman be attracted to me now?

The patients all left. Steve was still grinning, but he tried to soothe my feelings. "Hey, I'm sorry, but you've got to admit those pins are ugly. So what? Do you really think anybody is going to give you a ration of shit about them? Especially after they find out how you got so screwed up?"

"Hell, I don't know."

Crawford rounded the corner pushing the dressing cart. "OK, Eilert, let's rebandage your ugly legs." He seemed even rougher than usual on this change, mainly because he could now grip the legs and squeeze them. But with the casts off he could move from wound to wound quickly. The final wrap only needed to be done once, instead of several times as when there were windows cut in the casts. The pain still left me in an exhausted heap, but the time spent on the dressing change was cut in half.

"OK, Rick. Get your ass up to the Ortho Clinic. Doc Bone wants you fitted for a drop foot-brace," Crawford said as he cleaned up the dressing cart.

I was quick to oblige. I put on my robe and dropped down into my chair. As I was about to leave, Stumps pulled up next to me.

"Here, Rick, take these," he offered, holding out a pair of white socks. "I'm not going to need them." He smiled, then rolled away.

266

I felt a lump in my throat. Stumps, with both legs gone, knew how embarrassed I was with my horrible, scarred legs. He'd brought me a gift. Anyplace else it wouldn't have meant much. But here it reinforced a bond of friendship, one man's sincere concern for another's pain, both mental and physical.

Stumps had been sent to Philadelphia for prosthetic devices for his legs. But the infection in his left stump had flared up and he was returned to Great Lakes for treatment.

Because my knees wouldn't bend, I coaxed a student corpsman into helping with the socks. My legs had shrunk so much that the socks pulled up to mid-calf. I felt much more confident, though, and went up to the clinic undaunted. One consolation—I missed morning PT, and now I really had something to work on. The real rebuilding process was about to start.

I entered the clinic and was in a different world. There were real people here: women, children, and regular military personnel with common injuries, like broken bones from playing ball, skiing, or falling out of bed. As I passed through the crowded waiting room I felt as if all eyes were on me.

They were.

I checked in with the receptionist and was immediately admitted to one of the examining rooms.

There I found a huge, fat man slumped in a chair, dressed in civilian clothes, and looking as if he hadn't slept in years.

"Excuse me, sir. I'm Eilert. I was to report for a drop footbrace. I'm Dr. Boone's patient."

The man staggered to his feet, hampered by his excessive weight. "Yeah, sure. Get up here on the table," he said as he helped me up. I was astonished by the ease of movement I now possessed with the casts gone. I felt light as a feather and extremely strong.

The man examined the instruction chit from the doctor. Then he pulled out a tape measure and a measuring board for shoes. He pulled my socks off and my pajama leg up, gently made all the measurements, and logged them.

"That's it. Sweet and simple. I'll have the brace and new shoes for you in six to eight days. Good luck." He helped me back on with my socks and into the chair, then dismissed me.

I wheeled out quickly through the packed waiting room to the elevator. I tried hard to comprehend what was happening. Everything seemed to be accelerating faster than I could handle it. After the months of sameness, suddenly life was moving again. It was great.

As soon as I returned to the ward, I was sent up to PT to see Dr. Graham. I didn't mind at all. The way things were going I'd be walking in a few days, I thought.

"Well, Eilert, you got your cast off. How do you feel about that?"

"Great, sir. If you'll excuse the expression, out-fucking-standing."

"Have you been fitted for a brace yet?"

"Yes, sir, just a while ago. I was told I'd have the brace in six to eight days."

"Good, very good. All right, we are going to start you on a whole new therapy. While you're waiting for your brace, report to room number one. We want to start you working on moving those joints." He began to measure the degree of flection in my knees and ankles. "You're going to find that this will hurt some. It's been a long time since your joints have had any tension on them. One thing I want you to work on is standing. Do it at least once every two hours for about five minutes. You'll go to whirlpool for twenty minutes a session, but only submerge your feet, up to and including the ankles. I don't want any of your wounds in that water. Now, if you don't have any questions, get down to room one."

"One thing, sir. How long before I can walk on my own?"

The doctor looked puzzled. "We had this little talk before. You are always going to need crutches. Later, maybe only canes in each hand. I don't see you getting beyond that, and I don't want you to work beyond your ability. It's always conceivable that you can recover to where you ambulate by yourself, but I doubt it. Now, one step at a time. Get to room one."

I wheeled into the room, glancing at the terrible parallel bars.

"Hey, Rick. How did it go?" Steve yelled from a nearby table.

I held my thumbs up. From across the room, everybody's friend—Shultz—ambled up to my chair. "Well, looky here. The little cracker ass went and got his casts off. Get up on that table," he demanded as he yanked the chart out of my lap. Shultz read Dr. Graham's instructions carefully, then stood next to me. "I'm going to work your ass off. You're going to beg for mercy, but I won't care. You're just another smart ass, and I'm not going to take any crap from you."

Shultz pushed my shoulders down until my body was flat on the table. He pulled me to the end of the table so that my legs stuck out into space, with the edge of the table just under the knees.

"All right, bend your knees!" he yelled. He pushed down slowly but firmly on my ankles until the knees bent almost an inch. Then he let up.

I thought my legs would explode. It had been so long since I had bent my knees that they had frozen.

Steve looked on with sympathy. Shultz had been manhandling him for some time and he knew just how hard it was to bend the joints.

Shultz bent my knees down an inch four more times, then dismissed us to the whirlpool room. We got tubs next to one another. Steve's tub was ready for him. All he needed to do was turn it on and plunge his arm in up past the elbow. It was the one task he really enjoyed and looked forward to.

One of the corpsmen overseeing the tubs helped me sit on a wooden platform next to the tub. He pulled off my pajama bottoms and slowly lowered my feet into the warm, swirling water. I had used a whirlpool when I played football, but it had never felt as soothing then as it did now. After ten minutes I could feel some flexibility in my right ankle, and very slowly I worked it around in a circle. But the left ankle lay dead in the water. The only feeling was along the back of the ankle and the bottom of the foot.

After twenty minutes the machines were turned off and we prepared to leave. Steve wheeled me past the burn patients submerged in large pools of water. I'd seen badly burned men before, but these guys were severely wounded as well. Both Steve and I felt ashamed and embarrassed. Here we were bitching about moving joints, while these people suffered even when air touched their bodies. After seeing how they suffered, we remained silent.

I was determined to walk again. Now that the casts were off, my legs felt so light. I felt so mobile. But Dr. Graham had done all but tell me to hang it up, and Shultz had proved how weak and helpless I'd become. How could I walk on my own when I couldn't even stand alone? Questions filled my head . . . not just about my ability to walk. More frightening, I was sure I lost Cheryl—partly because of her decision to go to Florida, partly because of her less frequent visits to see me, but mostly because of my own feelings of failure. I'd recognized my physical shortcomings. Only now could I see what Cheryl had noticed months earlier.

The next five days were spent going back and forth to PT. Then Doc Bone took me back to the OR for another debridement of my right leg. Then there were another three days of shots and dressing changes. Fortunately, I was able to sleep between those changes.

Just as the prosthetics man had promised, my brace arrived. Steve pushed me up to the Ortho Clinic. I was like a kid getting his first bike. I hung my hopes on this brace. Maybe this would be the ticket to walking again.

When the big guy saw me enter the examining room, he staggered to his feet and put a huge suitcase on the desk next to the table.

I pulled myself up on the table. The big man opened the case and held up the brace, which had a shoe attached near the heel.

"Ain't that beautiful? Chrome all up on each side," he boasted.

"Yeah, real cute. I was kind of hoping for something a little less flashy. You know, a brace that doesn't look like a brace," I said with a tone of disappointment.

The brace man was disturbed. "Well, you have to wear a brace, so why try to hide it? This is real workmanship."

The fat man gently lifted my left leg, slid the shoe over the foot, and attached the top of the brace at my knee. He had me stand up to test its fit.

I smiled, "Great. I don't know how a brace is supposed to feel, but it fits fine. Thanks."

Steve helped me slip on the other shoe, which had been built up on the heel and sole about an inch. I had lost so much bone in the right leg that it was shorter than the left. I thanked the big man again and had Steve rush me down to the ward. When we got to our racks I hung my legs over the side of my rack and slid down to my feet.

The pain was terrible as the blood rushed to my toes, but I clenched my teeth and stood firm. I held on to the metal superstructure over my rack and slowly, painfully, moved one leg in front of the other as I walked alongside my bed. There was a terrible burning sensation, like knives, in my knees but I made it all the way to the foot of the rack, where I fell back on my mattress.

For the first time I had stood on my legs without casts or crutches. I got a loud round of applause from my friends.

"All right, Rick. Not bad. Not bad at all. With my help you can achieve anything," Steve laughed. But he knew what I was going through. Every day in the whirlpool he limbered up more. He had regained thirty degrees of flection in his elbow, and almost fifty degrees in his wrists in all directions. In addition he could raise his arm almost four inches away from his side. He could see improvement and wanted to help me achieve as much success.

The following day, after morning dressing changes, I convinced Steve to take me to PT earlier than scheduled. When we arrived I wheeled down to the torturous parallel bars. I pulled up between the bars, dropped my landing gear (the leg braces on the wheelchair), and pulled myself up with my arms. Slowly I shuffled the length of the bars, using my arms as much as possible until I got used to the pain of bearing my full weight on my feet.

When I turned for my return trip I lifted my hands up off the bars and, by sheer determination, began to move forward by dragging one foot, stiff-legged, in front of the other. I took five steps this way before the pain became so bad that I had to get Steve to help me to my chair.

"Damn, Rick, that was fantastic, but for God's sake take it easy." Steve was astonished.

Shultz appeared suddenly. He was irate. "What the hell are you doing, stupid? I never told you to pull anything like this. I ought to smash you, you asshole!" he yelled. That's all it took. Steve went crazy.

"You ass-wipe mother!" Steve screamed. "You so much as come close to him and I'll kill you. Do you read me, you chicken-shit son of a bitch? You've been strutting around here like a cock in a hen house. Well, that just stopped. Every swinging dick up here has killed better than you." His face reddened and the veins on his neck stuck out.

Shultz, a foot taller than Steve, started to move toward him when I rammed him broadside with my wheelchair.

"Do it, you duffus mother. Just do it. We're already hurt, it don't matter, but I'll pop your eyes out and squeeze 'em like grapes," I grunted.

By now a crowd was gathering: a few corpsmen, but almost twenty crippled marines. Dr. Graham came running up through the crowd and jumped between Shultz and Steve.

"Who do you people think you are? Up here I'm God and my people do as I say. You have nothing to do but listen. Do you read me?" he yelled at Steve.

"That asshole . . ." Steve started to say, but was cut off by the doctor.

"You watch your mouth. My people are worth ten of you. You just shut up," he snapped.

Someone in the crowd answered, "You're butt-fucking each other then. Cause you and these shit-for-brains ain't worth anything else."

The crowd cheered and laughed.

"That does it. You've had it, mister. Nobody talks to me that way. What's your name?" the doctor demanded.

"Louis, Harvey M., 2241142, corporal. What are you going to do, cut my hair and send me to Vietnam?" Everyone laughed.

"You'll be court-martialed, that's what."

"You think any of us care what rank we get out at? PFC, Proud Fucking Civilian, beats the hell out of any rank you've got. I'm boarded out, and there ain't shit you can do about it." The marine laughed.

"All right, all you people get to room one and the whirlpool. Break this up. You, Louis, come with me," the doctor ordered.

The group disbanded laughing and cursing. Shultz followed Steve closely into the therapy room, and I rammed the big corpsman from the rear, just behind the knees. Shultz spun around and took a swing but missed me by a foot. Then the two of us just stared at each other.

Two security people appeared in the hall carrying nightsticks and escorted Louis from the floor. He gave the doctor the international salute of defiance, his center digit raised high in the air. That brought applause from his comrades.

The rest of therapy and whirlpool was quiet. There were hard looks and gentle nudges exchanged but that was all.

When we returned to the ward, word of an uprising had preceded us and we were mobbed by the other patients. The nurses gazed sternly at us but said nothing. The patients laughed and cursed. It was something that was bound to happen, and it was just a matter of time before it happened again. Dr. Graham had looked the other way too long. Sooner or later our threats had to become action.

I returned to my rack exhausted by the day's activities and my short unassisted performance. Steve made his way around the ward telling everyone of my amazing display on the parallel bars.

Somehow the lid stayed on at Physical Therapy. Dr. Graham wasn't a bad man or a bad doctor. But he was new. He saw us battered marines as being lazy and always insolent. In reality, we were not satisfied with the low goals set by Therapy. So we took our rehabilitation as our personal responsibility, and we set our own goals. Shultz was an isolated case, like Crawford, but Dr. Graham took our actions as an indictment of his entire staff.

I was issued a pair of crutches that I used constantly, both in Therapy and on the ward. I left my rack once an hour to ambulate around the ward, just to build up stamina.

One day I decided to use the urinal in the head for the first time, but I found I couldn't reach my fly with the crutches under my arms. Fortunately Steve had followed me, and he held the crutches while I tried to urinate. At first the pain was so bad I couldn't do anything, but finally my animal needs triumphed and I let loose. Steve applauded while I held on to the pipe above the urinal for balance and buttoned up my fly.

I turned to Steve for my crutches, but he held them just out of my reach. I took a step toward him. He stepped back, still holding out the crutches. My face turned beet-red in anger and pain. I was so angry that I took three more steps after Steve, who kept smiling as he slowly retreated.

"Markley, if you value life as you know it, you'll give me those crutches!" I yelled. I shuffled forward some more. Steve back-pedaled again. He could see the anger in my eyes, and he told me later that I looked just like a man pulling the trigger to kill. He'd seen that expression before and now Steve was getting scared.

"Markley, I'll kill you. I'll pull your eyes out. I'll tear your lips back to your asshole." My voice was a blur of obscenities as I shuffled after him.

Finally Steve became afraid not only that I would catch him

but also that I would hurt myself. "Rick, Rick, listen to me . . ." Steve yelled as I came closer.

One of the cleaning ladies stood just inside the door to the head. Nobody else was around. She became so frightened by the look on my face that she started to sob.

"Rick . . . stop . . . listen! Rick, you're walking! Do you hear me? You're walking!" Steve screamed.

Suddenly I stopped and looked down. I had gone almost twenty paces on my own. I looked at Steve, then down at my terribly swollen, pounding legs. Huge tears welled up in my eyes.

"Oh, my God . . . oh, God, Steve, I'm walking. I'm really walking." Tears streamed down my cheeks. "Steve, I'm walking . . ." Then I froze as I began to get dizzy. Spots flashed in front of my eyes.

Steve held out the crutches so I could reach them, but he stayed back in case his life was still in danger.

I shored myself up with the crutches under my armpits. A huge smile crossed my face while the tears flowed. "I walked, Steve, I walked. . . . But I'm going to kill you, Markley. Don't ever fall asleep again."

# 15

AFTER FOUR MORE weeks of physical therapy, I was able to get around on crutches. I even tried standing without them. But after thirty seconds I needed something to steady me.

I'd been at Great Lakes for five months. My wounds were 90 percent closed. I was feeling much better, both physically and mentally, and I could feel my strength returning. I tried not to use the wheelchair at all.

"Steve, I've got a favor to ask. Cheryl and my parents are coming up here tonight. When they get here I want you to take them out in the hall by the windows on the other side of the elevators. Make sure they're sitting so they can't see me coming down the hall. I'm going to use my crutches out to the elevators, then I'm going to walk from there to where you're sitting."

Steve's eyes widened with as much apprehension as surprise. "Rick, you could barely take a step today. Don't press your luck. Besides, what are you going to sit on? You still can't bend your knees."

"Look, when I go to sit down just hold out your hand and I'll let myself down in the chair really slow. Maybe I won't bend my knees too much . . . OK? Promise?" I pleaded in a way Steve couldn't refuse.

When my folks arrived that evening Steve suggested they go out in the hall, just as a change. I excused myself to go to the head and said I'd meet them. As soon as they left I pulled out my crutches, which we'd tucked behind Slim's rack, put on my robe, and secured my brace, which was hidden in my bedside table. Slowly I stood up and waited a brief moment to get used to the pain and almost instant swelling. I moved as quickly as I could out of the ward and down the hall past the elevators. The distance was three times longer than any I'd done so far. By the time I reached the last elevator I was exhausted. At the corner I leaned my crutches against the wall and started to shuffle off toward the sitting area—fifteen paces away.

As soon as Steve saw me, he motioned to everyone to turn around.

"Hi, all. Mind if I join you?"

Everyone looked around and at first they didn't realize it was me. Then my mother's eyes lit up. "Good God. This is fantastic, just wonderful. I didn't even think that you could get up on crutches." She reached over and guided me to a chair.

Cheryl stood, unable to speak at first, tears streaming down her cheeks. "My prayers have been answered. I just can't believe it," Cheryl said finally. "After looking down at you in your bed for so long I can't believe how tall you are."

My father's mouth dropped and tears built up in his eyes. He stood up and walked toward me with his arms outstretched. Steve almost started to cry as we embraced. My father held me tightly, completely overcome with emotion and shock.

"God, Rick, I didn't know you could get up on crutches, let alone stand . . . but to walk . . . thank God," he sniffled, then embraced me again. "I forgot how tall you are, too. After all these months of looking down at you I just lost all memory of before. The doctors said you would never walk again. I just can't believe it." My father pulled out his handkerchief and wiped his eyes.

"Thank Doc Bone, Dad. He did the reassembly and Steve got me to walk without my crutches. Doc Bone really made me straight again. I'd follow him down the barrel of a howitzer," I vowed. Steve nodded. "Amen to that."

Steve was super happy. He knew how hard I had worked to build myself up. Now to see the expression on the faces of my parents and Cheryl made him feel the joy of the moment, too.

My father was speechless and spent much time staring at me. "Rick, how long have you been walking?"

"Not that long. Steve started me off a while back, but I still needed crutches for balance. I just soloed tonight to show you that I work at something during the day."

Steve helped me sit down on a chair, but halfway down my knees buckled with two loud pops. As I bit the inside of my lip, blood started to drip from the side of my mouth. My father's eyes opened wide. "Where's that coming from? Not your insides, I hope," he asked frantically.

"No, Dad, no. The dentist was working on my mouth. It must still be bleeding some. It's OK."

Steve rolled his eyes as he watched my face.

"Now hear this. Now hear this. Visiting hours are now over. Will all visitors please leave the hospital," a voice blasted over the PA system.

My father stood up and grabbed his coat. "Are you going back to the ward now?"

"No, Dad. Steve and I will stay here a while and have a butt," I said, softly praying that I wouldn't have to stand again.

"OK, son. See you soon. I'm so happy for you. Good night, you two." He shook our hands then left.

My mother bent over and gave me a kiss. She was still shaking with excitement. She said nothing, just squeezed my hand and walked over toward the elevator with my father.

Cheryl was in tears. I hadn't seen her that emotionally upset since I'd left for Vietnam. She bent over and gave me a wonderful hug and kiss, then quietly whispered in my ear, "I love you. I really do love you. This is the happiest day of my life. I'm so happy for you." Her voice quivered. She turned quickly and walked away.

My legs hurt so bad I couldn't move or stand.

We waited until we were sure they were gone before we spoke. "Man, am I glad they left. . . . I mean, my legs are killing me. I couldn't have lasted much longer. I didn't want to start crying in front of them," I sighed as I pulled my legs up and laid them on a nearby chair.

"I'm glad I don't have to walk on your legs. I'll go get your chair," Steve said as he got up and hurried to the ward and returned with Chief and my wheels.

Chief lifted me into the chair and got me back to my rack. He removed the brace and shoes from my swollen and bleeding feet. Then he got fresh washclothes and cleaned me up, while Steve lit me a cigarette.

"Woowee, Eilert, you sure don't know when to quit. Why not have Chief whip you before lights-out? Better yet, fix Shultz up with Cheryl. He'll be gentle," Steve joked as he watched Chief care for me, like someone washing a body for burial.

"Thanks, Chief. That feels so much better. Boy, if my girl

dumps me, will you marry me? I'm lousy in bed, but I can cook," I chuckled.

After lights-out neither of us could sleep, but rather than talk we closed our eyes and thought about the events of the day. After an hour of silence there was a muffled pop from outside. Minutes later O'Hara and McCarthy came running into the ward laughing. They went to Steve's rack, certain he was up.

"Hey, Markley, did you hear that?" O'Hara asked. "Someone shot Shultz. Ain't that something? I heard what you two went through up in PT . . . I just thought you'd like to know. Now, go to sleep."

The ward cheered and applauded. Nobody was at all surprised, except possibly Shultz.

Steve laughed, "I'm sure Shultz thought all those threats were so much hot air. If I had a marine tell me he was going to shoot me, I'd damn well believe him. These turkeys back here think all this is just a game. We're playing for real and they're just going through the motions."

"I wonder if he's dead," Turk growled. "I hope not. I'd like to see him live. If he does live he'll never pull his tough-guy stuff anymore. Shultz is like a lot of these athletic types. They think because they can punch you out they're rough. Everyone knows fighting is stupid—you just get cut and bruised—but if you got to fight, fight for real and blow them away."

The following morning at breakfast, the word went out that Shultz had been shot in the chest and was in Intensive Care. His wound was not severe. No vital organs had been hit—a few ribs were broken but nothing serious. Shultz never knew who'd shot him. He was sent up to Five South for three weeks, then sent home on twenty-day convalescent leave, and off to Vietnam. Nobody ever heard of him again.

Doctor's rounds were the usual grunts and groans but with a new twist. New casualties were pouring in. They required beds, so all patients who were recovering well and could ambulate were being discharged to Marine barracks. On my side of the ward Young was the first to go. He was nearly healed and could get around well on crutches.

The doctor studied Steve's wound very carefully. He seemed to be a marginal case. "Markley, do you want to get out of here today?" the doctor asked, as he continued to finger the small hole in Steve's shoulder.

Steve was completely surprised. He knew he was recovering, but for some reason he'd never really considered leaving the hospital till now.

Steve stammered as he answered, "Yes . . . yes, sir. That would be great. Does this mean I could like get liberty and all?"

"Sure does. You'll go to 38-H. It's a holding company just across the street. You still come here twice a day for PT and dressing changes, but they'll give you casual duty and you'll have to wear your uniform. How does that sound?"

"Great, sir, that's just outstanding, but I don't have any clothes. My uniform is crumpled up in my seabag," Steve said excitedly.

"No trouble. Get what you can from the people here and have the corpsman take your uniform to the cleaner."

Steve nodded and the doctor moved on to my rack. Steve scuttled to get his gear together.

I started doing the same.

"Hey, Eilert, you're not going anywhere. I still have to do some cutting on you."

"Oh, come on, sir. I need to leave. I can walk. I really can. Watch." I slid out of my rack and stood firm while my legs and feet swelled and turned from red to blue. I took two steps forward, then pulled myself back into bed. The doctor and his entourage applauded and smiled approvingly.

"That's great, Rick. Really good. Keep it up, but you're staying here." The doctor discussed it no further. He stripped the wound of its bandages and left instructions to continue as usual, then continued on to the next man.

I felt terrible. I wanted to get out so badly. Now my best friend was leaving. It was like the Nam all over again. You get tight with someone, he gets killed or wounded, or he rotates, and you're left all alone. I really needed those late-night discussions. Steve understood me. I felt abandoned.

Steve was too excited to think about anything but leaving. He got on the military shoes that he had stashed in his bedside table, then went from bed to bed to find something to wear. He found a pair of white socks, trousers that were three inches too short, and a shirt one size too large.

"I really look stupid," he laughed, "but I'm getting out of the hospital and that's all that matters."

His farewells were over quickly. He had to report in at Building 38-H. Meanwhile, I called home.

"Steve, after you get set in the barracks, give me a call. I got hold of Tuna. He said he'd bring up some of my clothes for you to use. You can go home with him this weekend. If nothing else, he'll get you drunk on your butt."

"Rick, that would be outstanding. My first weekend out in the world would be awful boring just wandering around. Just think, little buddy, tomorrow night Steve Markley will be let loose on an unsuspecting public. Lock your doors and hide your daughters, America." We both laughed. "Take care, Steve, and let me know what you do this weekend. I want the truth. See you later." Steve gave me a salty salute and left the ward carrying a plastic garbage bag full of goodies that he had saved from all the Red Cross visits.

Once Steve left, I started to feel low. We'd been such good friends and we had so much to talk about. Now I would have to find another gimp who had a sense of humor and something to say. I didn't have to wait long. Miss Bixby came to my rack and chatted for a few minutes, then announced that I was going into the solarium along with Hans.

"Hot damn, is that for real? Don't toy with me, Miss Bixby. I'm really going to have a home in the passion pit."

"Come on now, Rick, help me get some of this stuff out of here. Why call it the passion pit?"

"Why, Miss Bixby, just think about visiting hours and two young lovers who want to be alone. What better place in the whole hospital to be all by yourself than the solarium? As long as your roommates agree to give you some time."

"So that's why the door is always closed during visiting hours. No wonder that the boys are always in a good mood in there. Leave it to you guys to find something to use for sex."

"Miss Bixby, you cut me to the quick. Sex isn't all that comes with the solarium. There's no time limit on TV use. All you have to do is close the door and turn up the sound. I'm finally going south."

"What's that supposed to mean?"

"The solarium is the south part of the ward. The three men in the room are the most senior men on the ward and generally the ones closest to getting out. All the patients set their goal at being one of the 'three south.' Sounds kind of confusing doesn't it? Three South is the ward and the three south are the men in the racks in the south solarium."

"I get it. I never looked at it that way. I used to believe that you marines never thought about anything other than sex. I guess I was wrong . . . you think about sex in the solarium."

I was laughing as we piled my gear into a cart. Then I threw myself into a wheelchair and made tracks for my new home. Miss Bixby trailed after me with the cart, and set my personal items on my locker in the new room. Hans Corte had already moved in and was putting his gear away. Brandy, who had been there for two months, watched us moving in.

"Welcome, gentlemen, to your new home, one of the finer rooms available in this institution," Brandy said.

Hans had been hit with a mortar. It paralyzed his lower left leg, blew off his kneecap and elbow, and scarred the rest of his body. He'd been on the ward seven months by this time.

His girl, Pat, had moved from their hometown near Flint, Michigan, to the Great Lakes area. She got a job nearby and visited Hans at lunchtime and every evening. She was a wonderful girl. She was always enthusiastic and supportive. I was happy for them and envious at the same time. Both were nineteen years old, and they really knew how badly they needed each other.

Brandy had had a Claymore mine go off on him. It shattered both his legs below the knee and tore large chunks of flesh from his thighs. He was the opposite of Hans, loud, arrogant at times, and without a girl. He'd seen a lot of action in the Nam. He was twenty-two years old, with four years in the Marine Corps, and was an old man by our standards. Brandy proved to be a good counterweight to the other personalities in the solarium. Hans and I looked at our past and future with some degree of emotion. Brandy looked at everything clearly and logically. Common sense was his strongest trait. We soon became good friends.

That evening Tuna brought my clothes from home for Steve, along with two large pizzas. Hans, Brandy, Steve, Tuna, and I laughed the night away. We listened to Tuna detail where he was going to take Steve on liberty and what kind of girls they were likely to encounter.

I was happy to think about Steve's finally getting out on the town and even happier that he found someone to show him around. We were all going to live vicariously through Steve. He'd be visiting all the people and hangouts that I'd have been going to had I been out.

A few days later, Ron developed complications. His stump had become infected. The doctor took him to surgery. He was in the OR for four hours and the entire ward was very concerned. When he was brought up from the recovery room, all the people that could get out of their racks surrounded Ron's rack to see how he was doing. Ron joked around and waved his stump.

The following morning after breakfast, the corpsmen were searching for Ron. He wasn't to be found. One of the corpsmen who formerly had been on Three South had seen a patient, on crutches and wearing only his pajamas and a robe, making tracks for the front gate. He realized that it was rather odd, but then thought it was a bet or a prank. In truth Ron had gone AWOL, and couldn't be found anywhere.

Life settled down on the ward. The days and nights seemed to pass quickly. Hans, Brandy, and I would play cards all day, then watch the TV late into the night. It got to the point where what we watched wasn't important, only the fact that it made time pass. The Nam was still a big part of our lives. The constant reports, letters from friends still there, and our own wounds were constant reminders of the nightmare we had survived.

My wounds were very nearly closed on the surface of the leg, but inside, the holes still extended down to the bone. I now had osteomyelitis in both lower legs. This is a chronic infection in the bone. The area becomes extremely tender and the bone itself feels like it's throbbing. Drainage is constant, usually pus or a yellowish discharge. High fevers are common and continuous. This infection can become dormant and reappear years later, or it can stay active forever.

Dr. Boone's visits increased. When I first came on the ward, the doctor's visits had only been during the morning rounds. Now he visited every other afternoon, too. Although he didn't say so, I believed that the chance I would lose a leg was increasing. The infection wasn't going away and the wounds on my right leg were closing very slowly. The doctor decided to start a new treatment on the deep wounds. Twice daily during dressing changes, the corpsman was to ream them out with a Q-Tip and make them bleed, then pack the holes tight with sugar: regular, granulated, table sugar. The doctor said that it would promote tissue growth. The sugar turns into liquid and at each dressing change is washed out with Dakin's solution and hydrogen peroxide. Then the wound is caused to bleed and more sugar added. I was amazed. It seemed to me that medicine was going back to rattles and feathers. The doctor laughed heartily.

"Don't worry, Rick. We've used the procedure before, and it's been very successful. I'm still not certain about the left leg. It's not responding to any of the antibiotics except the Keflin shots, and then with only marginal results at best. You still may lose it. I'll do what I can, but I want you to know where we stand. In the meantime, one of the veterans' groups has an amputee that comes around and talks to the guys about losing their limbs. I think it would be a good idea for you to talk to him. Just so you've got an idea of what's involved."

"Yes, sir, I'd appreciate that. Hell, I like visitors anyway."

Actually, I'd come to depend on the idea that my leg would be saved. The idea of losing it, after all that I had gone through, took my breath away.

Steve was going to get liberty so he could spend the Easter holiday with me and my family. The anticipation of going home, even if only for a seventy-two-hour period, was wonderful. Over and over in my mind, I planned how to spend each and every hour with Cheryl. Just the thought of being alone with her, to talk to her without having forty people around me. There was so much that I wanted to say to her. I might even give her an engagement ring as I'd planned to do when we were on R&R in Hawaii. Of course, I forgot about Cheryl's plan for going to Florida with her friends. I wanted to forget. After her display of emotion when I walked, and during her later visits, I fooled myself into thinking that she wanted to stay home.

The day finally arrived. The doctor was giving out passes for the patients to go home on liberty, and as soon as I got the OK to go, I called Steve, who was in Patient Affairs, then phoned home to get a time for my mother to pick us up. After hanging up on my folks, I called Cheryl.

"Hello, Cheryl. This is Rick." I didn't even wait for her to say anything. I was just too excited. "Cheryl, I get to come home this weekend for Easter. Isn't that terrific? Maybe you could pick me up instead of my mother."

"Rick, that's wonderful, but I'm not going to be here this weekend. Remember, I told you before about going to Florida with my girl friends? I'm sorry but I can't change my plans. Rick, you didn't know for sure if you could get out of the hospital."

"You've got to be kidding me. I haven't been home and alone with you for a year, and now that I'm getting out you can't change your plans? You would rather be with your girl friends than me. That's just out-fucking-standing."

"Rick, I told you I was thinking of going down there. Don't get mad at me. I'll lose my deposit if I don't go."

"You mean to tell me that you're not going to be with me because you'll lose your deposit? No trouble, I'll give you the money you put down. Now you won't lose a thing."

"No, I can't do that. I've got to go. You don't understand. Rick, I have to get away. Even for a few days. I'll come home early so I can see you Easter Sunday. Just try to understand. I need a little time to myself—away from you, my home, my parents, and my job."

"I understand. Enjoy yourself." I hung up the phone. I felt as if my insides had been ripped out. I had to catch my breath. I knew I didn't have any right to believe that she really cared; I'd suspected all along that something was wrong. Still, it hurt. I didn't think anything could hurt me after what I'd been through. It was for Cheryl that I'd fought so hard to come back from the Nam, and from my wounds. Now, it was as if a rug had been pulled from under me. I felt lower than a snake's belly.

In a world full of people, I felt all alone. I lay back into my rack, closed my eyes, and tried to think of nothing but the pain in my legs. Steve came up from Patient Affairs with my pass to get out of the hospital.

"Here you go. Let's bug out. Have you talked to your folks about picking us up?"

"Yeah, Steve, my mom will pick us up in an hour. Chief went down to get my seabag, and my uniform is hanging in the closet there. I've been shining my shoes for the last five days."

"I bet Cheryl is going to shit when she finds out you're coming home. When are you going to call her?"

"I did. She shit, all right . . . on me. She's going to Florida with her girl friends." Steve sat down in the chair next to my rack, shaking his head.

"I can't believe it. After all this time putting on this big show, she goes with her girl friends, instead. Ain't love precious? Well, then we're both in the same boat. May as well get drunk. Tuna sure helped me forget my troubles before—I bet he could help us again."

"No shit. I'm going to call Fast Eddie. Maybe he can set us up with some ladies. I'll be damned if I'm going to cry over this. Somewhere out there is a woman who knows what love is. Maybe even a hundred of them. What's that saying? When you're not with the one you love, love the one you're with. Yeah, that's it—our platoon sergeant had that on his lighter."

"Let's get hot, Eilert."

I pulled my dress uniform from the closet and started to get dressed. I was surprised at how much weight I'd lost. I'd gone into the Marine Corps weighing 200 pounds, but after boot camp I was 175. Now, even after putting on a few pounds in the last couple of weeks, I weighed 145. Steve helped me get on my brace for the left leg.

"Steve, I feel like a walking skeleton. The damn medals weigh more than I do. By the way, did you get my ribbons for the uniform?"

"Yeah, right here. They're checking pretty close over at 38-H that your uniform is squared away. You're lucky you got this damn thing cleaned. I hear that they're making some guys go back and get the uniforms ironed. Hell, my whole time in the corps and this is only the third time I'll wear the damned thing off base."

"Steve, look at this. Talk about a squared-away marine. Look how this uniform fits. Man, it looks like I'm on leave from Auschwitz. Let's get out of here. Mom's already on her way."

The two of us went and picked up our passes to get off base, then returned to the hospital for the ride home. I used my crutches but I was still exhausted. This was the first time I'd been outdoors since the bus ride from Glenview. The excitement of the whole day made the pain seem mild, yet my leg had swelled up to twice its size. We didn't have to wait long before the car pulled up. My mother had never seen me in my winter uniform, and it had been so long since she'd seen me dressed in anything other than blue pajamas that she had to look twice to make sure it was me.

Once we were inside the car, my mother wasted no time in pulling out. It was a strange sensation, the smooth quiet ride of an automobile, the radio on. Both Steve and I were in heaven. Steve had already been out three weeks, but the newness of the world hadn't worn off yet. He marveled at everything. Every mile or two we would scan the tree lines and remark about how ideal the spot would be for an ambush. At one point a gust of wind shook a sign near the highway. The swish it made sounded like a rocket and the two of us started to dive to the floor. We looked at each other and started laughing. How foolish we must have looked. It happened five more times before the car turned down the tree-lined streets near home. When the car pulled up in front of my house, I thought I was going to cry. It hadn't been a dream after all. My senses came alive. I took in a clean, clear whiff of air untainted by the smell of gunpowder, pus, rotting skin, or burned flesh. I could hear the sounds of kids playing, laughter, babies crying. I could sense the spring-time. My sisters and brother came charging out of the house, screaming and crying. How could I ever have thought of leaving this place, as often as I'd thought of it in my younger years? As I stood up I didn't know who to grab first. I spread my arms and engulfed as many as I could touch.

I looked around at all the familiar sights that, as a boy, I'd explored and taken for granted. Across the street and set back a way was the field where I had played cowboys and Indians, hide and seek, and army. All the times I'd been shot there, yet re-covered in time to eat dinner.

I heard people talking around me, but I was so taken with the moment that no one person or thing had all my attention. I started to make my way to the front door.

"Mom, will you close the door and lock it, please?"

"You want me to close and lock the door?" I nodded. She did so without any further questions.

Many men wore the key to their front doors around their necks, next to their dog tags. I was no exception. I made my way up the front stoop and stood inches from the door, then pulled the key off my neck, unlocked the door, and pushed it open. How many of my friends would never be able to do this. But the joy of being home took over, and I wasted no time in going right to the kitchen and the refrigerator. The rest of the day was spent in phone calls and visits from neighbors and friends. When my father got home from work, the cycle started all over again with a thousand questions, and I was happy to answer them over and over again. Dinner was a feast. All the things that I loved to eat were there for Steve and me. We ate as if someone were going to take all the food away at a set time, as they did with the dinner trays. After dessert and coffee, Steve and I went to my bedroom, where we changed each other's dressings. My mother insisted that she watch. She'd never seen my wounds and was curious. She almost lost her dinner, excused herself, and returned to the kitchen. As Steve was finishing my dressings, he found that we had forgotten the sugar.

286

"Hey, Mrs. E, we could use some sugar up here." She came running up the stairs carrying the sugar bowl.

"I didn't see you bring your coffee up here."

Steve took the sugar away from her. "The sugar isn't for my coffee. It's for your son's leg." She almost died when she saw the sugar being jammed into the wound. Steve turned for another request. "Now could I have a glass of Scotch. Hold the ice, hold the water."

"Where are you going to put that?"

Steve smiled. "My mouth. I'm thirsty."

Once the dressing changes were over, we went to the front porch. Tuna was waiting.

"I wish that they could have taught me how to walk down stairs, too. That part doesn't start until next week. Come on Steve, quit falling behind."

"Rick, I draw the line at wearing my uniform from here on out. Let's get our goin'-to-meetin' clothes on."

Back up the stairs we went. Tuna had to do most of the dressing for us. There were some positions that we just couldn't do. Finally we were ready to take on the world. We decided to start by visiting the mother of a close friend of Tuna's and mine. We were only going to have a few drinks, then go looking for some ladies. When we arrived at the house, we already had a few in the car. I'd forgotten how easy it was to talk to Mommy, as she was called by all that knew her. She was a remarkable lady who'd lived as much as anyone I'd known. She could talk on any subject, and she knew how to tip her glass with the best of them. She'd been a frequent visitor to the hospital, but most of all, she was one person who'd stood by me during some of my hardest times before I'd entered the service. The night went on longer than expected. Steve and I both got very drunk. Tuna drove us home and helped us to my room. Then he got us undressed and put us to bed.

The next morning we awoke with ferocious hangovers. I sat up to investigate my legs. The left one had regular Band-Aids on it, about twenty of them. My right leg had a Q-Tip sticking out of it. We'd changed each other's dressings before we went to sleep. It was obvious someone had been drinking.

"Hey, Dr. Kildare, look what you did to me. Man, my legs are killing me."

"What the hell did you put in my back?"

ve turned around and I saw the end of a sock sticking out
s scapula, with the other sock taped over another hole.

)amn. I'm sorry, Steve. I thought it was gauze." We started laughing.

My mother stuck her head in the doorway. "Wow, this room smells like a liquor store. Hurry down, breakfast is almost ready, and the extra towels are next to the tub."

We finished changing our dressings, this time with some of that old-time pain. My leg was so swollen that the skin was tearing.

"Steve, how about we take it easy for a few hours. My legs look like I've got elephantiasis."

"I'm with you. Man, I need some coffee. I'll use the shower downstairs; you use the one up here. See you at the kitchen table."

After we'd both showered and eaten, we retired to the family room for some darkness and quiet in hopes that our headaches would shrink some. They eventually did.

That afternoon I got a phone call from Ed. We had gone through high school and college together. The only difference was that Ed didn't get booted out.

"Hi, Rick. How are you doing?"

"Great. I'm trying to recover from last night's visit with Mommy."

"Got you, you went for one drink and you left six hours later. Say, I've got just the girl for you. There's a party tonight, and she's free, in many ways. Do you like Julie Christie?"

"You're kidding. Who doesn't?"

"Well, this girl looks just like her—I'm not kidding. She'd be glad to go out this evening and said she looks forward to meeting you. Tell Steve that there's going to be some women there without dates, so there's a chance that he can hustle up something. Pick you up in an hour and forty-five minutes."

"You're really fast, Eddie. Sounds real good. See you in a bit. Thanks.

"Steve, listen to this, my date looks like Julie Christie. Now that's the way to start my new love life."

"You son of a bitch. If she is really that nice, you better not let her out of your sight. Tonight I take prisoners. There are going to be some stag women at this party, aren't there?"

"So he says. Anyway, we're all going in his car."

Ed arrived promptly. We wasted no time in picking up the girls. Beforehand, he prepared me for my date.

288

"I really wasn't kidding you. This girl is fantastic. It's a shame that I'm dating Sharon. It seems every time I get some time away from her, the girl I pick up is a friend of hers."

"Enough of that. You certain that there will be some extra ladies there? Steve said he felt funny going to a party where everyone has a date."

"I'm not sure how sociable the other girls are going to be. Military people aren't exactly popular right now. Steve, do you have a girl back home?"

"I did. . . . Right now I'm available. Not to mention being in heat. I appreciate your asking me to come along. I just hope I can still talk to girls like before."

Ed jumped out of the car and ran up the stairs. He and the two girls appeared in the doorway in short order. Steve didn't say a word when he saw my date. His mouth just dropped open.

She slipped into the car next to me. Steve wasted no time in moving close to her. Before any conversation started, we both had put our arms up around the seat in back of her. Ed made a quick introduction, while Sharon gave me a kiss and a hug. Ed and Sharon had double-dated with Cheryl and me several times during past years.

"Rick, it's so good to see you. Are you feeling well?"

"Sure am, Sharon, thanks." I quickly turned my attention to my date.

"Hi, Maria. It's nice to meet you. I really appreciate you coming along this evening. I know it was short notice."

"No, it wasn't any problem at all. Besides I've looked forward to meeting you. Ed and Sharon have said a lot of nice things about you." She then turned to Steve. In thirty seconds he was in love with her.

It was a short drive to the apartment where the party was being held. Everyone was able to get out of the car quickly, except for me. I hadn't any strength in my legs, and sitting in the backseat I was forced to bend my knees, which made getting out very difficult. It embarrassed me no end. Here I was barely five minutes with my date and I couldn't even get out of a car. My legs were still swollen and sore from the previous night, and I had to use my crutches for everything. Even the easiest maneuver was impossible without something to help bear my weight. Once out of the car, I ran into another obstacle. The apartment was on the second floor. Steve had to carry my crutches and stand behind me to help me climb the stairs. Once on the landing everything was fine. Ed knocked on the door and a young girl opened it to greet her guests. She stared at Steve and me, seeming annoyed at our presence. She wasn't alone. Once inside the living room all the other guests stopped talking and moved to one side of the room. Ed made the introductions and everyone was very cordial. But it was obvious that we were welcome only because of their friendship with Ed and Sharon.

Maria, Steve, and I took up one of the couches, Steve leaving only to freshen up the drinks. Maria was really a terrific lady. She knew how uncomfortable we were and how uneasy the rest of the people felt. She tried to get conversations started with some of the others, for the most part successfully.

As the evening went along and everyone had been drinking for a while, the people mellowed. Steve and I did everything to avoid the subject of Vietnam. But our luck didn't hold.

One guy that had been really putting the booze down jumped right into my shit. "How many people did you kill? Don't include the babies you killed, just the men and women."

The room went silent. Ed tried to get the guy to settle down, but couldn't. I was hurt by the accusation. I started to get up but couldn't because the couch was too low. That's when the people started to laugh at me. The remarks about our "murderous" behavior continued. Steve got up to kick ass, but was held back by Ed and our host.

"Come on, Rick, it's time to leave. Steve, help Rick up and let's get out of here," Ed suggested.

As soon as we left and got into the car Steve started to explode. It was all Ed and I could do to calm him down. I apologized up one side and down the other to Maria.

"I know this wasn't the kind of evening you had in mind. I'm really sorry. I had an idea something like this might happen. If not now, then later. I really like you, and I'd like to see you again when I get out of the hospital."

"I'm sorry, too. That idiot goes out of his way to make trouble. I used to go to high school with him. I like you, too. You're very easy to talk to. I'd like to see you again. Being with you and Steve tonight was really interesting. It's amazing that you guys are twenty years old. You seem as old as my father in some ways."

I put my arms around her and kissed her. What a kiss it was.

The car ride back to Maria's apartment seemed even shorter than the ride to the party. When the car rolled to a stop in front of her complex she planted another big kiss on me.

Steve got out on his side of the car to let Maria out. Just as he was about to get back into the car, he changed his mind and walked her to the front door. Then he ran to hold the lobby door for her. I knew what was going on and started cussing him out and then laughing. Fifteen minutes later he reappeared at the car door.

"Markley, you asshole. What were you doing with that innocent flower? What a friend."

"Come on, Rick, she could have been attacked in the hallway. I just wanted to thank her for talking to me. The other girls at the party didn't seem too interested. . . . OK, so I kissed her good night. So what."

"So, ass-wipe, when you kiss a girl her belly swells up." I began to laugh.

"She's got a terrific body, doesn't she?" Steve just nodded. Ed turned around, laughing.

"You two have a good time tonight, other than that asshole at the party?"

"Ed, you were right about Maria—she really is a great girl. She could have acted like all the others at the party, and I'm not too sure I would have blamed her. Instead she was really wonderful."

After Ed had dropped us off, we decided to sit on the porch and sober up a little before making the long journey of six steps to bed. Steve had Maria on the brain.

"Rick, I got to tell you, I really like Maria a lot. I asked her if I could see her next weekend and she said yes. Do you mind? I just don't want to date her behind your back. I know how busted up you are over Cheryl. Maria makes a love life seem possible—that's great for your ego."

"Hell, Steve, no telling how long I'll be in that damn hospital. There's no way I could get a romance going from my rack. Cheryl proves that. I just as soon have you taking care of her needs as lose contact with her completely."

"You're a prince, Eilert. I owe you one."

"You sure as hell do. I give you a queen, I expect nothing less upon demand, or two future draft choices, or cash. You *bich*?"

"What if I don't agree to those outrageous demands?"

"You don't get her phone number and last name."

Steve shook his head. "I've been in the jungle too long. I completely forgot to ask her. Rick, as a friend, a fellow marine, by all that is holy, what's her number? Listen, I've still got to change your dressings in the morning. Would you rather that Jody took over again?"

"Here it is. I wrote it down."

On Easter morning the whole family went to church. The last time either Steve or I had attended a service we were wearing flak jackets and helmets and carrying rifles. Even then there was a chance that Charlie might snipe at us, or drop in a rocket or two. We never intentionally hung around together in a group of people because that was a sure target. When Steve and I walked into the church, we panicked. It didn't matter that it was safe, that we were back in the world. We broke out in a cold sweat and retreated to the back of the church for the rest of the service. Afterward, we went home and waited out the day, loafing around until Easter dinner.

When we went to the table, we wanted to taste a little of everything rather than miss a single delicacy. We made pigs of ourselves, but my mother was happy to see it. She was a terrific cook and loved to see people enjoy her meals. After dinner, there was little we could do other than lie down. I had to psyche myself to return to the hospital the following morning. The pleasure of life at home was easy to become addicted to. Even the horrors of dressing changes didn't seem so bad when done at home.

I was tired, but still keyed up from the last two days' activities. I decided to sit on the front porch. No sooner had I sat down than Cheryl drove up in her father's car. I went up to say hello to her.

"Rick, get in the car. We can go for a drive."

"Sure, OK." I climbed in and she drove out to the local forest preserve, where she stopped the car and turned the lights off.

"Why aren't you still in Florida?"

"I felt terrible about your being here all by yourself. I'm just mixed up. I know I love you, but I'm not sure I want to get married. I still want to date other guys and I think it would be good for you to date other girls. I'm not trying to hurt you."

"I don't think that you're trying to hurt me, but it's impossible not to. I understand what you say. I don't believe it, but I understand it. You're right that we should date other people. I did this weekend and had a fantastic time."

"Who did you go out with? You don't waste any time, do you?"

"You made it clear that you wanted no part of me. You chose

to spend the time with your girl friends rather than be with me. I've been dealing with pain for a long time now. One thing is certain, I'll get over you."

"But I don't want you to get over me. I can't blame you for being angry—what I did was really selfish. I'm not trying to hurt you, but it seems that all I do lately takes me further and further away from you. Try to understand."

"Hey, I understand. If I was well and you were all gimped up, I'm not certain that I would want the years of taking care of you. It's not an easy decision. And I don't think that I could take just dating you in between other boy friends. I'd rather find a girl who wanted what I had to offer." She started to cry and laid her head on my shoulder. We started to make up for all the time that we had been apart.

"Cheryl, I've missed you so much. I can't count the number of hours I've spent thinking of this moment. What to say? How to act? This very minute has been my dream for almost a year. Now that I'm with you . . . I'm nervous. God, I've missed you." I held her and kissed her gently. I kept my eyes open just to make sure she didn't disappear.

"Rick . . . I couldn't take it if you went away again. I had the same dreams. I constantly worried you would be killed. I never thought about your being wounded. I love you. Please be patient."

Little else was said. Cheryl brought me home. We said our good-byes and she quickly backed out into the street and sped away. I stood in the driveway for a few minutes, thinking of the things we had talked about. Steve came out when he heard the car leave.

"Where were you?"

"Cheryl came by a while ago. We just went out to do a little talking and a little getting-to-know-you stuff. She wants to see me, but still date other guys."

"Oh, I've heard that somewhere before. Is she still going to come up to the hospital?"

"So she says . . . most likely to go to the Rathskeller. I don't blame her, though. I'm not sure I wouldn't do the same thing if the roles were reversed. Let's finish that quart of Scotch."

"Good idea. We've got to be back at the hospital by six tomorrow morning. Would you rather go back tonight or in the morning?"

"Need you ask?"

Several times that evening we pondered the idea of going over the hill, but decided against it . . . we didn't have enough money. We got to sleep at two. No sooner had we closed our eyes, it seemed, than the alarm went off at five. It was dark outside, the sun just starting to come up. We shaved, brushed our teeth, grabbed a cup of coffee, said our good-byes, and made tracks for the base. My father drove like the devil was after him. We arrived at 38-H with five minutes to spare. When I got up on the ward and signed in, I saw bodies all over their racks, still in uniform. I looked at the other times noted on the sign-in sheet. Almost everyone had come back within the last thirty minutes.

I made my way back to the solarium. Then I sat my crutches up against the wall, kicked off my shoes, and crawled into my rack with my uniform on. I was so tired. It felt so good to have my feet up for a change. I pulled the sheet up over me and fell asleep.

The next three weeks went quickly. Steve continued to see Maria. He bought a used car and made mid-week and weekend trips to the hospital. Every time he returned he came to my room to taunt me.

"Hi, Rick. Guess where I've been?"

"You son of a bitch. The thought drives me insane."

"Listen, I need some clothes. Do you mind if I go by your house and pick up a few things?"

"Go ahead, but don't ruin anything."

Steve put on a wide grin. "One more thing, can I borrow twenty bucks?"

"You got more balls. What have you been doing with your paychecks? Is there anything else?"

"Listen, it's rough out there. I've got to take Maria out once in a while. She's getting tired of me coming on Friday afternoon and camping out in her bedroom until Sunday. By the way, she told me to say hi."

"Markley, you're an animal. What does she see in a guy that could breed on an ant farm?" Hans and Brandy laughed themselves sick.

Cheryl came by much more frequently. Easter break had given us a chance to be alone, to talk candidly and reaffirm our feelings. Ever since I'd returned from that liberty, the days had been filled with renewed anticipation of going home for good.

Then the days seemed to go by slower. Sometimes it was easier when I forgot all the little things that went along with being home.

The twice-daily trips to Physical Therapy helped a lot. I was now able to bend my knees without much discomfort. The mobility of my ankles had also improved.

I had two more surgeries—two weeks in a row. The second laid the main wound on the right leg open again. This time the hole was the size of a golf ball, and just as before it had to be packed with sugar. The dressing changes were just as bad as when I'd first come on the ward, and I had to use pain shots. It was even more difficult to sleep. So I went through the same routine as before—late-night visits to the head with the phonograph and records.

Ron had come back from being AWOL for six weeks. Everyone was surprised to see him. They were equally amazed that his leg hadn't become infected.

"Ron, what the hell did you come back for?" I asked as I watched him hop around the room on his good leg.

"Hell, I ran out of money. If they pay me, I'll take off again."

Ron had gone to a private doctor for bandages, antibiotics, and pain medication. He was never court-martialed for his absence without leave. He was soon to be discharged anyway.

"How are you, Rick?"

"Pretty good. My wounds are closing fairly fast. I had the last operation a week ago. The doctor said I may never really heal because of this bone infection. On the other hand it could stay away for years."

We continued to talk. Now that Ron was back there was another hand for cards, another soul to joke around with. The faces on the ward had begun to change and almost everyone I knew well had gotten out. Now that summer was in the wind, all the patients wanted to go outside. The ward was so stuffy and the stench of infected skin and dry blood was so strong that fresh air was a treat.

The following days went by swiftly. The schools had all let out and all of my friends that had been away were now making frequent visits. It felt good for me to have my close friends Tuna, Ed, Mike, and Brian all come up together. It had been so long since we were in the same room together, with all the joking around and talk of women past and present. They began to plan a party for the end of the summer to welcome me home. With each passing day I began to feel better and better about myself and my future.

It was mid-June and a sunny clear day when the doctor came around to announce that I could go home. I was caught completely off guard.

"Good morning, Rick. How are you feeling?"

"Pretty good, Doc. Say, can I go outside with Ron today? Just down to the sun deck. We won't stay out long, I promise. This place is getting to me. Sometimes I think I'm going nuts."

The doctor smiled. "Then why don't you go home today?"

I was shocked. "You mean I can have liberty for a few days? That's fantastic."

The doctor shook his head. "No, not liberty. Convalescent leave until your discharge comes through." I was speechless. "I've already cut your PEB, the Physical Evaluation Board report. You have to be over at Building One to see the board this morning. They read your PEB to you, and if it all sounds good and nothing has been left out, you sign it and then check out of the hospital and go home."

"*Oh, my God,* you're serious. My God . . . I, ah . . . I . . . *thank you* . . . ah, thanks, sir. I never thought I was ever going to hear that. What happens at the board in Building One?"

"They just review your disabilities and determine how disabled you are, and that determines how much of a pension you're going to get. Then they'll explain how you go about getting future medical care from the Veterans Administration. You'll also be told what you're entitled to as a retired serviceman. You have to be able to walk on crutches all the way to the board. They feel if you can't make the hike over there, then you're not well enough to get out. After that you come back here. Check out at Security, the Cashier's window for any phone calls you've made and not paid for, and Patient Affairs. Then go over to Marine barracks and get your picture taken, get fingerprinted, sign a whole slew of forms, get your orders. Then come back here and clean out your locker and scrub down your rack with Betadine solution. Now that sounds pretty easy, doesn't it? Oh, one more thing. I'll make up prescriptions for you. You'll need medication plus dressing changes to hold you for a while. Don't forget to come by the 'scrips.' This stuff is very expensive on the outside."

"Yes, sir, I'll be back. How far is this Building One?"

"About six blocks away. Now get going. This is going to be a long day."

"Thank you, sir." The doctor then continued his rounds.

I asked the corpsman to get me a phone to call my parents. Mother went crazy with joy that I was coming home for good. She then called my father at work. He, too, was excited. He called me.

"Hello, Rick. This is Dad. You're getting out today?"

"Yeah, isn't that terrific? I've got a bunch of things to do, so don't come up until this evening around five. I'll be waiting in the lobby for you. I've got to get going, so I'll see you later."

"Good-bye, son. See you in a little while." After we hung up I went about cleaning up and getting my uniform on. I'd never been this excited before. It was all happening so fast. Steve came in as I was putting my tie on.

"Hey, congratulations. I saw your orders being cut this morning. If you need a ride later on today, let me know. You're going to be beat by the time you have to go over to Marine barracks. I can get away for a few minutes. If you need a ride home tonight, I get off at seven. We got an inspection today after work, so I have to sit around for that. Have you called your folks yet?"

"Yeah, my dad is going to pick me up about five o'clock. They're really excited, too. Just think of it—I'm going to have dinner at home tonight. Regular old dinner. I can't believe it."

"You're lucky, Eilert. I've got to work till my discharge. You get to lay around at home."

I got my crutches out, said a short farewell to Hans and Brandy, and set out for Building 1. It was all the distance that the doctor said it was. Halfway there I had to lean against a tree and catch my breath. After a five-minute break I started out again. Finally I had the building in sight. It looked a thousand miles away. My hands started to hurt from the crutch handles, and I could feel my legs swelling and the wounds ripping with each step I took. I finally reached the steps in front of the large, red-brick building. At first I tried to climb the stairs as I'd been taught at Physical Therapy. I tired of that quickly and threw my crutches up to the top of the stairs, then pulled myself up, step by step, with the railing.

Once at the top, I picked up my crutches and entered by the huge doors. The building was very old. It was probably used in the French and Indian Wars. I spied a long line of marines sitting on benches on each side of the corridor. I went up to the front desk, checked in, then took my place in line.

It was a very long wait. I was getting very uncomfortable, but knew that if I complained they'd just send me back to the ward until it didn't hurt, and that could be a long time. I could see the pain on all the others' faces as well. After four hours I was finally called. I hurt so bad I could barely move, but move I did.

Once inside the office, I had to stand in front of two officers who read my entire medical history to me. When that was done, I was asked if anything had been left out. When I shook my head no, they signed the forms, then I signed. I was dismissed!

I made my way back out of the building. I gazed out over the parade ground and spotted the hospital off in the distance. Then I started back to the ward. I knew that if I didn't lie down I'd soon pass out from the pain. A half hour later I found my rack. I was exhausted. I pulled my legs up and waited until the swelling went down.

"Hans, will you do me a big favor?" Hans nodded. "Would you please get all my gear together and put it in a plastic bag? I've got a bunch of places to go before I even get to Marine barracks—I'll be back later."

Off I went again. First to Security, where they cut off my identification bracelet, then off to the cashier. I waited in line there for forty-five minutes, standing up, before I had my papers stamped RELEASED. Then to Patient Affairs. Fortunately Steve was working there. He was able to get my papers put through in a matter of minutes. Normally the wait was two hours.

Steve excused himself for a few minutes so that he could take me to Marine barracks.

"Steve, could you go to the ward later and bring down all my gear? Hans is getting it all together. I've got to pick up my seabag, too."

"Sure I will, but right now I've got to get back to the office. We're really swamped, and if they find out I left the hospital, my ass is grass. I'll get your gear and see you in the lobby around five, right?"

"Yeah, great, and thanks for the ride. I'll see you later."

I made my way into the barracks, only to find there were five different stations I had to clear. First they took my picture, then sent me to be fingerprinted for a "discharged" ID card. Then I took a trip to the paymaster to pick up any money I had coming. There I found out that my pay records were gone. I'd have to wait for my money until they were recovered. Then I was sent on to have the officer of the day sign my orders, then to another station to sign some more papers. I looked at my watch. It was four o'clock and the storage department closed at four-thirty. I had to get my seabag before I could leave.

I moved as fast as I could. It started to rain and my crutches sank into the ground every few steps, almost knocking me off balance and sending me into the grass. My hands were swollen, my legs pounding. I was completely exhausted.

I finally arrived at the hospital entrance. The clock on the wall read 4:25. I hurried as best I could to the elevator, which seemed to take forever to come, then I took it to the basement. There I followed the crowds of men moving through a tunnel that led from the hospital to Building 38-H. Everyone was using the tunnel to avoid getting wet. I arrived at the storage compartment just as they were closing the doors.

"Please, please, wait one more minute. Just get my seabag and I can go home." At first the clerk wasn't going to do it, but after seeing the exhaustion on my face, he relented.

The seabag weighed all of forty pounds. I had to shove my hand through the handle on the side, grab the hand grip on the crutch, then try to move with the handle of the seabag digging into my wrist and its weight twisting the crutch. I made my way to the lobby, where Steve was waiting with the gear from my locker. Hans, Brandy, and Ron were also there to say good-bye.

"Well, Hans, best of luck to you and Pat. I've really enjoyed having you around. I thought that you would be getting out long before me. Take care of yourself and write if you get a chance. You only live on the other side of Lake Michigan. Keep in touch."

"I'll do that, Rick. I hope things work out between you and Cheryl. It sure is getting boring around here. Did you know that Doc Bone has been transferred to Five South?"

"No, I didn't. That's a shame for all you old guys on the ward."

"Took me by surprise, too. Come back up if you get bored. I'll still be here." I shook Hans's hand and smiled.

"Brandy, you watch out for yourself, especially with a new doctor. You got away with a lot of shit before, but this new guy might not be the kind of man Bone is. I hope everything at home works out."

"Thanks, Rick. You take care, too. It's been a lot of fun being sick with people like you around." We shook hands, then Brandy and Hans returned to the ward. The dinner cart was coming.

"Ron, stay out of trouble. If things get any worse at home, come over to my folks' place. There will always be someplace for you to hang your hat."

"Thanks, Rick. But I'm not going to be around that long. Payday is next Monday and I have places to go. Thank your mom for me. She's always really nice to me. See you around."

"I hope I will see you. Say good-bye to Smitty for me. He hasn't been around the ward for a while, since he went to 38-H."

"Sure will. I'll get going, got to get some chow."

I watched Ron leaving until I lost sight of his wheelchair. It was hard to say good-bye to friends who had meant so much for so long.

It had been difficult to say good-bye to friends in the Nam. The hospital was very much the same. It's possible to see the best and worst in people when they're very ill. The bond that we formed in Ward Three South was very personal and would last a lifetime. Later on, hardly a day went by when the sight of one of my scars didn't make me recall how they got there and the men who helped pass the time and heal the wounds.

Steve was still standing there. "Well, Rick, take care. I'm not going to say anything nice since I'll be coming to your house every weekend, at least. Maybe we'll get that apartment we've talked about. I've got to get going. I'll see you in a few days. Say hi to your folks."

"Will do. See you soon, and thanks for everything." Steve gave me a salty salute and made his way to the elevator.

My father walked into the lobby.

"Hey there, Mr. Soon-to-be-civilian. Ready to go home?"

"Hi, Dad. Yeah, let's get going." I went to the car and climbed in on the passenger side. My father put all my gear into the trunk. I stared up at the hospital. From where the car was parked, I could see the window of the head, where I'd spent so many nights dreaming of this moment. But there was so much of my life yet to be lived. As the car pulled away, I didn't look back.

The war had brought men as close together as any friends could ever be. But our friendships in the Nam were dissolved by death, time after time. In the hospital, we made friendships based on a common denominator of pain and a different kind of courage, which up to that point none of us had ever needed before. It was frightening to go into combat. Sometimes, the journey home required far more bravery.

# Epilogue:
# January 4, 1983

THE WEATHER WAS surprisingly mild and the sun was shining brightly as Cheryl drove me up to the hospital. We'd left our ten-month-old son, Scott, at home with my mother. Our five-year-old daughter, Kerrie, was sitting on my lap. As we pulled to a stop, tears streamed down Kerrie's face. She held me tightly.

"I'm going to miss you so much, Daddy. I hope the doctors don't hurt you."

"I'll miss you, too. Don't worry, I'll be fine."

I kissed her forehead, then leaned over and gave Cheryl a gentle kiss. "I'll give you a call as soon as I see Dr. Dangles. I love you," I said as I got out of the car and gathered my baggage. "See you soon."

"Take care, Rick. I'll call you later tonight. I love you, too," Cheryl shouted as she pulled away.

I turned and entered the lobby of Great Lakes Naval Hospital. I smiled and shook my head as I made my way to a ward. The hallways hadn't changed in all the fifteen years since I'd first been there.

I checked in and a young corpsman took my vital signs and medical history. I was amazed at how young he was. It was hard to believe so much time had passed. I was issued a pair of pajamas and assigned a rack. Then I changed quickly and got in bed. As I lay there I thought about the thirty-nine operations I'd been through since I was wounded and the one I had to face the next day.

I still had a considerable amount of shrapnel sprinkled around inside me, plus bone fragments that caused new infections. This time a metal plate in my lower right leg was going to be removed, and I'd have a big dose of antibiotics, given intravenously, for the osteomyelitis in my left leg. It wasn't going to be anything life threatening. Nontheless, each operation seemed to take more out of me at age thirty-five, and my recovery time was increasing.

My doctor, Dangles, was a new breed. He was a civilian, since the abolition of the draft had left the Navy short of qualified medical personnel. But I was more than happy to be in his hands. He'd served some of his residency under Dr. Boone Brackett in a Chicago hospital, so I had total faith in him.

A lot had happened since my discharge back in 1968.

Steve and I rented an apartment together and went back to college. Steve managed to finish. But after I'd had to go back to the hospital three times in three semesters, I knew that my college career was over. It also seemed that my civilian life wasn't going to be much of a success. In 1969, I applied for twenty-three jobs and was turned down for all of them. One prospective employer told me that his firm didn't hire professional killers. The others cited my disability and said they couldn't afford to have me on the payroll.

Meanwhile, Cheryl and I broke up. She started working as a flight attendant for Eastern Airlines and I decided to try to find work in Europe. It was a difficult time for both of us.

I went to Ireland and then the Continent, moving around until I got a job washing dishes and making egg rolls in a Chinese restaurant in Hamburg, West Germany. Staying on my feet all day was too much. My legs acted up and I had to get crutches from the local U.S. Army hospital. I quit and went to Madrid to work for a Spanish export company. I began to write the manuscript of this book there. But most important, Cheryl and I began writing each other.

It was now two and a half years since I'd been wounded, and Cheryl was able to look at our relationship more objectively. We knew that we loved each other and that our love would endure any future tests. So in November, 1970, I returned to the United States and on December 4, we were married.

Our marriage has been fabulous. We've had some difficulties, but compared to life at Great Lakes during 1968 everything is a cakewalk. Cheryl and I both have drawn strength from that experience. I've had to be hospitalized every year since 1972, but not once has she complained.

I finally landed a job with Union Oil Company in 1973, and I worked there for seven years doing accounting and commercial credit representation. Continuing operations and recurring hospitalizations caused me to leave. Meanwhile, Cheryl was working for Eastern Airlines, so there was always some income to supplement my disability pension, and our children were born. They're the pride of our lives and they've helped us become closer as a couple and a family.

Ward Three South is empty now. The beds and all the furnishings have been stored or scrapped. The doors to the ward are locked and the heat is turned off to conserve energy, but oh, the ghosts that fill that place.

Dr. Boone went to Vietnam in 1969 and worked for several months in a field hospital. He now has a successful practice in Oak Park, Illinois, where he and his wife, Jean, and their five children live. He's chief of orthopedic surgery at several Chicago hospitals, and he still sees me and other men from Ward Three South as patients and friends. He's always available to us for medical assistance without charge, and we've all benefited from his wise counsel and special friendship.

Steve married after he finished college. He has a farm in Minnesota and he and his wife have adopted two children. He went to China on an agricultural trade mission and was considering going back there to sell farm equipment until the economy went sour.

Smitty went home to Michigan, got his college degree, and started a flying school.

Hans married Pat. They have two children and live in Michigan.

Cox and Smith, those two fine corpsmen, went to Vietnam. They were both killed there.

Crawford also went to Vietnam. He was reported killed in action.

Snyder and Cole went to Vietnam. Each man lost a leg there.

Blind Al went to live at home with his parents. He never married.

Chief went to Vietnam and was shot twice in the chest. His strong physique saved his life. He's married now and lives in Indiana with his wife and daughter. He works for a railroad

and, in his spare time
man. He's still dedica

Brandy went home

Ron married his ol
track of him after tha

Miss Bixby went to

I looked up. A nur
"Mr. Eilert, I'm Miss
understand you were

"Yes, ma'am. Were

"Yes. Not on these
nity. Every once in a
Three South and Thr
many terribly wound

"Do you remember
threw a bedpan on tl
surgery?"

She smiled sudden
yes, I do. That was a

She took my hands
hospital . . . the way
that went on here.
found a reason to la
was when I found ou
me a lot about coura
bed and hot food, an
God bless you." She
away.

I felt a lump in my
pered.